Marketing Semiotics

Signs, Strategies, and Brand Value

Laura R. Oswald

OXFORD
UNIVERSITY PRESS

OXFORD
UNIVERSITY PRESS

Great Clarendon Street, Oxford OX2 6DP
United Kingdom

Oxford University Press is a department of the University of Oxford.
It furthers the University's objective of excellence in research, scholarship,
and education by publishing worldwide. Oxford is a registered trade mark of
Oxford University Press in the UK and in certain other countries

British Library Cataloguing in Publication Data
Data available

Library of Congress Cataloging in Publication Data
Data available

ISBN 978-0-19-956650-1

Printed in the United Kingdom by
the MPG Books Group Ltd

Marketing Sem

Signs, Strategies, and Brand Value

For Nicolas and Julia

■ CONTENTS

■ ACKNOWLEDGMENTS

Marketing Semiotics originated in an espresso café in Evanston, Illinois, in 1991. I had become weary of writing on hair-splitting topics in postmodern critical theory and asked a neighbor, Mary Ann McGrath, to share with me her academic interest in shoppers at the local farmer's market. In the course of that conversation, I realized that the marketplace formed a living and breathing laboratory for semiotic inquiry, and that consumer research would take me out of the library and into life. I also left the café with the names of three people who would, over the next decade, help me bring this idea to fruition— John Sherry, Rita Denny, and Jerry Cole.

John Sherry, a marketing anthropologist, introduced me to the interpretive consumer research literature during a seminar at Northwestern University. Without thought for reward, Sherry guided me through my first published ethnography with consumers, where I applied semiotics to a cross-cultural setting. Rita Denny, an anthropologist and consultant, handed me my first business project, the luxury perfume case that I discuss in Chapter 2. And Jerry Cole, a senior vice-president of strategy at the D.D.B. Needham Agency, hired me to conduct exploratory research in the automotive category and walked me through the steps of the strategic planning process.

From the very beginning, I was struck by the generosity and creativity of the marketing professionals who were willing to take a risk on an academic who was cobbling together an approach to branding that is not taught in business schools. I took the next ten years off from teaching and built an enthusiastic clientele comprising blue-chip companies such as Ford, McDonald's, Coca-Cola, and General Mills. I am indebted to Sally Lombardo, from the Ford Motor Company, Malachy Walsh, a senior vice-president of strategy at J. Walter Thompson, and Brenda Williams, a consumer insights expert at Leo Burnett, for their enthusiastic support in the early days of the business.

I am also grateful to Virginia Valentine and Monty Alexander, who are responsible for making semiotic research standard practice in the United Kingdom. I was fortunate indeed to have been included in many international projects for their company, Semiotic Solutions, and to have enjoyed their friendship and creativity for many years.

The Marketing Semiotics approach draws energy and creativity from balancing semiotic theory and business practice. I have been inspired by notable academics, Russell Belk and Douglas Holt, who in writings, conferences, and edited books have challenged the rigid boundaries separating academic research from the realities of the marketplace. They have helped forge a new paradigm in business education that thrives on the tensions between theory and practice, art and science.

This book might still be an idea in my mind were it not for Simon Nyeck and Marie-Laure Djelic, who invited me to teach marketing semiotics at ESSEC Business School in Paris from 2005 to 2006. I developed lectures for MBA students that would become the framework for *Marketing Semiotics.* I also thank the many talented students at ESSEC for putting these ideas into action in class projects and research.

Balancing theory and practice formed at once the greatest impetus and also the greatest challenge to writing this book. Ellen Neuborne became the sounding board for my ideas at various stages of the writing, and provided me perspective and direction when my pen faltered. I am also indebted to Lynn Childress, whose exacting and tireless work on copyediting the manuscript was indispensable to the coherence and readability of the book.

My acknowledgments would be incomplete if I failed to mention French semiotician, Christian Metz, who agreed to direct my research on semiotics while I completed a Ph.D. at New York University, without any material reward. Metz inspired me to tackle the big issues and to challenge the status quo without losing the rigor and precision of the scientific process. At his untimely death in 1993, he had already formed a worldwide following that included another prominent marketing semiotician, Jean-Marie Floch.

Since a book on visual semiotics necessarily demands reference to actual marketing images, the author is grateful to the copyright holders of the following images for their specific permission to use their images from the text:

Figure 1.12: reproduction of René Magritte, *La Trahison des images/Ceci n'est pas une pipe,* courtesy of the Artist Rights Society, NY, the Art Resource, NY, and the Los Angeles Museum of Art, Los Angeles, CA.

Figure 3.2: the Kodak logo, courtesy of the Kodak Company, Rochester, NY.

Figure 3.6: photograph of Nicole and Etienne Emery courtesy of Patrice Lucenet, France.

Figures 4.5 and 4.6: drawings created by Tonik Associates, London, UK.

Figure 5.1: *Freedom from Want* by Norman Rockwell, courtesy of the Norman Rockwell Family Estate.

Figure 5.3: Olympic Games logos, courtesy of the International Olympics Committee.

Figure 6.2: *Angry Landscape* (1967) by Karen Appel, courtesy of the Appel Foundation and Van Lennep Producties, Holland.

Figure 6.3: *Untitled* (1950) by Beauford Delaney, courtesy of the Minneapolis Institute of Art and Les Amis de Beauford Delaney.

Figure 6.4: *Music Pink and Blue II* (1918) by Georgia O'Keefe, courtesy of the O'Keefe Museum, the Artists Rights Society, and the Whitney Museum, NY.

Figure 6.5: *White Center* by Mark Rothko, courtesy of the Estate of Mark Rothko, Los Angeles Museum of Art, Los Angeles, CA, Art Resource, NY.

While every effort was made to contact the copyright holders of material in this book, in some cases we were unable to do so. If the copyright holders contact the author or publisher, we will be pleased to rectify any omission at the earliest opportunity.

Chicago, Illinois
December 2010

■ LIST OF FIGURES

■ LIST OF TABLES

Introduction

"Consumers shop for meanings, not stuff."

Brand equity is the financial value of goods derived from intangible brand benefits that exceed the good's use value. Brands deliver these benefits to consumers in the form of meanings, such as the perception of quality, a symbolic relationship, a vicarious experience, or even a sense of identity. The extent to which consumers recognize, internalize, and relate to brand meanings is not an academic question; it has tangible impact on the firm's financial performance.[1] In other words, brand meaning is not merely a value added. It is the condition of possibility for creating brand value. Therefore, managing brand equity demands first and foremost managing brand meanings or semiotics.

In this book, I introduce the reader to semiotics, a social-science discipline that extends the laws of structural linguistics to the analysis of verbal, visual, and spatial sign systems. I demonstrate the application of semiotics to marketing by presenting a step-by-step methodology for organizing and focusing meanings associated with the brand, the consumer, and the culture in order to achieve strategic goals. Semiotics exceeds the rhetorical or content analysis of meaning because it sheds light on the cultural codes that structure the phenomenal world into semantic categories and implicates consumers in the brand world.

The marketing semiotics approach can be used to refocus, extend, or reposition the brand, or to develop new products or new segments and markets. It can be used to create clear, impactful, and relevant brand communication and find communication channels that align the brand message with media preferences of the target market. This book provides the reader with actionable direction for steering brands through technological and cultural change, differentiating brands in the competitive environment, and counteracting the natural depletion of brand meaning over time.

In North America, semiotics research is typically commissioned at the end of a strategic decision-making process to develop creative communication strategy, which limits the powerful potential of semiotics for growing brand value. Semiotic research should form the cornerstone of brand equity management, since brands are essentially sign systems that contribute to profitability by distinguishing brands from simple commodities, differentiating them from competitors, and engaging consumers in the brand world. In *Marketing Semiotics*, I propose a strategic reorganization of the brand-building hierarchy that moves semiotic research to the front of the planning process.

The Semiotic Paradigm in the Brand Management Research

Since Sidney Levy published the groundbreaking paper, "Symbols for Sale" in 1959, many experts have written on the impact of brand meanings on market value. Although authors may disagree on the particular theory, methodology, or measurement tool used to gauge brand equity, they agree with the principle that brands have value for the firm and for investors to the extent that consumers associate the brand with meaning or "semiotic" value. For example, in their legendary book on brand positioning, Al Ries and Jack Trout ([1981] 2000) underscore the role of meaning in growing brand equity, insisting that the battle for market share is in fact a battle for the mind of consumers.

THEORY AND PRACTICE

The purpose of this book is to demonstrate how semiotic concepts and research methods can be used to solve business problems. I guide the reader through the application of semiotic concepts to marketing practice. I also advance marketing science by introducing readers to a methodology that is standard procedure in the strategic brand management process in Europe. Although other researchers have used semiotics to interpret the meanings in advertising that has already been produced, in this book I demonstrate how semiotic concepts can be implemented at all stages of the planning process to build, strengthen, and clarify brand meanings. Semiotics can be applied systematically to the full spectrum of brand management processes, including research, market segmentation, brand positioning, creative strategy, and the design of products, packaging, and retail sites.

I highlight real business cases where brands succeed or fail to the extent that management monitors brand meanings. I ask, for instance, how did a blue-chip brand like Kodak fall prey to the perils of category leadership, blindsided by success? I use plain language and clear examples to provide answers to questions such as: "Can we save this brand?" "Can we reach this target?" "Can we stir passions?" "Can we brand a retail experience?" I clarify complex concepts by means of figures and grids.

Marketing Semiotics is based upon twenty years of teaching, writing, and consulting experience. In the course of my work, I have applied semiotics to dozens of business cases in order to refocus, reposition, or extend the brand to new products, customers, and markets. And I have worked with advertisers and planners to align communication and media strategy with the brand positioning and the culture of consumers.

MANAGING BRAND MEANINGS

David Aaker (1991, 1996) is responsible for articulating the brand equity system on the basis of brand meanings, including consumer perceptions for quality and reliability; their emotional, cultural, and personal associations with the logo and other brand symbols; and the loyalty that these affective associations produce. He makes direct links between these intangibles and the brand's value for the firm and investors. Strong and widely recognized brand associations also support the brand's trademark ownership and retailing clout. It is much more difficult to violate with impunity trademarks for widely recognized brands than those associated with local, relatively unknown brands. And furthermore, retailers are more likely to give shelf space to brands that consistently draw customers into the store.

Jennifer Aaker (1997)[2] probes further into the symbolic dimension of brands by focusing on the brand personality—the set of human characteristics consumers associate with brands as the result of advertising associations. She develops an instrument for measuring the scope and depth of brand personality. Her research into the symbolic meaning of brands for consumers derives to some extent from McCracken's account (1986) of advertising as a mechanism for transferring meanings from culture to goods and brands.

Susan Fournier (1998) extends the brand personality concept into the notion of consumer–brand relationships. She finds that consumers engage in multiple types of relationships with brands in their personal "brand portfolios," ranging from practical to intimate. Fournier also draws direct links between marketing activities that affect the brand personality and customer loyalty. For example, inconsistencies or ambiguities in the brand personality due to activities such as line extensions or inconsistent creative strategy would disrupt consumers' affective involvement with brands the same way they would disrupt any interpersonal relationship.

The effective management of brand meanings has measurable consequences for brand value, as evidenced by the kinds of measurement tools used by researchers to measure brand equity. The Interbrand Group gives a value to the range and depth of meanings consumers associate with brands. This value may surpass the entire material equity of a company, such as buildings and products. Interbrand values the Coca-Cola brand at nearly $70 billion.[3] In advanced consumer culture, even the most basic marketing functions, from line extensions to media planning, must be scrutinized in terms of what they communicate about the quality, distinctiveness, and relevance of the brand for consumers.

Even pricing strategy has a meaning. Luxury companies such as Prada would rather destroy inventory surplus than sell it at discount because the perception of rarity and inaccessibility associated with Prada contributes more to the long-term value of the brand than to the potential short-term income generated from discounting.

A SEMIOTICS-BASED STRATEGY

In this book, I extend the brand strategy literature by focusing in detail on the mechanics of meaning production, consumer engagement, and research design that enable marketers to manage brand meanings. I introduce marketing semiotics, the science of signs and meaning in the marketplace, to the strategic brand management toolbox. Semiotics adapts linguistic theory to the study of nonverbal signs and symbols and anchors them in the culture of consumers. Semiotics transcends the analysis of communication per se and can be used strategically to align the brand with its heritage and positioning and clarify competitive distinctions. From one chapter to the next, I develop the discussion of semiotics from smaller to larger systems of meanings. I propose research protocols designed to elicit symbolic associations, brand fantasies, and stories from consumers. I use semiotics to position brands on competitive grids and link brand identity to the culture of consumers. I apply semiotic analysis to various activities in the marketing mix from consumer research and advertising to retail design.

Semiotics in the Critical Theory Paradigm

In addition to its place in the brand strategy literature, this book also extends a long tradition of scholarship on critical theories of meaning production. We owe the very notion of symbolic consumption—consumers' use of goods to create personal identities, identify with groups, and "extend" their selves—to foundational studies in consumer behavior and marketing by Sidney Levy (1959), Mary Douglas and Baron Isherwood ([1979] 2002), and Russel Belk (1987, 1988). However, the current book advances the extant scholarship by focussing specifically on the impact of brand meaning and consumer perceptions on brand equity—the material value of the brand for the firm.

The following, cursory overview highlights some of the current trends in the current literature on meaning in the marketplace.

ADVERTISING RESEARCH

The early scholarship on meaning in the marketplace focuses on advertising research. Since Marshall McLuhan (1951) and Vance Packard (1956) drew popular attention to the impact of advertising persuasion on consumer behavior, scholars have pondered the social and psychological implications of advertising for consumer culture. The advertising research literature roughly follows two streams: literary theory and culture studies.

Literary Theory

The application of literary theory to advertising includes a spectrum of approaches from the formal analysis of texts and advertising rhetoric to reader response theory. French critic Roland Barthes (1977*a*) inaugurated this tradition in his famous structural analysis of an Italian pasta print ad. He investigates the manner in which rhetorical figures, cultural references, and symbols free the photographic signifier from its literal meaning and structure the connotative dimension of an Italian pasta ad. Barbara Stern (1989) extends this tradition. She analyzes narrative structure and "voice" in advertising (1991), draws parallels between Frye's classification of cultural myths and four styles of advertising messages (1995), and applies deconstructive methodology to advertising, illustrating something of the polyvalent nature of advertising meanings (Stern 1993*b*, 1996*a*, 1996*b*).

As the art of persuasion, advertising is a ripe field for the study of rhetorical figures. Linda Scott (1994*a*) examines the role of visual metaphors in the construction of meaning in advertising. Edward McQuarrie and David Glen Mick (1996) expand the advertising rhetoric literature by compiling a taxonomy of classical rhetorical figures in advertising language. They suggest that rhetorical language may have more impact and memorability for consumers than the literal meaning, since rhetorical figures "deviate" from consumer expectations.

Reader response theorists filled a growing need in the literary criticism stream when they developed a methodology to account for the implication of consumers themselves in the production of advertising meanings. David Mick and Claus Buhl (1992) account for the different responses of four brothers to the same set of advertisements by drawing comparisons and contrasts between the brothers' life projects and the lifestyles and values represented in the ads. Linda Scott extended reader response theory by examining the ways consumers read the actual form of advertising—the graphics and language of the message—according to shared reading processes, such as rhetorical figures, literary genres, and narrative.

Literary theory provides a rich field of enquiry for understanding how meaning is produced in advertising. However, its proponents do not suggest how literary theory contributes to the strategic brand management process. It falls short of accounting for the codes that link advertising meaning to the brand positioning and implicate consumers in the brand world. Nor does it contribute to other marketing processes such as strategic positioning, market segmentation, or aligning creative strategy to the culture of the target market.

Culture Studies

The culture studies approach includes application of content analysis, structural anthropology, and semiotics to advertising content rather than consumer behavior per se. It is based on the assumption that advertising is a window onto the culture of consumers.

Content analysis is a methodology used by social scientists to develop hypotheses about a market or social group, track changes in social trends over time, and draw attention to the underlying attitudes, values, and political tensions within a culture (Kassarjian, 1977). Researchers sift through a representative sample of advertising texts associated with a product category, a historical period, or a consumer segment, for example, highlighting and quantifying patterns of information that recur across the data set. Researchers draw from these patterns the evidence to support generalities about a culture, a social practice, or a product category. For example, Belk and Pollay (1985a, 1985b) paint a picture of contemporary consumer ideals, both in North America and in a cross-cultural comparison of North America and Japan, by exposing consistent themes in a large sample of advertising. Tse et al. (1989) extend this approach to the China market in a study of advertising in three Chinese markets (Hong Kong, Taiwan, and the People's Republic of China) over several years time. They develop hypotheses about the evolving culture of Chinese consumers in relation to their more "open" counterparts.

Anthropologists such as Grant McCracken (1986) and John Sherry (1987) suggest that the structure of meaning in advertising reflects deep structures in the organization of culture into semantic categories. Advertising is nothing less than a "conduit" for transferring meanings from the world of culture to the world of consumer goods. When McCracken relates the structure of meaning in advertising to the structure of culture, but he stops short of accounting for the semiotic operations structuring culture, advertising, and the minds of consumers.

Sherry (1987) extends this research stream by highlighting the dialectical relationship of advertising to culture. He calls advertising a "cultural system" that is regulated by conventions structuring the way consumers read meanings, perform rituals, and perceive the world. Advertising plays a role in creating consumer culture and influencing the ways consumers interpret the marketplace, adopt consumption rituals, and even form identities. Sherry and Camargo (1987) illustrate this idea by means of a cross-cultural analysis of Japanese packaging that mixes English and Japanese words on the label. In addition to communicating something of the worldliness and modernity of the brand, this promotional tactic also legitimizes to some extent the incursion of Western consumer culture into Japanese social life. Sherry (1998) continues this kind of exploration in an analysis of Niketown as a Servicescape, a term he coins to describe the impact of design semiotics on the retail experience. Authors such as Kozinets et al. (2004) extend this approach in the examination of the interplay between retail design and consumer agency—the choices they make in co-creating the retail experience.

More recently, anthologies such as the *Handbook for Qualitative Research Methods in Marketing* (Belk, 2006), and proceedings from the Consumer Culture Theory conferences (i.e., Sherry and Fischer, 2009), offer a range of research perspectives on marketing meanings and consumer behavior.

In recent years, there has been renewed interest in structural semiotics as a means of accounting for social change. In a recent paper, Xin and Belk (2008) draw upon Barthes' semiotics of myth to account for the ideological tensions between communism and consumerism in advertising in the People's Republic of China. In another paper, Humphreys (2010) employs a semiotic analysis of dozens of newspaper articles to account for the influence of symbolic structures in the mass media on the long-range evolution of consumer values as they relate to gambling.

"MARKETING" AND "SEMIOTICS"

Of the few books written on marketing and semiotics, most focus on the mechanics of meaning production in advertisements and cultural texts.[4] Advertising copy is an understandable focus for the field of semiotics, since advertising is the mechanism marketers use to transfer meanings from the world of consumers to the brand.[5] For example, consumers associate Coca-Cola with the family Christmas because of legendary advertising imagery that embeds the brand in scenes with Santa Claus and Christmas trees. They associate the Apple brand with innovation because the brand name, logo, and advertising emphasize creativity and countercultural values.

As Eco (1979) states, semiotics extends to all aspects of culture, so the potential for applying semiotics to consumer research has yet to be realized. Consumer culture includes not only the artificial signs created by advertisers and designers but also the lived environments, social rituals, and ideological tensions structuring daily life. Jean Umiker-Sebeok's anthology (1987) suggests something of the diversity and richness of this field, and includes essays on the application of semiotics to a broad range of marketing topics, but do not address specifically the role of semiotics for managing brand equity.[6]

Jean-Marie Floch's book, *Semiotics, Marketing and Communication* (2001), is an exception to this rule. Floch, who coincidentally shared with me the same research director, Christian Metz, at the École des Hautes Études en Sciences Sociales in Paris, applies semiotics to a range of case studies, from developing positioning and logo design for a bank to redesigning Paris metro stations. The influence of Metz,[7] the founder of cinema semiotics, is evident in Floch's sensitivity to the visual, spatial, and narrative codes structuring meaning in the marketplace.

Floch's book is clearly targeted to specialists who are already familiar with the terminology of semiotics. Floch may also focus too narrowly on the "semiotic square," an analytical tool developed by Algirdas Greimas ([1966] 1984). The semiotic square reduces signification to three oppositional relationships that underlie propositions and narrative structures, including contradiction, complementarity, and contrast. Like a mathematical formula, the semiotic square provides a tidy model for understanding the elementary structures of discourse but does not account for the influence of the cultural context on meaning production.

Marketing Semiotics

In *Marketing Semiotics*, I integrate the structure of meaning into the broader consumer culture in which it is embedded. Drawing upon the intersections between structural semiotics and anthropology, I claim that brands grow in value to the extent that they resonate with the structure of myths, archetypes, and rhetorical operations at work in the cultural environment. I also include in every chapter a tutorial in basic semiotic concepts. I walk the reader through the step-by-step analysis of a case study and provide a methodology that readers can learn to apply to their own business problems.

TERMINOLOGY

The word "semiotics" derives from the Greek word *semios* or "sign," originally a medical term for "symptom." I use the word "semiotics" throughout the book in two ways. I use "semiotics" to refer to the social-science discipline devoted to the study of signs in cultural perspective. I also use "semiotics" to refer to the ensemble of signifying operations at work in a sign system, such as a brand, an advertising text, or a retail setting. For example, the "semiotics" of a retail setting refers to all the sign elements in that environment, such as the merchandising elements, the traffic flow, and the arrangement of the furnishings and product displays.

I use the word "semiosis" in a broad sense to refer to the dynamic of meaning production. It is dialectical in nature and describes the implication of cognitive processes in the consumer—or reader or spectator—in the structure of meanings they encounter in culture. The word "semiology" has been used interchangeably with "semiotics" to refer to the science of signs. In this book, I use it in a very narrow sense in relation to a philosophical perspective on the world. The semiological perspective transcends the metaphysical orientation of phenomenology and interprets reality in terms of cultural codes that structure phenomena into signs and meanings.

THEORETICAL FOUNDATIONS

The approach outlined in this book draws upon European developments in structural semiotics and linguistics represented by authors such as Lévi-Strauss ([1958] 1967), Barthes ([1964] 2000), Benveniste (1971), Metz ([1971]1991), ([1977] 1981), Eco (1979), Greimas (1984), and Jakobson (1990). These authors all draw upon the structural tradition of Ferdinand de Saussure ([1916] 1998), a Swiss linguist who developed a structural theory of signs at the end of the nineteenth century. The distinctive feature of the European literature stems from the dialectical nature of structural semiotics and the key role of binary analysis in the production and interpretation of meaning.

The dialectical foundations of structural semiotics have particular and urgent implications for marketing semiotics, because they account for the ways codes articulate the world of noise and chaos into systems of relationships characterized by distinction and difference. For instance, the binary distinctions between brands form the basis of positioning strategy, persuasion, and consumer choice in the marketplace.

Readers may wonder why Peirce ([1955] 1988), an American philosopher who founded the pragmatic tradition in semiotics, does not figure prominently in this book. Though a lengthy debate on the relative merits of Saussure and Peirce is beyond the scope of this book, it is worth noting that contemporary semiotic theory and practice do not rigidly conform to one tradition or another. Semioticians such as Jakobson, Eco, and Benveniste draw upon the traditions of both Peirce and Saussure to advance the science of signs. However, it may be useful to understand the basic differences between these two traditions in semiotics and explain why the Saussurian tradition has particular application to strategic brand management theory.[8]

Peirce was a contemporary of Saussure's living in the United States. His work on semiotics was limited to a brief but significant discussion of "logic as semiotics" in a book on Pragmatism. He viewed sign theory as a key to understanding phenomena in what we call the real world. He proposed a triadic model of the sign, which included the materiality of the sign or the "representamen"; the logical framework in which the sign could be interpreted or the "interpretant"; and a third term, the "object," a concept to which the sign refers. He also created a taxonomy of the possible types of signs, as defined by the logical relationship between the sign and its object. They include the iconic (based on similarity), indexical (based on contiguity), and "symbolic" (based on convention). Perhaps the most important feature of Peirce's semiotics for the philosophy of language is his notion that a sign is not a discrete unit of meaning but can itself become a signifier for another sign in an infinite dynamic of *semiosis*, or meaning production (Eco, 1979).

The limitations of Peirce's approach for marketing semiotics are threefold:

- Although Peirce's triadic model gives an account of the formal implication of meaning, perception, and reality in meaning production, it abstracts the process of meaning production from a theory of cognition, which would implicate the consciousness of the speaker in that process.

- Furthermore, Peirce suggests that the conventional or codified aspect of semiosis is limited to certain types of signs, rather than identifying the code as a fundamental property of semiosis as a cultural activity.

- As a result, Peirce's theory does not account for the dialectical structure of meaning, which implicates any particular sign or statement in broader cultural discourses, such as myth.

By contrast, Saussure viewed semiotics as "a part of social psychology." His orientation of structural linguistics to the dialectical relationships between units of meaning, rather than on relationships between signs and their referents in the real world, marked a revolution in the science of language. Before Saussure, the study of language was left to philologists, who studied language and literature in historical or "diachronic" perspective, highlighting ways that the sounds and meanings of words changed over time. There was an almost naïve assumption in philology that language was a given, the natural legacy of our ancestors, rather than a form of social and cultural production. There was very little study of the structure of language—its "synchronic dimension" and its roots in culture and cognition.

Structural Semiotics

Therefore, when Saussure developed sign theory in the late nineteenth century, he sought to dramatically break from the philological tradition. Saussure emphasized that language is made up of signs and the codes that organize signs in discourse. Signs are themselves structured by the "arbitrary" association of a material signifier, such as a sound, with an abstract concept. For example, the association of the sounds for /car/ and the concept "car" is not intrinsic to the object itself (the car), but is entirely dictated by semantic codes in the English language. The theory of codes anchors semiotics in the study of culture and dispels notions such as the universal or "natural" meaning of things. This insight prompted Eco (1979: 61) to claim that "the codes, inasmuch as they are accepted by a society, set up a 'cultural' world which is neither actual nor possible in the ontological sense. Its existence is linked to a cultural order, which is the way in which a society thinks [and] speaks."

By drawing attention to the role of social codes in the production of meaning, Saussure emphasized that meaning is a cultural construction, not a product of nature. The arbitrariness of the signifier/signified relationship is important not only for understanding the way meaning is produced in language but also in nonlinguistic systems. The "arbitrariness" feature of images or objects, for example, can be interpreted metaphorically to account for the role of codes and social convention in meaning production. For example, the precise meaning of brand logos for consumers is codified by habit and convention. The logo/brand relationship can change as the logo is exposed to consumers in other cultures.

Some critics claim that the codified nature of the signifier/signified relationship limits application of structuralism to the study of extralinguistic sign systems, such as consumer goods. Grayson and Shulman (2000) argue, for instance, that in many cases the subjective meanings consumers attach to goods are not dictated by code but by consumers' idiosyncratic interpretations, based on personal experience. However, brands would not have universal appeal at all if they did not communicate a core identity and message shared by a large audience. Once we move beyond the individual consumer and their private world of meanings into the fray of social communication and the world of brands, it becomes clear that even nonlinguistic sign systems are codified to some extent. It is only in the realm of connotations and nuances that consumers take liberties with brand meaning in order to incorporate them into their identity projects.

Semiotics and Culture

If we agree with Umberto Eco (1979: 26) that culture and signification are interdependent systems of knowledge, then culture and signification are both subject to codes that articulate the inchoate mass of phenomena we call reality into cultural categories and meanings. Structuralism is founded on the assumption of a dialectical organization of phenomena into binary pairs. The binary analysis of consumer data, whether a set of advertisements, interviews, or cultural texts, provides access to the distinctive features of competitive brands in a category, it sheds light on the underlying value system structuring culture, and accounts for the production of cultural myths and archetypes.

METHODOLOGIES

The structural approach to meaning in the marketplace has important implications for strategic brand management because it enables researchers to cut through the clutter and noise in a market and identify the broad cultural paradigms structuring a product category, such as young and old. The semiotic perspective influences all aspects of the research design, from constructing an interview protocol to data collection and analysis.

Data Collection

The marketing semiotics research process involves collecting and decoding data from consumers, popular culture, and the brand history. Data is then classified into groups ordered in a hierarchy of larger to smaller units of meaning, beginning with the broad cultural categories associated with the consumer target, such as gender or power. The cultural categories are analyzed further into emotional territories that bind the brand to the lifestyles and values of consumers. Then the material signifiers or "semiotic cues" associated with these meanings, such as images, words, and stories, are identified. The results are organized into a system of interrelated elements on a Consumer Brandscape, which reflects the integration of culture, consumer experiences, and the communication function for the brand. For strategic positioning purposes, the brand is then positioned along with competitors on a double-axis grid representing the binary relationships among elements of the brand category.

Binary Analysis

To give a very simplistic example, let us say we want to understand the cultural categories consumers associate with soft drinks and then understand how a specific brand is positioned in relation to them. Research would identify the key benefits consumers associate with soft drinks, such as refreshment or fun. Refreshment and fun structure the overall category, but to identify distinctive features of individual brands, the researcher may segment the respondent pool by demographics, lifestyles, and values. Findings may suggest that younger, more trend-sensitive consumers associate refreshment and fun with Pepsi, and more mature, traditional consumers associate these terms with Coke. By plotting the binary pairs tradition/trendiness and maturity/youth on a binary grid, we not only identify the two quadrants in which these two brands are positioned but also reveal unoccupied spaces of meaning in which competitive brands or brand extensions might be positioned (Figure I.1).

In addition to clarifying the positions of brands in the competitive arena, binary analysis also articulates the inchoate world of phenomena and sensations into systems of relationships characterized by oppositions (such as good and evil), contrasts (such as apples and oranges), and complements (such as factors that are neither good nor evil in a given circumstance). When applied to secondary data or consumer research, this process also draws forth the

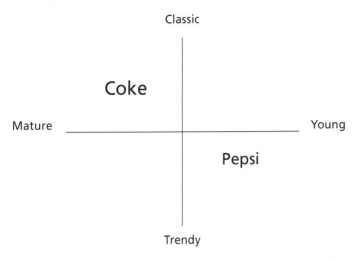

Figure I.1. A Binary Competitive Analysis—Soft Drinks

broad myths and archetypes structuring culture and reveals the underlying value system organizing social norms and consumer beliefs into categories of meaning.

Culture "makes sense" because it is structured by these kinds of contrasts and distinctions, and because these distinctions are codified by long-standing tradition. Take gender, for instance. The signs for "masculinity" are meaningful by way of contrast with the signs for "femininity" in a given culture. For example, a society may associate masculinity with physical strength and femininity with caregiving. Although consumers play with the conventions associated with gender in fashion and behavior, semiotic play is rooted in the conventions structuring gender in a given society.

The binary analysis of cultural data provides a window onto the myths and archetypes that structure the collective unconscious. Myths are the stories societies perpetuate in order to resolve, in symbolic terms, social tensions and conflicts that cannot be resolved in reality. For example, the Marlboro Man represents freedom and individuality for an America of shrinking frontiers, increasing conformity, and the automation of daily life.

Chapter Summaries

The content of this book stems from academic articles, lectures, and client presentations I developed over a twenty-year period. I structured each chapter in three parts, including the presentation of a marketing problem, discussion of a semiotic principle related to that problem, and a case study that resolves the problem and suggests managerial recommendations. I analyze concepts on strategic grids and include images drawn from advertising, popular culture, and consumer research to support and bring to life the writing.

All of the detailed case studies were drawn from first-hand experiences consulting to clients in North America, Europe, and Asia. In some instances, I disguised brand names or modified the strategic recommendations of a study in order to protect the proprietary claims of clients. I have also substituted graphic likenesses for copyrighted brand imagery to illustrate a concept when permissions to reprint were not granted by copyright holders.

In Chapter 1, I present an overview of the contributions of structural semiotics to the study of symbolic consumption. I examine not only marketing communication per se but also investigate parallels between the psychic, cognitive, and structural operations that motivate the symbolic function of goods and brands in the first place. I then show how these insights contribute to the strategic function of meanings in the marketplace at the levels of consumer insights, brand positioning, consumer loyalty, and communication strategy for a global diaper brand.

In Chapter 2, I introduce the reader to the basics of structural semiotics and its application to solving an identity and positioning problem for a new brand of perfume developed by American designer Halston in the early 1990s. Semiotic analysis of advertising for the luxury perfume category revealed cultural tensions between two distinct interpretations of the feminine in Western culture—the Goddess and the Girl Next Door. Research revealed that advertising for the new brand had not resolved these tensions, which explained why the campaign failed in consumer testing. The ambiguous advertising signaled deeper, strategic problems upstream in the positioning process. Research also uncovered an opportunity in the luxury perfume category for the new perfume brand to symbolize an emerging cultural interpretation of the feminine.

In Chapter 3, I draw attention to the multitude of influences structuring brand meaning that form the brand system or Brandscape. This symbolic terrain is constructed by means of an ongoing give-and-take between the brand heritage, consumer culture, and the competitive environment. By means of case studies for two blue-chip brands, Kodak and Blue Cross, I show that brands succeed or fail to the extent that management systematically calibrates the Consumer Brandscape to the evolving needs of consumers and trends in the environment.

In Chapter 4, I introduce discourse theory as a means of identifying a recurring subtext in a set of advertisements that transcends any given campaign. The subtext communicates the brand positioning, the ideological and cultural perspectives of management at a given time. I present an overview of discourse theory and present increasingly complex levels of discourse analysis. These include everything from the micro-discourses structuring meaning in a single image or logo to the macro-discourses that communicate the positioning over multiple campaigns, time frames, and markets. I summarize a case study for Kraft Singles that demonstrates how discourse theory can be used to help management to track the evolution of the brand positioning and consumer culture over time, and align new advertising with this evolution.

In Chapter 5, I show how discourse theory can be used to manage brands in multicultural contexts, where consumers may speak a common language, such as English, but view the world through unique social and cultural lenses associated with their ethnic subculture. Multicultural brand strategy relies on semiotics to "translate" brand values from one cultural context to another. I begin with a theory of cross-cultural consumption, showing how ethnic consumers rework the rituals and meanings of mass consumer culture in order to integrate them into their own culture and worldview. By means of illustration, I walk the reader through a strategic ethnographic study of African-American drivers that led to new product design and advertising for Ford F-150 truck. Researchers translated the primary positioning into the signs and symbols of ethnic subcultures while retaining the essence of the brand message.

In Chapter 6, I look at the ways consumers "read" and experience dwellings and branded retail sites as *Signscapes*. I use the term "Signscape" to refer to a semiotic system that structures consumer space as a form of discourse. Signscapes transcend the blueprint or design of the physical environment because they are multidimensional sites of meaning production. These dimensions include everything from the floor plan and décor to the disposition of furnishings and traffic flow. I introduce semiotic principles structuring consumer space and illustrate these principles with reference to two case studies. The first examines how consumers' subjective experiences of chronic pain are communicated in their lived environments. The second case applies these principles to the design of a fast food restaurant.

In Chapter 7, I conclude with an overview of new directions for marketing semiotics in the areas of Internet marketing and global brand strategy. I provide examples from two business cases to illustrate the potential of semiotics for marketing, public policy, and intellectual property on the Internet. Semiotics can be used to understand the unique interface of consumers with the computer hypertext, which is dynamic, multimedia, and performative. I also draw attention to the importance of semiotics for calibrating brand meanings to the culture of consumers in developing markets. Early-stage findings from a comparative study with affluent French and Chinese consumers suggest that marketers take for granted the ability and willingness of consumers abroad to learn the "rules of the road" necessary to participate in brand culture in the first place, let alone become loyal to one brand or another. I map the dual dimensions of brand meaning and highlight the different ways consumers East and West respond to luxury brands.

The implications of semiotic theory and methodology for understanding consumers, managing brands, and probing the values and beliefs structuring culture are broad and deep. The following chapters introduce readers to this rich field and provide theoretical resources and methods of analysis to readers interested in pursuing marketing semiotics research as practitioners, students, and scholars.

▧ ENDNOTES

1. See Ries and Trout ([1981] 2000), Biel (1993), Aaker (1996), and Keller and Lehman (2006)
2. See also Aaker et al. (2001) and Aaker et al. (2004).
3. Genelius (2009) reports on the Interbrand Group's Report on the 100 Best Global Brands.
4. Goldman and Papson (1996), Scott and Batra (2003), and Gaffey (2004), and Holbrook and Hirschman (1993)
5. McCracken (1986) emphasizes the role of advertising in transferring meanings from the realm of culture to the realm of brands.
6. For example, see the essays by Belk (1987) on identity formation, Sherry on culture (1987), Hoshino (1987) on product design, and Kehret-Ward (1987) on the syntax of product use.
7. Metz developed the theory of cinema semiotics from a structural analysis of the narrative film ([1971] 1991) to a postmodern interpretation of cinema as a site for the psychic construction of the spectating subject ([1977] 1981).
8. For a detailed comparison of these two traditions, see Mick and Oswald (2007).

1 Semiotics in the World of Goods

"You are what you eat!"

Marketing semiotics is a field of investigation that is based on the proposition that goods often transcend their functional purpose and have symbolic value for consumers. For example, when grandmother's cookbook stores more family memories than useful recipes for the grandchildren, we could say that the symbolic, emotional value of the cookbook has surpassed its practical value for the family. In similar fashion, brands are defined by their symbolic value for consumers, since brand meanings differentiate competitors in the marketplace and target the unmet symbolic needs of consumers.[1] The semiotic value of the brand name, the logo, and other proprietary assets forms the cornerstone of brand equity.[2]

In this chapter, I provide an overview of the contributions of structural semiotics to the study of symbolic consumption. I examine not only marketing communication per se but also investigate parallels between the psychic, cognitive, and structural operations that motivate the symbolic function of goods and brands in the first place. I then show how these insights contribute to the strategic function of meanings in the marketplace at the levels of consumer insights, brand positioning, consumer loyalty, and communication strategy.

Theories of Symbolic Consumption

Consumers engage in symbolic consumption from the moment they use goods as signs. Anthropologists have long established that consumers choose goods to embellish or extend their identities, identify with a group, and mark transitions from one life stage to the next (see Douglas and Isherwood, [1979] 2002; McCracken, 1986; Belk et al., 1989; Deshpande and Stayman, 1994). A bride might measure her status by the size of the diamond in her engagement ring. The boss might throw a lavish office holiday party to show off his success. The meaning of goods for consumers may be tied to the material value of the goods themselves, such as precious jewels and state-of-the-art technology. It may be associated with the memories or emotions consumers attach to special goods over time, or dictated by cultural norms, such as Christmas trees at Christmas. Symbolic consumption has social and psychological dimensions that account for the consumer's ability to project meanings onto goods and integrate the meaning of goods into their lifestyles and social networks.

CONSUMPTION IN THE SOCIAL ORDER

The literature on symbolic consumption stems in large part from the seminal work of anthropologist Douglas and economist Isherwood ([1979] 2002). In *The World of Goods*, they propose an alternative to the prevailing utilitarian account of why people want goods. They make the case that consumer demand is implicated in a social economy structured by the quest for meaning rather than subsistence per se. The authors question the validity of traditional supply and demand economics and offer instead an interpretation of the marketplace as the site for cultural production and social exchange, moderated by goods.

In the first place, they draw attention to the social and psychological meanings of goods that dictate consumer demand, not material needs alone. And in the second place, they propose that the meaning and force of consumption are woven into the shared values, beliefs, and relationships that structure society.

Imagine, for example, a world without birthdays or holidays, when seasons, births, and deaths would go by without acknowledgment. Furthermore, imagine birthdays and holidays without rituals involving the production, exchange, or preservation of possessions of some kind. And finally, imagine giving or receiving gifts, preparing the holiday meal, or inviting guests without collective guidelines about the meaning of goods, the traditions, and social classifications involved in these rituals. The way that consumers use goods not only reflects but also regulates the cultural conventions, myths, and social order of a society by anchoring them to the collective unconscious as signs. Douglas and Isherwood state, "Consumption is a ritual process whose primary function is to make sense of the inchoate flux of events" ([1979] 2002: 43).

Douglas and Isherwood thus underscore the need to look beyond subsistence and ostentatious display to explain economics as a social economy of consumption. In this social economy, consumers interpret goods as signs in a symbolic activity that marks and regulates social organization, cultural production, and value. However, the authors stop short of providing a theory of symbol formation to account for the manner in which objects take on meaning. Nor do they explain how culture becomes organized into conventions and laws. To answer these questions, I submit their anthropological project to structural theory and analysis, and draw upon psychoanalysis to understand how consumers make meanings of things at all.

STRUCTURALISM

Structuralism is based on the metaphysical assumption that meaning production is a system of relationships codified by culture and that these semiotic relationships actually structure, rather than mirror, phenomenal reality. This interpretation of meaning distinguishes structuralism from empirical approaches to meaning, exemplified in the work of Peirce (1955) and Austin ([1962] 2005).

Structural Semiotics

Structural semiotics is a form of critical analysis based on the proposition that the world as we know it is structured, like language, into smaller to larger units of meaning that relate to each other in an organized system.

Semiotic analysis provides an account of symbol formation and its extension into nonlinguistic semiotic structures such as social organization, ritual behavior, and the mass media. Since marketing relies on collective perceptions and behaviors in the marketplace, this information can be important for developing products, positioning brands, and creating advertising.

To explain the underlying processes responsible for the articulation of culture into meaningful units, and for projecting these meanings onto goods in the first place, I refer in the next sections to Lévi-Strauss's structural anthropology and Freud's psychoanalytical theory of symbol formation.

Structural Anthropology

Claude Lévi-Strauss draws parallels between language and culture, using structural linguistics as a model for analyzing cultural phenomena (Lévi-Strauss, [1958] 1963). His work has led to the current understanding of semiotic systems as cultural systems, and every unit of meaning a unit of culture (Eco, 1976: 76). As Levy (1959) pointed out in his pathbreaking paper, Lévi-Strauss's findings apply not only to remote cultures but also to contemporary consumer behavior, since cultural codes also structure the meanings consumers attach to goods and rituals. They structure the myths consumers perpetuate about their lives, consumption rituals, and brand preferences.[3] I will expand further on the structure of consumer mythology in the case study presented at the end of this chapter.

Three Principles of Structural Anthropology. Lévi-Strauss introduced three structural principles to anthropology: (*a*) the role of the collective unconscious in the production and preservation of cultural systems; (*b*) the role of deep structures or universal laws organizing the social world; and (*c*) the importance of the system—the notion that every unit of culture is linked systemically to other units, so that changes at any level of culture will also entail changes in the rest of the system.

Principle 1: The Collective Unconscious. Conscious phenomena are the product of unconscious, universal structures or codes. The dialectical implication of unconscious structures and material representation is a foundation principle of structural linguistics, as illustrated in the Saussurian sign. Rather than focusing on the empirical analysis of individual statements, Saussure focused on the codes that regulate the association of material signifiers, such as phonemes, with abstract meanings. By defining the sign as a dialectical association of *signifier* and the *signified*, Saussure emphasized the metaphysical structure of meaning production and the unconscious codes regulating the organization signs in discourse (see Figure 1.1).

This metaphysical interpretation of linguistic behavior revolutionized the social sciences because it focused attention on the unconscious, universal constructs responsible for the shared beliefs, values, and behaviors we call culture.

Principle 2: The Deep Structure of Culture and the General Codes. Lévi-Strauss proposed that culture resembles language inasmuch as it is organized by means of codes structuring the collective unconsciousness. He states, "The kinship system is a language. . . . In the case of kinship as well as linguistics, the observable phenomena result from the action of laws which are general but implicit" (Lévi-Strauss, [1958] 1967: 32–46). These deep structures account for the formation of the universal myths that structure the meaning of social life. They can be traced in the repetition of binary patterns in the visible signs of culture, such as rituals, artefacts, and social organization.

Second, the object of anthropology should be the general laws that regulate cultural phenomena, not the phenomena taken at face value. Lévi-Strauss

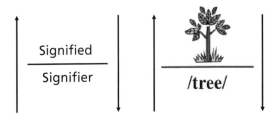

Figure 1.1. The Dual Structure of the Sign

broke with tradition when he switched the focus of analysis from empirical observation to the quest for the universal laws or codes responsible for cultural phenomena. These laws articulate the vague outlines of phenomena into a conceptual grid that regulates social life in the same way that grammar regulates language. The conceptual grid is responsible for structuring the cultural categories that organize social life. These codes account for the shared rituals and meanings organizing social behavior, from traffic signals to dining etiquette.

Principle 3: The Cultural System. In line with Saussure, Lévi-Strauss changed the focus of anthropology from the study of individual phenomena (such as meal preparation) to the unconscious mental structures organizing the cultural system (such as myths). Defying anthropological tradition, Lévi-Strauss claimed that culture structures social life, rather than being the product of social necessity. He privileged meaning over empirical reality and claimed that culture gave rise to social structures, rather than the other way around.

He states, "Like phonemes, kinship terms are elements of meaning; like phonemes, they acquire meaning only if they are integrated into systems. 'Kinship systems,' like 'phonemic systems,' are built by the mind on the level of unconscious thought" (Lévi-Strauss, [1958] 1974: 31–2).[4] Furthermore, inasmuch as kinship structures are codified like language, Lévi-Strauss's binary oppositions form categories of culture in the same way that phonetic oppositions structure meaning in linguistic discourse. Binarism, he claimed, formed the universal structure of thought and was responsible for the organization of culture into paradigmatic systems. Consequently, to uncover the broad paradigmatic systems structuring culture, the anthropologists submit cultural data to binary analysis.

The Structure of Myth. Lévi-Strauss began with analysis of a large set of cultural myths, the stories that social groups perpetuate to explain the mysteries associated with life, death, and sexuality. For example, the culinary practices of the population he studied could be divided along a preliminary opposition between raw and cooked food. Raw food falls to the side of Nature; cooked food falls to the side of Culture. This binary pair gives rise to a series of oppositions moving from the concrete, that is, raw and cooked food, to the abstract, that is, status hierarchies, knowledge production, and the interpretation of the sacred. Furthermore, Lévi-Strauss identified extraordinary, anomalous elements of myth that subvert to some extent the binary stability of the cultural system by providing a middle ground between the two terms. For example, the Genesis story accounts for the mysteries of life and death in Creation myth.

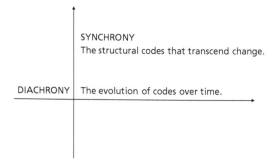

Figure 1.2. Double Axes of Cultural Organization

Synchrony and Diachrony. In addition to binary analysis, Lévi-Strauss adopted the two-dimensional analysis proposed by Saussure for linguistics. It includes the diachronic analysis of phenomena over time and the synchronic analysis of phenomena in a single time period. By tracking the recurrence of meanings and structures associated with cultural phenomena over time, the researcher identifies recurring themes in the data in diachrony. The synchronic analysis identifies the abstract code system that transcends cultural change (see Figure 1.2).

The researcher thus separates the wheat from the chaff, as it were, and uses the findings to induce the existence of general "laws" or codes regulating meaning production over time, laws that transcend cultural change.

Furthermore, the synchronic and diachronic analyses complement each other. The code system, like the grammar of a language, emerges from the identification of recurring semiotic structures over time. Likewise, a preliminary analysis of a single phenomenon can provide a guideline for tracking the evolution and consistency of cultural codes in a data set.

CROSS-CULTURAL SYMBOLIC CONSUMPTION

For example, the initial interview with an ethnic family can suggest hypotheses about the ways ethnic consumers navigate the cultural borders structuring multicultural societies. In a Haitian-American household that I studied in Chicago, the grandparents spoke the colonial French language; the middle-aged daughter spoke Creole, and the children responded in English (Oswald, 1999). The oppositions French/Creole and Creole/English generated a paradigmatic set of oppositions structuring the way Haitians in America defined their identities, their relationship with the mother country, and their participation in American culture. These binaries also regulated the consumer behavior of the family, such as food preparation. The housewife served ethnic

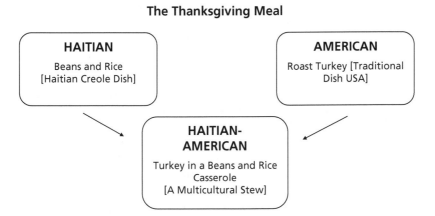

Figure 1.3. Code Swapping in a Multicultural Society

foods involving the extended family; she reserved American dishes and products interactions with mainstream social groups, such as birthday parties with neighbors. Moreover, to mark their dual participation in mainstream and ethnic cultures, they blended traditions on occasion. For example, they served turkey at Thanksgiving in a beans and rice casserole (see Figure 1.3).

Similar forms of code mixing appear with increasing regularity in global marketing campaigns, in which references to the West in word and image appeal to consumer aspirations to modernism and internationalism. For example, Sherry and Camargo (1987) found that the mix of English and Japanese in packaging and advertising represents tensions within Japanese culture between the forces of globalization and the deeply rooted antagonism of the Japanese toward foreigners.

PSYCHOANALYSIS AND STRUCTURALISM

Although the existence of unconscious structures in the construction of meaning is a foundation principle of structural semiotics, it was Sigmund Freud, Saussure's contemporary, who developed an actual theory of symbol formation based on psychological operations in the human psyche. By the time Lévi-Strauss wrote *Structural Anthropology* in 1958, Freudian psychoanalysis was already deeply embedded in the popular culture. Although Freud's interpretation of the unconscious was more oriented to physical drives in the body than the cognitive structures inferred by the Structuralists, Freud's work doubtless influenced the Structuralists' focus on an unconscious structural system at the root of meaning production and cultural organization. For this reason, I will summarize Freud's psychoanalytic account of symbol formation.

The Theory of Symbol Formation

Freud's interpretation of the unconscious is nothing less than a structural theory of the ways human subjects communicate psychic concepts through symbolic behavior. In *The Interpretation of Dreams*, first published in 1899, Freud explained the symbolic function in terms of the psychic drives, defined as energy flows in the body that regulate the movement between emotional states and cognition. They include displacement and condensation.

Displacement defines the drive to displace meanings and emotions from the mind to external representations from children's toys to language. Condensation defines the drive to condense multiple thoughts into a single, polyvalent symbol. Children may use dolls, for example, to stand in for real love objects, such as the mother. Here the symbolic replacement of the mother by the doll resolves, in the imaginary order, the tensions arising from the mother's absence (see Freud, [1909] 1955; Lacan, [1953] 2002). They may condense the ideas of dolls, mother, and sexual fantasy in dreams (see Figure 1.4).

The theory of the drives has roots in metaphysical philosophy, most notably the phenomenology of Hegel and his followers in the nineteenth century (Hegel, [1807] 1977). Put simply, phenomenology focuses on the structure of consciousness itself, rather than pondering the nature of reality as a separate entity. In this perspective, notions such as reality or truth are simply functions of the dialectical implication of one's perceptions and the structure of consciousness. In other words, neither mind nor matter constitutes the origins of being or meaning, because meaning and being are productions resulting from this dialectic. Thus, Freud shares with Saussure an understanding of meaning as a construction rather than an imitation of transcendent realities.

The Structure of Meaning

Freud also identifies secondary drives that structure the specific organization of texts such as dreams and fantasies. The secondary drives of displacement and condensation are responsible for the shape of meaning and originate in

Figure 1.4. Mind and Meaning

the body as psychic drives. In this sense, they parallel rhetorical structures in discourse. Displacements and condensations, at the level of the signifier, are often motivated by the unconscious censor that conceals or disguises unpleasant thoughts or painful truths. Hence, speakers employ euphemisms to censor language associated with bodily functions, replacing the word "toilet" with W.C. or "the ladies' room," for instance. They may also make a Freudian slip of tongue, unwittingly uttering a truth buried in the subconscious mind. If a person states, "I'm planning the funeral," when they intended to say, "the wedding," their unconscious fear has broken through to consciousness and revealed the speaker's latent feelings about the event.

Displacements also motivate the condensation of multiple paths of meaning in language and image on the basis of similarity. For example, though cars do not resemble babies, the comparison can be motivated by displacing the focus of attention from the entities themselves to the consumer's relationship to them (see Figure 1.5).

Freud's theory influenced developments in the theory of symbol formation throughout the twentieth century from Klein to Maslow and Lacan, who proposed that the unconscious is structured like a language (Lacan [1953] 2002; Maslow, 1943; Klein (1975)). For Lacan the emotional world of the individual is in fact regulated by semiotic structures that link the mind of the individual subject to the collective unconscious (Freud, [1898] 2010). Furthermore, Freud's interpretation of the unconscious as a symbolic system and his articulation of this system into binary pairs parallels trends in linguistics and the social sciences in his time. He sought universal structures and unconscious processes that would account for the ability of humans to project ideas onto symbolic representations, to organize those meanings according to universally accepted codes, and to share those meanings with a wide group of people.

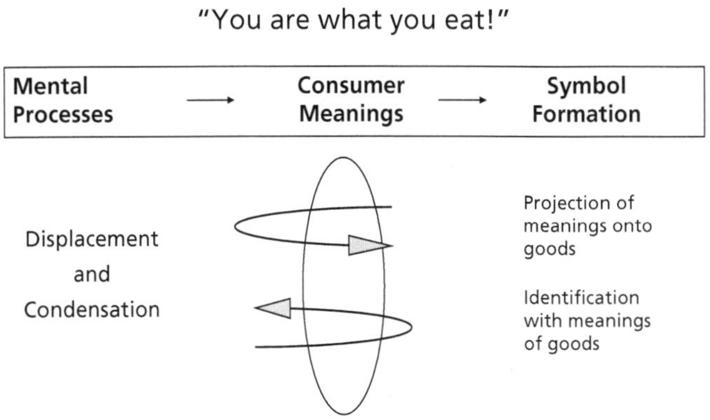

"You are what you eat!"

Figure 1.5. The Dialectic of Symbolic Consumption

Implications for Marketing

Freud's theory of symbol formation also has important implications for consumer behavior and advertising response, since the drives of displacement and condensation also motivate the transfer of meaning from one semantic category to another in symbols. Psychic projection accounts for the ways consumers personalize goods and brands, and use them as symbolic extensions of themselves. These insights give new meaning to the adage, "You are what you eat."

The theory of the psychic drives gives an account of the process that enables consumers to attach memories, beliefs, or mood states to national flags and heirlooms. Displacement and condensation also account for the polyvalent associations consumers make with brands. They are responsible for the rich polyvalence of consumer fantasy, advertising imagery, and brand logos, and are responsible for the transference of these meanings to products and services.

In his theory of the psychic drives, Freud hypothesizes that unconscious mental operations are responsible for symbol formation by projecting thoughts onto external representations. Freud also points to the role of the drives to move meanings from one signifier to another within these representations, as in the transfer of meaning from one term to another in metaphors. Projective displacements prevail in consumer culture from the metaphors consumers make to describe their experiences to the advertising messages that communicate emotional associations between branded products and the unmet needs of consumers.

When consumers describe their cars as their "babies," they may also be seeking a symbolic resolution to an emotional tension, perhaps the need for someone to nurture. By means of psychic displacement, the car becomes an emotional bridge between the two terms and the two semantic fields they represent, the human and the mechanical.

The Interpretive Research Paradigm

When applied in the field of marketing, semiotic analysis is an interpretive methodology that makes hypotheses about a consumer segment or category based on the analysis of recurring patterns and behaviors in a set of data. By articulating the codes structuring these patterns in consumer data, advertising, and other phenomena, the marketing semiotician seeks the essence of a brand, a product, or a consumer segment that transcends any particular ad campaign, consumer interview, or trip to the store.

Unlike empirical research, experimentation, and statistical surveys, which rely on the literal meaning of consumer statements, hypothesis testing, and rational consumer choices, semiotic research begins with the identification of a corpus of texts, which may include interview transcripts, competitive and historical advertising for the brand, and/or secondary data such as the texts of popular culture.

Semiotic analysis begins with the identification of a text or sign system, such as a package. This is followed by a binary analysis of the cultural codes structuring the text into a discourse, such as sacred and profane. The researcher then teases out the unique implementation of the codes that come to the surface in semiotic practice. Consumers and marketers draw upon universal codes to communicate meanings because these codes form the social scaffolding, the sine qua non, of communication. When implementing these codes in day-to-day consumption and marketing activities, consumers and marketers then manipulate these codes to communicate a distinct point of view or internalize a personal interpretation of the message.

THE TEXT

The text is the minimal unit of semiotic analysis. Unlike linguistics, which focuses on the mechanics of combination and selection to make meanings from phonetic sounds, semiotics focuses on the codes organizing meaning production in complete messages. Put differently, linguistics focuses on microstructures, semiotics focuses on macrostructures of meaning. Although macrostructures such as a novel may be constructed from language, the text cannot be reduced to its linguistic components. Likewise, poetics concerns the way meanings are organized in poetry by the integration of sound patterns, rhetorical figuration, and the meanings of words. Linguistic structures, such as syllables, form the material of poetry, but are not the specific object of analysis.

The boundaries of the text are finite—an ad, an interview, etc. Furthermore, multiple texts usually comprise the complete data set under analysis for any given study. For consumer research, the data set includes but is not limited to consumer transcripts. Although made up of speech, consumer responses are not analyzed for their linguistic components per se but for the stories, emotions, and symbolic associations consumers make with regard to the research question. Semiotic analysis would examine the structure of individual texts, such as consumer narratives.

The data set may include analysis of narrative structures across a set of consumers in the same target group or subculture. When the data set includes multiple texts, analysis serves to uncover general patterns of meaning that prevail from one text to the next and therefore reflect the collective myths, values, and beliefs consumers associate with the brand or product category. The data set might also include multiple advertisements for a category. The semiotic analysis would outline the broad binary oppositions that structure the deep collective values and myths consumers associate with a product category and a specific brand.

In the study of the paper diaper category discussed below, researchers gathered competitive advertising for the category for a five-year period, and collected cultural data drawn from store visits, popular culture, including movies and television shows, and blogs. In the early stages of analysis, themes emerged that guided the analysis of the rest of the data. From this process, researchers identified the dominant codes responsible for attaching certain meanings to the product category and competitive brands, and paid attention to "outliers" that signaled changes in the category that may lead new trends moving forward.

The text may also consist of the consumer's home environment. The dimensions would include the layout, the organization of private and public spaces, the placement of goods in the home, and the implications of this placement for social interactions and roles within the home, and so on.

THE BINARY STRUCTURE OF DISCOURSE

After identifying the data set, which may include consumer narratives and behaviors, advertising, and other secondary data, researchers look for patterns in the data that give rise to the broad semiotic tensions and paradigms structuring the category and the consumer segment. For structural semiotics, binary analysis is the fundamental operation for encoding, decoding, and classifying the sea of phenomena into semantic categories, rhetorical nuances, and discourses. The binary analysis of the textual system is based on the premise that semiotic operations reflect the dialectical structure of thought (at least in the West). Thus, binary analysis of the data is the first step in identifying the codes structuring a product category, a consumer segment, or a competitive set of brands.

So far we have discussed the relation of signifier to signified, diachrony to synchrony, condensation, and displacement. These binaries cannot be collapsed into a single overarching paradigm, but structure, at various levels of analysis, relationships between signs and meanings, and between one sign and another.

In this section, I focus on the binary relations that structure verbal and visual discourse. They include the cognitive processes of substitution and combination, the discursive structures of paradigm and syntagm, the rhetorical operations of metaphor and metonymy, and the epistemological play between the meaning and reference of discourse. Since these binary operations structure dialectical relationships between units of discourse, they contribute to the dynamic nature of semiosis or meaning production.

Semiosis builds upon the tensions between opposing terms of a binary. The semiotician is interested in the ways consumers (and marketers) mix and match these terms in new ways. Binary analysis thus accounts for both the regularity and creativity of semiotic systems.

CONSUMER PERFORMANCE

Codes determine the guidelines for interpreting signs. However, in day-to-day communication, individuals manipulate or "perform" structural codes in two ways. First, they make choices from the set of possible replacements for a given cultural unit. Second, they align these choices in statements and other sign systems, such as rituals. The substitution and combination of the terms in meaning production can operate at the level of discourse, structuring the axes of paradigm and syntagm. They can also operate at the level of rhetorical figures on the axes of metaphor and metonymy.

Selection and Combination

Based on research with aphasics, patients who are losing speech function, Jakobson identified two fundamental relationships that influence the way we organize and read signs. They include the mental operations of selection and combination, and the formal relations of similarity and contiguity. On the following grid, I organize these binary pairs into two basic aspects of semiosis. They operate at the level of mental operations, which accounts for the ability of consumers and speakers to encode and decode messages, construct figures of speech, and project meanings onto symbolic representations (see Figure 1.6).

Selection and combination account for the infinitely generative capacity of semiotic systems to serve the communication needs of speakers or consumers in everyday life. They structure the relation of discursive elements on the linear and vertical axes of language, and the relation of poetic signifier and signified in rhetorical figures. These operations are not restricted to literary activity. Consumers substitute and combine units of meaning in order to create and interpret meanings in the endless communication events of daily life.

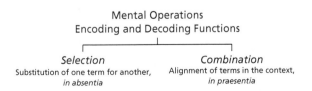

Figure 1.6. Selection and Combination

Paradigm/Syntagm

The linear, syntagmatic dimension of discourse is dialectically related to the vertical, paradigmatic dimension of discourse. In order to communicate meanings, consumer-speakers must choose a term from a set (i.e., the dictionary) that best fits with the grammatical and semantic structure of the sentence. For example, to complain to the waiter about my tea, I might say, "This tea is bitter." If I want to thank him for bringing me a replacement, I might say, "This tea is better." The choice of one distinctive feature or the other on the paradigmatic axis, of /i/ or /e/, influences the meaning of the statement, on the syntagmatic axis.[5] Furthermore, the choice to use one or the other is entirely driven by the intention of the statement expressed on the syntagmatic axis (see Figure 1.7).

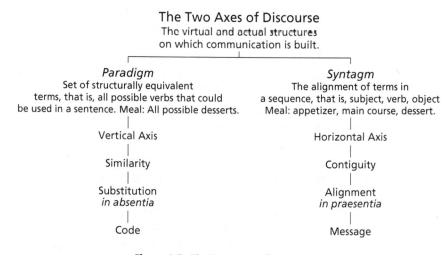

Figure 1.7. The Two Axes of Discourse

Consumers constantly make choices and combinations on the basis of similarity and contiguity from their choice of words to their choice of menu options. A *prix fixe* menu provides a good illustration of how selection and combination operate in other semiotic systems. The diner is presented with a fixed sequence of services—appetizer, main course, and dessert. These service categories form the syntagmatic order of the meal. Each of these service classifications includes a paradigmatic set of possible choices. The main course might include the options of chicken, beef, and fish; the dessert course might include cake, pie, ice cream, and tarte. To form a complete combination of main course, side dishes, and dessert, the diner has to select dishes from several sets of options on the menu.

The substitution and combination of meaning units are regulated by cultural conventions or codes structuring language or other semiotic systems.

For example, the order in which dishes are presented on the menu is culture-specific. In the People's Republic of China, for example, appetizers and main dishes are placed on the table at the same time. Cultural codes also dictate what kinds of foods are served at different times of the day. In China, breakfast may consist of smoked duck, grilled vegetables, pickled eggs, and sautéed noodles, whereas ham and eggs, pancakes, or cereals would be appropriate in the West. Holiday meals are also structured by cultural codes inherited from one generation to the next.

Consumers usually do not behave in lockstep with cultural codes, but mix and match rituals such as the family meal according to their needs and lifestyles. They may engage in "paradigm busting" behaviors by trying Chinese "dim sum" for breakfast or dine on cereal and milk to break out of the mold. Holiday rituals such as Thanksgiving allow for a certain amount of consumer choice and creativity as outsiders marry into the family or individuals begin following dietary trends, such as vegetarianism. Ethnic consumers may adapt mainstream holiday rituals to their own cultural practices, using food preparation as a means of negotiating their participation in and distinction from the dominant culture.

Metaphor and Metonymy

The operations of selection and combination also structure the poetic function of discourse, which is responsible for rhetorical figuration. By contrast with the referential function, the poetic function of discourse subordinates the linear logic of the sequence to the polyvalence of the paradigm. For this reason, Jakobson (1960: 358) claims that "the poetic function projects the principle of equivalence from the axis of selection to the axis of combination". The comparison of a runner with a turbo engine, unlikely as it may seem, can thus form the impetus for creating a brand discourse about the energizing effects of a running shoe. The poetic function sets up an ongoing tension between two terms of a comparison, playing with the differences and similarities between the two. On the other hand, the referential function simply replaces one term for another on the basis of the logic of the statement. Is the tea b/i/tter or b/e/tter?

Jakobson subsumed the plurality of rhetorical tropes under the broad binary opposition of associations by similarity (metaphor) and associations by contiguity (metonymy). By focusing on the mental operations structuring rhetorical statements, rather than the form of individual figures, Jakobson challenged the Aristotelian notion of rhetoric as a decoration or deviation from the "proper," literal sense of a statement and emphasized rhetoric's role in the poetic function of discourse. Rhetoric not only adds pleasure and beauty to a literal statement, but actually expands knowledge by forming correspondences between disparate semantic fields.[6]

Metaphor links *signifiers* by means of their shared characteristics, or similarities. Metonymy links *signifiers* by means of their logical or spatial contiguity. By interpreting rhetoric in terms of the broad binary opposition of associations by similarity and contiguity, structural semiotics integrates figurative operations within the overall process and structure of *semiosis*. Metaphor and metonymy thus work in tandem with the mental processes of displacement and condensation, and the discursive structures of paradigm and syntagm. The interplay between these two forms of association in figurative discourse supports the integration of the emotional and rational dimensions of brand discourse and engages consumers in that figurative play.

As I show in the example below, rhetorical operations both expand the semantic field of a statement and also inscribe the judgments of the speaker and reference to the context into the statement (see Figure 1.8).

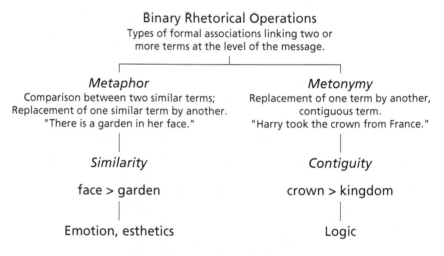

Binary Rhetorical Operations
Types of formal associations linking two or
more terms at the level of the message.

Metaphor	*Metonymy*
Comparison between two similar terms; Replacement of one similar term by another. "There is a garden in her face."	Replacement of one term by another, contiguous term. "Harry took the crown from France."
Similarity	*Contiguity*
face > garden	crown > kingdom
Emotion, esthetics	Logic

Figure 1.8. Metaphor and Metonymy

Meaning and Reference

Benveniste advanced structural semiotics in the 1960s by introducing the notion of discourse as the minimal unit of semiotic analysis. He claimed that limiting analysis to the individual sign or its distinctive features reduced meaning to mere abstraction (Benveniste, [1966] 1971). Furthermore, Benveniste traced the reference and subjectivity of discourse in specific codes for "voice" and "reference." He claimed that any semiotic operation that pointed to the point of view or creative hand of a narrator inscribes subjectivity in discourse. He finds that demonstrative pronouns such as "this" or "that" refer the reader/consumer to the context of a statement. The play between meaning and reference defines *semiosis* in action, when consumers have to manipulate these deep structures to consume and produce meanings in the marketplace.

IMPLICATIONS FOR SYMBOLIC CONSUMPTION

Rhetorical operations enable consumers to violate the semantic codes structuring a statement, mixing and matching semantic categories in order to emphasize the mood, look, or emotional force of an idea or to create an image of the idea in the mind. They also transcend the traditional function of advertising persuasion by bridging two or more fields of meaning, creating a brand world that satisfies the emotional needs of consumers. Consumer statements such as "My (Ford) truck is my husband" are motivated by a chain of intermediary associations linking brand consumption to desire in the Consumer Brandscape. The Ford brand is positioned as reliable, stylish, masculine, and powerful, all of which would make for an ideal partner. The consumer in question divorced her unreliable, unsupportive husband and relied on her Ford to back her up, carry heavy loads, and look good on the road.

Although rhetorical figures grant individuals a certain degree of license with the code, they are nonetheless limited by the semantic compatibility of the terms. For example, the statement "Mary eats shoes" fails as a metaphor because it attempts to join two mutually incompatible semantic categories, edible and inedible. Metaphors succeed when motivated by an underlying logic associating diverse semantic categories, as in the verb "devour." Defined by Webster's dictionary as "to consume voraciously," "devour" can embrace both edible and inedible objects under the rubric of consumption in general. It also supports tensions between these two categories, giving emotional force and imagery to the idea of Mary's consumer behavior.

As I illustrate below, visual metaphors are somewhat more forgiving than language, since images are already much more polyvalent, as well as less rigidly codified, than words, and can bridge dramatically different semantic fields.

IMPLICATIONS FOR ADVERTISING

Advertising Rhetoric

It might be asked what advantages can be derived from using metaphor, a fairly complicated intellectual process, when the literal statement "Mary buys lots of shoes" would suffice? Rhetorical figuration has the advantage over literal statements by communicating more than concepts. It broadens the semantic field of an idea and communicates visceral and visual associations that transcend the facts per se. For this reason, metaphorical figures contribute to the breadth and depth of brand meanings when they are used in advertising.

The rhetorical dimension of discourse has important implications for growing brand equity. Rhetoric expands the emotional breadth, depth, and semiotic value of brands and fosters visceral connections between the brand world and consumers. In the next example, I illustrate how metonymical associations between semantic units support and "motivate" even the most far-fetched metaphors by emphasizing the linear connections between these contexts through time and space.

Take for example, the following advertisement for Nike Shox Turbo running shoes. The headline itself—"This is not a running shoe!"—invites us to think beyond the literal meaning of the product and engage with the emotional message of the brand. To emphasize the power of their new Shox running shoe, Nike created a print ad showing a turbo engine with the running shoe in place of the piston (see Figure 1.9)

"This is a super-turbo blast of go-fast under the hood and big breath of Nitrous when you need it. With pure Nike shoe responsive cushioning technology to harness every last bit of horsepower to be ready when you put your foot to the floor. The Nike Shoe Turbo and other tools for better running at nikerunning.com."

Figure 1.9. Brand Rhetoric

The tagline boldly announces that the brand benefits transcend the mundane realm of product benefits and satisfy consumer needs for inspiration and poetry. The piston/shoe substitution is then implicated in a chain of metonymies linking the piston to the engine and also the shoe to the runner. In this way, the brand rhetoric equates the performance of the Shox-shod runner to a turbine-driven engine, reinforced in the text, which compares Shox to "a super-tuned blast of go-fast under the hood." In other words, the shoe drives the runner in the same way that the piston drives the engine. The implication of metonymy in the shoe/piston metaphor supports the poetic "logic" of the rhetorical system (see Figure 1.10).

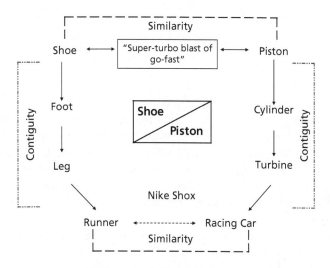

Figure 1.10. The Logic of Metaphor

The piston/shoe metaphor expands the semantic scope of the brand by bridging differences between incongruous semantic contexts—cars and runners—along the lines of the shared meaning of "engineering."[7]

Meaning and Reference in Advertising

Advertisements are not simply icons to be looked at. They are discourses aimed at communicating the brand meaning and engaging the consumer/spectator into the brand world. This discursive dimension of advertising takes us into the realm of yet another binary opposition between the meaning of a statement or representation and reference to the context and subject-address of the message—the "speaker" and "receiver" of the message.

I devote Chapter 4 to a lengthy study of discourse theory. The current, brief discussion serves to illustrate how tensions between the meaning and reference of representations accounts for the cultural nuances communicated in marketing discourses and the engagement of consumers in marketing texts such as advertisements (see Figure 1.11).

In the Nike Shox advertisement mentioned above, the brand plays on the tensions between the meanings communicated in word and image and references to the brand world and the culture of consumers. First of all, Nike appropriated the form and meaning of the dictionary term "shocks" in order

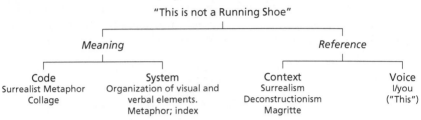

Figure 1.11. Semiosis in Action

to communicate the unique and original experience of the Shox brand running shoe. The brand name also extends the literal meaning of "shocks" mentioned into hyperbolic claims. *Webster's Dictionary* defines "shocks" as "violent shakes or jars" and "sudden stimulations of the nerves and convulsive contraction of the muscles caused by the discharge of electricity through the animal body." In the Nike lexicon, Shox defines "a super-tuned blast of go-fast under the hood."

In addition to referencing the brand meaning, the Nike ad references the Generation X target in word and image. For example, by replacing the conventional spelling of "shocks" with the homophone, Shox, the brand name references the X in extreme sports culture, X men heroes, and extreme adventure.

The tagline itself "This is not a running shoe" directly implicates the consumer/spectator in the visual discourse. Use of the demonstrative pronoun "this" implies the presence of a narrator and receiver of the discourse. Furthermore, the tagline references Magritte's famous Surrealist painting of a smoker's pipe, emblazoned with the assertion, "This is not a pipe" ["Ceci n'est pas une pipe"] (see Figure 1.12).

Like his contemporaries in the Surrealist Movement, Magritte insisted that the object of painting, like the object of semiotics, is the representation itself, not the phenomenal real. In other paintings, Magritte deconstructs the visual world into disparate signifiers that lack an anchor in the phenomenal world. Mirrors, windows, and landscapes reflect back on the act of painting, suggesting that reality falls within the tensions between the image and the creative imagination.

What does Magritte have to do with runners? Judging from the number of blogs, websites, and software created in his name, Magritte is a kind of cult hero for the Gen X generation, who may identify Magritte's humorous, disoriented world with virtual space–time context of the Internet. There is even a website software system named after him. Furthermore, the reference to Surrealism and deconstructionist philosophy may form an inside joke with more elite members of the target market, whose shared cultural capital would be a source of personal identification with the brand.

Figure 1.12. Magritte, "This is not a pipe" (1928)

Applications and Case Study

So far I have reviewed the basics of structural semiotics at the levels of the psychic drives, discursive structures, and rhetorical operations producing meaning in consumer culture. I have analyzed these structures in examples from consumer research and advertising communication. In this section, I show how semiotic theory and analysis can contribute to the strategic function of brand meanings. This level of analysis is where "the rubber hits the road" because it is at this level that marketing semiotics actively contributes to the value of brand meanings in the marketplace.

The design and analysis of the research for this case study highlights the distinctive characteristics of structural semiotic research, at the levels of data collection, analysis, and reporting.

THE SEMIOTICS RESEARCH PROCESS

Data Collection

- Saussure defined the object of linguistic science as "language in all its manifestations, an object of the broadest possible scope." Likewise, the object of semiotics includes all manifestations of meaning production or *semiosis*. First, semiotics does not privilege primary research with consumers because consumer verbatims form only a narrow component of the semiotic context of a category.

- Next, semiotics examines artifacts from popular culture to identify the dominant and emerging codes structuring the meaning of a category, such as the binary analysis of the diaper category in terms of nature vs. culture.

- Furthermore, semiotics does not structure the investigation according to narrow marketing objectives, such as concept testing, but develops hypotheses based on the recurrence of semiotic structures in an extensive data set. This broad approach to data collection leads to the discovery of emergent codes and trends in a culture that can be leveraged for purposes of innovation.

- When primary research with consumers is called for, consumers are interviewed in situ at home or at work. Consumer ethnography provides context and authenticity to consumer speech, attributes that are missing from research conducted at a research facility. I once interviewed a housewife who prided herself on "never buying fast food" and "only preparing fresh meals" for her family. A quick look inside her refrigerator proved otherwise. Leftovers from Burger King and frozen meals from WalMart were the telltale signs that consumers do not always say what they mean or mean what they say.

The Semiotic Analysis

Consumers draw upon cultural myths to negotiate these kinds of tensions between cultural ideals and the demands of day-to-day life. Semiotic analysis stakes out the broad tensions that structure these myths in a product category and identifies ways that a brand can resolve these tensions by means of strategic positioning, new product development, and creative strategy.

Myths structure culture into constituent units (such as morality and gender) and structure these units into binary pairs (such as good and evil, masculinity and femininity) (Lévi-Strauss, [1964] 1969). Because myths structure the collective unconscious, they also structure the meaning of consumer possessions and behaviors in all kinds of marketing texts and rituals from the retail setting to the brand website.

Semiotic analysis identifies the constituent units that structure a category (such as motherhood) and analyzes these elements into binary pairs (such as good mother and bad mother). If messages in the marketplace consistently associate motherhood with the sacred, the analyst infers that its opposite, the profane, is associated with the "bad mother." These kinds of oppositions structure the competitive space of a category and provide guidelines for brand positioning.

BEYOND CONSUMER MYTHOLOGY: POSITIONING BABY DIAPERS

In 2005, a supermarket conglomerate in the United Kingdom decided to market their own brand of disposable diaper, which I will call *Baby's Best*, that would be marketed worldwide in their various retail chains. Management commissioned a semiotic study of the diaper category in order to create a competitive positioning and creative strategy for *Baby's Best* that would compete with the category leader, Pampers. Working with the advertising agency, our team mapped the semiotic dimensions of the diaper category, identified the cultural myths that consumers associate with babies and motherhood, and found a new cultural space for *Baby's Best*.

The data set was limited to cultural artifacts for the category and did not include primary research with consumers. We collected messaging from retail sites, advertising, packaging, and new products related to baby care in general. We examined popular self-help books, magazine articles, and blogs related to parenting, baby care, and motherhood. Researchers visited specialty shops in Chicago and Los Angeles, surfed websites, and examined new products, technologies, and fashion for this segment. Researchers also looked for these codes in popular television programs, movies, and magazines devoted to mothers and babies.

The Good Mother

Consumers obviously purchase diapers to avoid the inevitable mess created by babies who have not yet been toilet trained. What is not obvious is the way that these product benefits are associated with ideological and moral standards in the marketing media. In a manner reminiscent of Lévi-Strauss's raw and cooked dimensions of culinary culture ([1964] 1969), the wet/dry binary in diaper messaging is linked to a series of oppositions including nature/culture, chaos/control, and profane/sacred in the culture of babies.

The diaper category is embedded in an ideological discourse that privileges control and even denial of the bodily functions. The category leader, *Pampers*, epitomizes this positioning. *Pampers* advertising for a ten-year period embeds new product claims in messaging that elevates dryness to the level of godliness. By improving absorption and preventing leakage, the brand not only keeps baby dry but also represents the victory of Culture over Nature. By implication, mothers who use this brand are "Good Mothers." As the guardian of Culture, the "Good Mother" controls the liquids, flows, accidents, and messes associated with Nature. The "Bad Mother," by implication, is out of control.

Furthermore, brand symbolism for the dominant discourse supports this myth by censoring, in the Freudian sense, references to the real toilet functions of baby. Packaging and advertising messages displace the profane meanings associated with the toilet onto representations of mothers and babies insulated from reality in a timeless, luminous radiation. The repetition of these themes in the data set contributes to a kind of Mommy Myth that masks the real struggles of mothers. They satisfy, in the imaginary–symbolic realm, unmet consumer needs to meet the standards society expects of them as the gatekeepers of culture.

The Baby Industry

The Mommy Myth also structures meaning in the broader context of baby culture in North America. News stories and other media from the period revealed a growing gap between the lives of women and the myth of the Good Mother. A 2005 cover story in *Newsweek* said it all: "The Myth of the Perfect Mother: Why It Drives Real Women Crazy" (Warner, 2005*b*). A young mother with an infant in her lap is depicted as an eight-armed wonder juggling the duties of parenting, work, marriage, and housekeeping. The story was based on a popular book on modern motherhood, entitled, *Perfect Madness: Motherhood in the Age of Anxiety* (Warner, 2005*a*). Popular reality shows such as "Nanny 911" and "Super Nanny" fueled mother's insecurities by highlighting the superior talents of the British nanny. Such examples reflect the widespread angst experienced by mothers who strained to live up to the Good Mother ideal.

Although women's lives were out of control, the baby business marketed products that would satisfy, on a symbolic–imaginary level, mothers' need to succeed. The baby business preyed on mothers' insecurities with a dazzling array of new products, technologies, and self-help books. They included designer prams sturdy enough for combat and stylish enough for Beverly Hills, self-feeding contraptions for baby, sound machines to quiet baby, tools for developing genius baby, and baby-carrying slings with poetic brand names such as *Parents of Invention, Hotslings, Maya Sling,* and *Mamma's Milk.* Such brand names masked the real needs for women to have time and space for themselves with emotional appeals that idealized the mother–baby relationship.

Self-help books offered mothers tips for controlling, managing, and silencing their babies "in three easy steps." The titles themselves reflect both the tensions facing mothers and the extremes to which consumers would go to master the mommy game: *Busy but Balanced, Motherhood in the Age of Anxiety, 10 Principles for Spiritual Parenting* (as seen on Oprah), *Secrets of the Baby Whisperer,* and *The Off-Switch.* No one was willing to expose the Mommy Myth for what it was: a collective fantasy that masked the social and cultural tensions associated with motherhood in the postfeminist age.

The Strategic Challenge

Given the prevalence of the Mommy Myth in the culture, it was a dangerous game for marketers to move brands out of the "Good Mother" positioning. They faced the dilemma of competing head-on with *Pampers* with an even "better Mother" image or hovering dangerously at the edge of the opposite pole, the "Bad Mother." Even generic and store brands imitated the *Pampers* positioning in package design, leaving consumers with a bewildering array of identical products at the point of purchase.

The strategic challenge facing *Baby's Best* was to differentiate the brand from the dominant brand without falling to the side of wet babies and the "Bad Mother." In order to create a distinctive positioning for the brand, we chose not to challenge the dominant discourse head on or try to develop an even "Better Mother." We looked instead for a new cultural space that transcended the Good Mother/Bad Mother binary altogether. We began by plotting the constituent units of the dominant discourse on a Semiotic Square, a strategic tool derived from structural semantics that breaks down the binary structures within a category into more complex relationships. By means of this exercise, we deconstructed the dominant discourse into more nuanced interpretations of motherhood and the role of diapers in that interpretation.

The Semiotic Square

Algirdas Greimas ([1966] 1984) developed the Semiotic Square in order to advance structuralism beyond the oversimplicity of binary analysis. The Semiotic Square organizes the constituent elements of a semantic category on a double binary grid, comprised of three relationships: contradiction [S = S1 > S2], contrariness [−S = −S1 > −S2], and implication [−S = S1 > −S2 and −S1 > S2]. This three-dimensional structure accounts for the nuances and ambiguities that fall within the two poles of the paradigm and extends the semantic complexity of the semiotic analysis (see Figure 1.13).

The dialectical opposition of "wet" and "dry" baby frames the dominant semiotic space for the diaper category, as represented by the solid arrows joining the contradictory terms of Wet and Dry [S = s1 and s2] on the inner square. In order to account for the implication of wet and dry diapers in the ideological opposition of Nature and Culture, we projected another square on top of the first one, structured by the contradictory relation of Nature to Culture, represented by a solid arrow [S1a and S2a]. This approach both anchored the physical attributes, Wet and Dry, in the cultural context and increased the number of quadrants in which to position the *Baby's Best* brand.

Pampers and its clones were positioned in the upper-right corner of the grid and associate dryness with order, tidiness, and the "Good Mother." In order to move *Baby's Best* out of the "Good Mother" quadrant and build a unique brand positioning, we deconstructed the contradictory relations structuring the category into secondary and tertiary binaries. We traced secondary relations of contrariness, that is, not Wet and not Dry [−S = −s1 and −s2], associated by dashed arrows. We then traced tertiary relationships of implication, Wet and not Dry [s1 and −s2], and Dry and not Wet [s2 and −s1], using a dashed line.

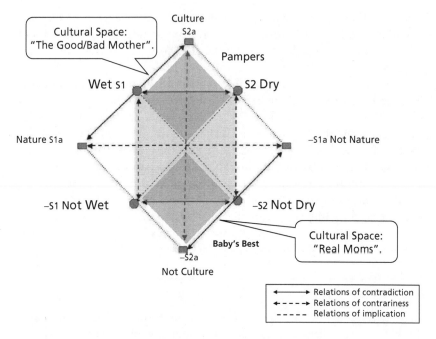

Figure 1.13. The Structure of Myth in the Diaper Category

A New Market Space

This exercise led to the development of a new cultural paradigm for the category based on oppositions between a cultural ideal and the real of motherhood. This paradigm emerged in a two-stage process. First, by breaking down the primary binaries (Wet/Dry, Bad/Good, Nature/Culture) into their contrary terms (i.e., Not Dry, Not Wet, etc.) analysis opened up an alternative to the rigid bifurcation of the category into moral absolutes such as Good and Bad, Nature and Culture. Second, by implicating these contrary units in each other at the lower end of the Semiotic Square, analysis identified a countercultural space in the diaper brandscape that called into question the Mommy Myth and its underlying beliefs and values.

For example, the implication of "Not Wet" in "Not Dry" emphasizes the role of diapers in the real transitions between these two states. In this neutral space, diapers moderate the accidents and uncertainties associated with baby's body, Nature, and mother's busy life—they do not erase them. Furthermore, the implication of "Not-Nature" (−S1a) in "Not-Culture" (−S2a) places in question the assumption that Nature, that is, the messy bodily functions, transcends Culture. In fact, baby's toilet functions are not intrinsically "bad." They are censored from the dominant brand positioning in response to cultural biases in the marketplace.

The countercultural space of diapers also defined a new market space for positioning *Baby's Best* targeted to busy moms, as they negotiate the tensions between society's ideals and the realities of modern motherhood. It also led to the development of a creative strategy derived from contemporary countercultural representations of motherhood. We recommended characters and situations based on popular comedies from the period, such as *Roseanne* and *The Simpsons*. These programs demystified motherhood and gave vent to the frustrations of mothers in the marketplace. These programs used irony to mask a social critique, making light of the dominant ideology without violating the sacred sanctions protecting family, mother, and apple pie in American culture. By drawing upon themes, characters, and situations from the popular counterculture, we provided a context and a style for developing a unique positioning and creative strategy for the *Baby's Best* brand.

In this chapter, I reviewed the various dimensions of symbolic consumption and gave an account of theories from the social sciences that account for the meaning of goods, brands, and communication in the marketplace. In the following chapters, I draw upon this information to investigate in more detail the contributions of marketing semiotics to the science and practice of consumer research and brand strategy.

■ ENDNOTES

1. Sid Levy mainstreamed this idea in a 1959 article in *Harvard Business Review*, "Symbols for Sale."

2. Aaker (1991) and Keller (2007) agree that brand associations directly influence consumer loyalty, brand distinction, and value—the primary components of brand equity.

3. Sid Levy (1981) introduced Lévi-Strauss's analysis of myth to marketing research.

4. Lévi-Strauss ([1958] 1974: 31–2) cites his debt to the structural linguist Troubetskoy for these findings.

5. For more on distinctive features, see Jakobson et al. ([1956] 1990).

6. Lotman (2000) defines rhetoric as a "mechanism for meaning generation." See also Jakobson (1956), Genette ([1972] 1982), and Metz ([1977] 1981).

7. Scott's analysis (1994) of advertising metaphors emphasizes formal structures associating one term for another in advertising imagery but does not discuss underlying discursive structures that link two semantic universes.

2 Marketing Semiotics

"What's wrong with this picture?"

As I said in Chapter 1, brands consist of meanings, not just the "stuff" that consumers use. As a result, brand value is not merely *enhanced* by the meanings consumers associate with brand name, the product, the logo, and other brand assets (Aaker, 1995; Keller, 1993; Kapferer, 2003). It is a *function* of those meanings, and contributes to the brand's "semiotic value." This is why companies such as the Interbrand Group measure brand equity by means of surveys that gauge the breadth, depth, and durability of meanings consumers associate with brands in the marketplace, not just the number of products sold or the number of clicks on a Web site. In this chapter, I introduce the basics of structural semiotics, and demonstrate how the marketing semiotics method can be applied to a business problem related to the identity and positioning of a new luxury perfume. I begin analysis with the advertising campaign, the very tip of the iceberg of the brand system. I begin with a statement of the problem, I move on to an overview of semiotic concepts, and then bring theory to bear on solving the business case.

Semiotics and Brand Equity

A brand is a sign system that engages the consumer in an imaginary/symbolic process of need-fulfillment, differentiates the brand from competitors, and adds measurable value to a product offering. This understanding of brands derives from the general theory of symbolic consumption, which emphasizes the role of goods to communicate social and emotional benefits that satisfy consumer needs, such as the needs for status, self-image, and love (see Douglas and Isherwood, [1979] 1996; McCracken, 1991). Added value can take the form of a vicarious experience, a symbolic relationship, or some other emotional benefit.

THE BUSINESS PROBLEM

The American fashion house, Halston, developed a new luxury perfume in the early 1990s aimed at reviving the brand. To protect company information I will call the perfume, "Woman." The company had created a new scent, innovative package design, and an advertising campaign featuring Cindy Crawford, the super model. Marketing Semiotics became involved when the advertising agency discovered that the new ad campaign for "Woman" failed in audience testing. A likeness of the campaign is shown in Figure 2.1.

Although the combination of the Halston brand name, new product innovation, and Cindy Crawford seemed like a formula for success, the campaign communicated ambiguity about the kind of woman that would use the brand, suggesting that the brand positioning itself was unclear. As a result, the new advertising campaign failed in prelaunch testing. On the front side of the page, the model is represented as a "Universal Goddess," a nude figure against a timeless background photographed in black and white. On the reverse side of the page, the model is represented as "the Girl Next Door," a casually dressed figure in living color, seen with her husband in a lived environment. Contrasting visual codes in the image, such as lighting, color scheme, camera position, and perspective, reinforce these conflicting cultural interpretations of the feminine.

Ambiguity at the level of brand communication usually signals deeper, strategic problems with a brand. Ambiguity or inconsistency in the message over time undermines the integrity of the brand, fosters distrust, and even threatens it with extinction (Aaker et al., 2004). The "Woman" campaign failed in testing because it unwittingly communicated ambiguity and inconsistency about the values and beliefs of the company, the culture of the target market, and the overall brand positioning and message.

Figure 2.1. A Likeness of the Two-Page Perfume Ad for Halston

A marketing semiotics approach to this case both diagnosed the communication problem in the campaign and also provided strategic direction for repositioning the brand and developing a unique and coherent brand message.

A SEMIOTIC STRATEGY

Brands sometimes fail to touch the hearts and minds of consumers because their internal structure is inconsistent or their message lacks relevance for the target segment. In the case of "Woman" perfume, the brand positioning communicated on the front side of an ad was contradicted by the positioning communicated on the reverse side. For other brands, the message communicated in print advertising may be contradicted by communication at the point of purchase, or brand messages are out of sync with the external culture of their target market. In brief, using a celebrity or a creative advertising campaign cannot remedy faulty positioning strategy.

To align the brand with the category and the culture of consumers, semiotics research belongs upstream in the strategic planning process. For consumers to incorporate brand meanings into their lifestyles and emotional worlds, the brand message must reflect a deep and nuanced understanding of the multiple cultural categories in which the brand is embedded, from the brand legacy, to consumer culture, to the popular culture. Iconic brands such as Nike, for example, succeed because of management's consistent efforts to calibrate brand strategy to the evolving needs and aspirations of athletes at all levels of participation. The challenge and purpose of advertising, then, is to integrate all communication vehicles around this positioning and these consumer needs and wants.

Semiotics has traditionally been relegated to downstream processes such as advertising execution, package design, and naming (Sherry and Camargo, 1987; McQuarrie and Mick, 1992; Scott, 1994a, 1994b; Beasley and Danesi, 2002; Aaker, 2007). A frequently overlooked function of semiotic research is the ability to develop coherent brand strategy. When executed upstream, semiotics research can integrate consumer insights, brand legacy, and cultural creativity into a platform from which other marketing functions spring, such as product development, pricing strategy, retailing, and advertising strategy.

By managing brand semiotics at all stages in the development, execution, and communication of the brand, marketers create a code system that structures the consistent and enduring association of the brand with specific icons, language, and symbols in consumers' minds. The marketing function thus serves to create a unique brand "language" that speaks for the brand over its lifetime.

Semiotics can be incorporated into the planning process at the stages of research, analysis, and advertising communication. They include:

- Decoding the consumer culture of the target market;
- Plotting the semiotic dimensions of the category on a strategic grid;
- Positioning the brand on that grid;
- Identifying emergent cultural codes and trends; and
- Aligning creative strategy with these emergent codes.

The Structural Semiotics Paradigm

In the words of Umberto Eco, the Italian semiotician, semiotics is a social science discipline that takes into account "everything that can be taken as a sign" (Eco, 1979: 7). A related term, semiosis, defines the process of meaning production. A sign, simply stated, is something that stands for something else, and semiosis is the cognitive activity that underlies communication activities, whether verbal or nonverbal. As Eco (1979: 66) claims, signs not only mirror culture but they are "units of culture," and their meaning and structure are entirely regulated by cultural convention.

Although grounded in the study of language, semiotic analysis is a trans-linguistic activity (Barthes, 1964: 11) that accounts for the systematic organization of culture and society by means of structural codes. It is a multidisciplinary field of inquiry that engages with culture, consumption, and communication in the marketplace. It would be easy to confuse semiotics with textual analysis or rhetoric. While it is true that semiotics provides tools for analyzing the formal functions of verbal and visual texts, semiotics is essentially a social science and builds upon the formal analysis to understand human behavior. Semiotics seeks to understand how the codes structuring meaning production in sign systems— from ritual behavior to social organization, from shopping to advertising— influence the ways humans respond to messages in their environments. Take the traffic sign system, for instance. The meaning of the stop sign is codified by means of a set of universally accepted symbols, including a red octagonal sign, inscribed with the white letters S T O P. If the semiotician were to limit analysis to only the formal aspects of signs, they would fail to account for the most important function of the traffic sign system, that is, to regulate how drivers interact with other drivers on the road.

THE STRUCTURAL SYSTEM

The structural orientation of semiotics discussed in this book is rooted in structural linguistics, founded by the Swiss linguist, Ferdinand de Saussure ([1916] 2000) in the nineteenth century. Saussure revolutionized the study of language by isolating the formal codes, "la langue," that are responsible for meaning production in language use, "speech." These codes define the timeless structural system of language—its synchronic dimension—that transcends evolutionary change, its diachronic dimension. The formal characteristics of language resemble the rules of chess, the monetary system, or the rules of etiquette. These code systems dictate the conventions for play, value creation, and social behavior, and have the potential to generate an infinite number of games, transactions, and social interactions bound by formal conventions.

Unlike his counterpart in the United States, C. S. Peirce ([1884] 1955), Saussure emphasized the dialectical nature of the sign as the codified association of a material *signifier*, such as the sounds in a word, with a *signified* or concept, as exemplified in the Figure 2.2. (For further discussion on Saussure and Peirce, see Mick and Oswald, 2006.)

From the binary structure of the sign into material signifier and signified, to the articulation of discourse into narrative voice and consumer response, structural semiotics interprets the world as a system of tensions and relation ships, rather than a fixed and static lexicon of meanings. By exposing the dual structure of the sign, Saussure highlighted the arbitrary nature of the relation between signifier and signified—there is nothing intrinsically "car-like" in the sounds /car/. Nor are these associations subject to the whims of individual speakers; they are regulated by cultural convention. Such codes regulate meaning in all kinds of sign systems from the syntax of language to the laws of visual perspective. It is precisely this, the conventional nature of the Saussurian sign, that embeds structural semiotics in the culture of consumers and frames the study of signs within the disciplines of sociology, psychology, and anthropology.

A SEMIOTICS OF CONSUMPTION

As discussed in Chapter 1, the symbolic function of goods transforms ordinary things into signifiers for abstract concepts such as status and group affiliation (Douglas and Isherwood (1979). Goods then become nonverbal sign systems. The symbolic function of goods is moderated by cultural codes and conventions. For example, the diamond ring does not signify commitment to wed in all cultures. When the De Beers Company entered the Chinese mainland market, diamond rings did not figure in the wedding plans; after several years and many ad campaigns later, the engagement ring is now

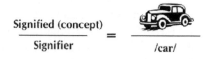

Figure 2.2. The Dual Structure of Signs

entering into the popular culture. When symbolic associations become entrenched in culture by means of habit or convention, they form codes that regulate behavior, perception, and social organization in cultural contexts.

For instance, cultural codes determine social hierarchies and relations of power in a group. Compare the social organization of a boardroom in Japan with one in the United States, for instance, and one finds distinct codes for marking the social dynamic of the organization. In Japan, the power structure is hierarchical; in the United States, it is more lateral. In recent years, Americans have even eliminated the corner office, a traditional symbol of the corporate hierarchy. To understand the impact of gender on consumer behavior, the semiotician identifies the codes for gender identity in a culture and examines how these codes govern the behavior of men and women, including the ways they dress, the professions they enter, their functions in the household, and their behavior with members of the opposite sex.

Marketing Semiotics

This chapter focuses on the way semiotic codes structure marketing discourse and influence consumer perceptions and behaviors. Marketing semiotics draws upon analytical tools and theories from academic disciplines such as the social sciences, art history, and film theory. Academics and marketing semioticians alike seek themes, structures, and rhetorical operations that create imaginary worlds in word and image. However, marketing semiotics differs from the academic discourse in very important ways. The academic is concerned with theory building, hypothesis testing, and the cultural critique as ends in themselves. The marketing semiotician, on the other hand, uses theory, method, and the cultural critique to align brands with the culture of consumers and inject creativity into strategic brand management.

THE FIELD OF SEMIOTICS

At the most superficial level, semiotics is a hermeneutic practice that seeks to uncover the formal codes structuring meaning. However, unlike rhetorical or content analysis, semiotic analysis embeds the interpretive process in the cultural context of the message. Semiotic analysis focuses less on the meaning of individual texts than on the recurring binary structures underlying meaning production in a group of texts. Semiotics can thus unveil the paradigmatic dimensions of a product category and map the strategic relationships among competitors within the category. For example, a binary relationship between the cultural categories of Man and Machine structures brand meaning in the personal computer category. Semiotic analysis can then identify distinctions among brands in the competitive set, based on the various interpretations of the Man/Machine relationship, such as intimate, distant, or complex.

Furthermore, semiotics is a social science discipline (Eco, 1979), inasmuch as it defines an independent field of study, can be used to generate hypotheses, carries a unique toolbox of methods for analysis, and can be repeated in multiple settings by multiple stakeholders, from medical researchers to zoologists (Sebeok, 1972). Unlike communication science or rhetorical analysis, semiotics provides a systematic way of extracting the general codes of a signifying system from the meanings of any single text. Semiotic analysis begins with a data set, such as a group of ads for the brand and the competitive set, or a set of consumer interviews and observations, and identifies the underlying system of codes that structure meaning for the brand, the category, and the target market. This system of codes acts like a kind of grammar that marketers can then use to manage brand extensions or reposition the current brand. In this way, structural semiotics organizes the world of noise and chaos into systems of relationships characterized by distinction and difference.

This approach has important implications for brand strategy research because the distinction and difference of brands within a competitive arena stand at the foundation of strategic brand management. Brands have value for consumers to the exact degree that they communicate a clear, distinctive, and relevant system of core brand meanings and relationships that can be repeated, extended, and communicated consistently over time, across a range of discourses from advertising to the corporate annual report.

THE BRAND SYSTEM

Although semiotics is concerned with the structure of meaning, it does not stop with a structural analysis, but identifies ways brand meanings are embedded in the broad cultural myths, social organization, and beliefs of the target market. The brand system resembles *la langue*, the term that Saussure (op. cit.) gives to the system of linguistic codes that defines the range of possibilities for producing discourses but is not reduced to *la parole*, the message itself.

Semiotic analysis aligns the brand meaning and positioning with consumers' personal, social, and cultural needs and expectations. As an example, let us suppose Volkswagen realized that the "cute car" is no longer as relevant as the "green car" in the current environmentally conscious culture, but did not want to lose the equity they have in the Beetle. If management could discover mutually compatible codes structuring both the meaning of "cute car" and "green" in the automotive category, they could incorporate "green" meanings into the current brand positioning without sacrificing the core brand message and equity of the Beetle.

To summarize, brands are multidimensional sign systems that can be analyzed in terms of their material, conventional, contextual, and performative structures. In order to be owned, perceived, or available for analysis at all, sign systems must be available to the senses and so have a material dimension. Next, in order to be understood, sign systems must be codified by conventions that all the members of a group share. Next, sign systems form social discourses whose meaning is modified by the communication context. And finally, sign systems are performative inasmuch as they engage two or more interlocutors (the speaker and receiver; the marketer and consumer) in a communication event. All of these dimensions are at play in brand discourse, where they contribute to brand recognition, emotional associations, cultural relevance, and the relationship to consumers (Table 2.1).

Table 2.1. The Semiotic Dimensions of Brands

Material	Conventional	Contextual	Performative
Words, images, spaces, forms	Codified by tradition or rules	Cultural nuances	Intersubjectivity reference
Logo, package, ads, etc.			

The Material Dimension

The material, intelligible dimension of marketing signs includes signifiers such as logos, brand names, jingles, trademarks, and taglines. It includes anything that stands for the brand in the marketplace. The material dimension also includes subunits of meaning, such as the unique colors, forms, styles, and fonts associated with the brand. The McDonald's logo shown in Figure 2.3 references the brand through a variety of formal elements: the trademark golden arches and brand name, the unique font used in the text, and the red background. The material dimension of marketing signs defines what the company owns when it files for a trademark—it is one of the company's intangible assets. The company's proprietary brand assets can be described, repeated in many formats, and extended or leveraged to accommodate new contexts, segments, and strategies over time (Mick and Oswald, 2007).

The Conventional Dimension

Brand communication is an entirely social phenomenon. As a sign system for communicating the brand's positioning and promise, brand communication is structured by means of social conventions or codes shared by consumers in a market. Codes structure the relationship between a brand signifier and the brand and structure the product category in terms of binary distinctions. Binary codes articulate the phenomenal world into distinct units of meaning. For example, the concept of "darkness" is meaningful only in relation to its opposite, "light." The binary structure of communication enables humans to differentiate units of meaning from each other and to create logical classifications for sorting and combining these units in discourses.

Brand Codes. The binary structure of the linguistic sign is instructive for accounting for the ways marketing signs link a material signifier, such as a logo, to a set of associations in the consumer's mind. Just as the sounds for the word car, /car/, signify the concept of a car, so brand signifiers such as the golden arches, signify the concept of McDonald's. The logo/brand relationship is codified by tradition and protected by trademark ownership. To the extent that the brand signifier/signified relationship has become universally codified within a market, brand awareness, loyalty, and perception of quality increase, since consumers will consistently think of the brand when they are exposed to its signifiers, such as the logo.

Advertising plays a key role in creating and sustaining the association of a marketing signifier and signified over time. Advertising also regulates the organization of brands in social space, where they influence behavior and experience. A McDonald's sign viewed from the highway may welcome the traveler who is far from home and seeks a familiar and predictable dining experience.

Thus, while the brand logo stands for the company in a literal sense, the logo is a sign for the broader world of cultural codes, rituals, and consumer experiences associated with the brand (Figure 2.3).

Brand Logos as Signs

Signified (concept)	McDonald's
Signifier	Golden Arches Logo

Figure 2.3. Logos as Signs

Category Codes. Codes structure consumer expectations about product and retail categories. They influence consumer perceptions of brands and guide their purchase decisions. For example, because of repeated shopping experiences, shoppers can quickly discern healthy from unhealthy snacks, without looking at the ingredients, by identifying the semiotic cues in the packaging. Packaging communicates "healthy" by means of the material, the color scheme, and the design of the package. A cursory look through the snack food aisle shows that unhealthy snacks, such as potato chips using chemicals such as non-fat olestra, are packaged in loud colored aluminum bags; products that claim to be healthy, such as Pepperidge Farm crackers, are packaged in muted tones in paper bags. Other design dimensions such as packaging shape, font, and imagery reinforce these meanings. The binary association of healthy with paper and muted tones, and unhealthy with foil and bright tones, references a code system that consumers understand through repeated experiences with a product category. Shoppers "read" these kinds of distinctions as they walk down the grocery store aisle as clearly and intuitively as they read traffic signs.

Category codes also determine the shopper's navigation of retail space. Category-specific merchandising codes regulate design elements such as the traffic flow, the disposition of furnishings, the placement of the cashier, and product displays. These codes manage consumer expectations of retail settings so that consumers do not have to learn an entirely new store layout every time they shop at a different location. These codes also influence consumer perceptions of the retail space and guide them through the shopping experience.

Cultural Codes. Cultural codes also contribute to consumers' interpretation and experience of marketing communication. For example, the codes structuring the illusion of linear perspective in the retail setting derive from artistic traditions handed down since the Quattrocento School in Italy. They structure the branded retail experience and influence the degree of comfort, understanding, and pleasure consumers experience with the brand as they navigate the retail space. At theme parks, such as Disney World in Orlando, Florida, visual cues—from markings on the pavement to signage and the strategic placement of the live Disney characters—guide visitors imperceptibly through the park in a kind of staged performance (Oswald, 1989).

Counterfeit Codes. Unfortunately, the universality and power of iconic brand symbols, such as the Burberry plaid, also make iconic brands more susceptible to counterfeit. In the 1990s, Burberry sold licenses to reproduce the famous check pattern to manufacturers all over the world, and the plaid was duplicated on cheap merchandise, available to anyone (Moon et al., 2003). Counterfeiters trying to cash in on the Burberry brand equity could easily copy the plaid pattern. Since luxury brand value depends on the rarity and exclusivity of the brand name and logo, the cheapening and proliferation of the Burberry plaid lost equity, and by the late 1990s the brand was on the verge of extinction.

To confront this problem, Burberry bought back many of the licenses and repositioned the brand. Even more recently, a radical move to transcend the plaid altogether has led the brand in new, exciting designs, textures, and nuances associated with the hip London youth culture. In other words, to gain authenticity, management had to reinvent a sign system for the brand that captured the spirit and essence of the brand while replacing the plaid icon with new signifiers for the brand. The counterfeit problem seems to have sparked innovation at Burberry, where bold new designs and countercultural styles carry forward the British brand legacy in visual cues that are more difficult to copy than the plaid.

The Contextual Dimension

Marketing signs are context-sensitive, so the precise meanings consumers attach to marketing signs is apt to change from one market to the next. They are perceived through the filter of the social and cultural codes that shape meaning in the consumer's world, such as status markers and gender identity. Alternatively, marketing signs may become incorporated into the culture itself over time, as with the generic association of the Kleenex name with the paper handkerchief category or the association of a personal philosophy with the Nike tagline, "Just Do It."

Brand signifiers participate in a much more complex semiotic system linking brand symbolism to cultural codes structuring meaning production in a given market. They include language and the meanings attached to color schemes, shapes, and symbols. This truth is particularly relevant for marketing Western brands in emerging markets. In the same way that linguistic codes determine the meaning of Chinese texts for speakers of Chinese, so do Chinese cultural codes contribute to the way Chinese consumers "read" meanings of nonverbal messages in advertising, such as logos and pictures. Conflicts between local cultural codes and global advertising can create negative brand perceptions and even political resistance. This explains why Nike's 2004 ad, "Chamber of Fear," drew fire in China from the SARFT (State Administration of Radio, Film and Television). The ad depicted a US basketball player, LeBron James, defeating cartoon characters of a kung fu fighter, two women in traditional costume, and a pair of Chinese dragons (BBC, 2004). Since *kung fu* is a spiritual practice and martial art, not an instrument of violence, this ad contributed to misunderstanding and cultural conflict indeed.

Denotation and Connotation. The cultural interpretation of marketing signs belongs to the *connotative* function of sign systems, in contrast to the *denotative* function. The *denotative* function of discourse resembles the dictionary meaning of a word—it simply indicates the concept as a matter of fact. When drivers on the highway see the golden arches from a distance, they infer that there is a McDonald's restaurant nearby. At this level of analysis, the logo is a simple identifying function. It distinguishes one brand from another at the point of purchase, for instance.

However, the *connotative* function of discourse endows signs with nuances and shades of meaning that people associate with the brand or any of the brand signifiers and is highly dependent on the context of the message. Connotations may be culturally based, such as the interpretation of symbols and colors. Connotations may also be highly personal. For instance, some people will see the McDonald's icon and think "clean, predictable place to eat" and others may think "cheap, fattening food."

The Performative Dimension

The performative function of discourse refers to the ways interlocutors use semiotic codes to communicate with each other. The performative function involves two kinds of semiotic operation: subject address and reference. I use the word "interlocutors" in place of "speakers" or "individuals" because the participants in a communication event could include any number of agents involved in meaning exchange, such as a spectator and the transparent narrator of a film or advertisement, anonymous participants in a blog event, or the Internet shopper interacting with an automated system. The time and space of the communication event—its context—contributes to the specific meaning, nuances, and intentions understood by the interlocutors. For instance, the irony of a statement such as, "What a great deal!" would only be apparent if the interlocutors recognized that the sale price was actually too high.

Subject Address. As a form of discourse, sign systems communicate something for someone. In this sense, discourse involves the operation of subject address. "Voice" is the symbolic marker for tracing subject address in discourse. Pronouns such as "I" and "you" are some of the many ways "voice" is traced in verbal communication (Benveniste, [1966] 1971). A different set of codes traces voice in nonverbal discourses, such as photography and film. Voice is a kind of virtual narrator that can be traced in rhetorical devices, camera angles, perspective, and the looks of characters, if any, in the image (see Stam et al., 1992: 117).

Meaning and Reference. Marketing signs, such as the logo, resemble linguistic signs by linking a material signifier to an abstract concept. Furthermore, marketing signs are amplified and nuanced when they are framed within contexts. For example, in a limited sense, the McDonald's logo stands for the brand in the marketplace. It also evokes the brand mythology and the broader popular culture in which the brand communicates to consumers. While McDonald's spells "American" in global consumer culture, the precise interpretation of this meaning changes over time and from one market to the next. A brand like McDonald's might mean indulgence in the developing world, though it communicates inexpensive meals in the United States. The logo is also linked to a range of other marketing elements from advertising and retail design to online programs and corporate sponsorships.

THE STRUCTURE OF BRAND DISCOURSE

Although individual signs, taken on their own, have meanings, as in the association of /car/ = car, they do not operate on their own. It is by virtue of their relationship to other signs and their organization into discourses, such as a sentence, a film sequence, or an advertisement, that signs take on their precise meaning and serve the larger communication function. Structuralists such as Roman Jakobson (1956) contend that two fundamental semiotic operations in the mind—substitution and alignment—account for the ways signs are organized into discourses, regardless of the medium.

Paradigm and Syntagm

Substitution and alignment structure the organization of semiotic units into discourses and structure the relationship between two semiotic units in rhetorical figures. Substitution structures the organization of signs into paradigmatic sets; alignment structures the alignment of signs in a syntagmatic set. The operations of substitution and alignment are critical to human communication because they enable humans to form infinite combinations of signs in order to express themselves. I will begin with a discussion of discourse.

Alignment. The syntagmatic axis of a representation does not have to be linear, as in language. The syntagmatic axis includes any configuration of contiguous terms in a text. The text could be a logo, an advertisement, a retail environment, or an Internet event. This alignment, while not dictated by universal rules of syntax (subject, verb, object), is codified within the brand system. Take the McDonald's logo as an example. The alignment of the golden arches, the McDonald's brand name, and the color red is anything but arbitrary. This particular arrangement of color and line stands for the brand in an infinite number of contexts because it is invariable or codified. Furthermore, this arrangement has become embedded in the broader culture as a sign for the McDonald's brand.

Another example would be the arrangement of product categories in a department store. Knowing how very little time men traditionally spend shopping as compared to women, retailers place the men's section on the first floor with easy access to the front door, and the women's section on the second floor and above. These arrangements have come to be expected—they have been codified by habit.

Substitution. The axis of substitution includes the virtual set of all possible variations on the elements of a sign system. This mental operation accounts for the human capacity to replace one sign for another, more appropriate sign, that is, using the word "bet" instead of "pet," to describe a casino operation. Alignment structures the consumer's ability to string signs together on the syntagmatic axis, in a statement such as, "I bet three dollars." The act of substitution draws upon terms that belong to a paradigmatic set, such as all the words in English that sound like "bet," or the set of all deciduous trees in North America.

Cultural norms and socially constructed expectations set the limit of possible substitutions for elements of a sign system. The McDonald's logo, like most logos, has been modified to meet the demands of modernization and globalization. The semiotic structure of McDonald's logo consists of a stable set of elements that identify the company throughout the world, including the golden arches, white lettering, and bright red background. Over time, the brand identity has become so strong that consumers think "McDonald's," whether all of these signifiers are present or not. As with other iconic brands, the key figure of the golden arches comes to stand for the brand on its own. Although the red background may give way to a white background or the McDonald's name may be translated into a local language, the golden arches remain an unchanging characteristic of the McDonald's brand, the *sine qua non* of the McDonald's identity throughout the world (see Figure 2.4).

Figure 2.4. Brands in Translation

The intersection of alignment and substitution governs the way other marketing elements are structured in a company, such as their core competencies or products. The grid in Figure 2.5 demonstrates the range of products that can be associated with the Starbucks' experience. This kind of analysis can be very useful in developing brand extensions and new markets that are consistent with the brand's core competencies.

Figure 2.5. Alignment and Substitution

The rules of alignment and substitution also structure relationships of inclusion and exclusion between a category and other categories, and between brand and other brands within a product category, as illustrated in Figure 2.6. First of all, the category is itself defined with reference to other categories in a hierarchical order. Take the beverage category, for example. As I show in Figure 2.6, the beverage category can be subdivided into alcoholic and nonalcoholic beverages. The nonalcoholic beverage category can then be subdivided into carbonated and noncarbonated, or hot and cold beverages, and so on. Within any of these subcategories, competitive brands can be positioned in binary opposition to each other in order to test for their distinctiveness from each other.

Coke and Pepsi, for example, can be classified into the broad category of soft drinks, which is differentiated from other categories of beverages in terms of binary oppositions such as carbonated/still, cold/hot, sweet/dry. Coke and Pepsi also form a binary opposition between two positioning strategies, identities, aesthetic styles, and target segments. A binary analysis might include oppositions such as traditional/trendy, mature/young, classic/changing, red/blue, and so on.

The binary organization of sign systems is a key concept for organizing products into meaningful categories, mapping a product category in terms of product benefits and associations, and differentiating brands in the competitive set in terms of intangible benefits such as personality, lifestyle, aesthetics, and symbolic relationship. Although this type of analysis could be extended into much more detailed analysis and complex relationships, this grid illustrates a method of analyzing the semiotic structures that contribute to the intelligibility of brands within a product category and differentiate brands from other brands.

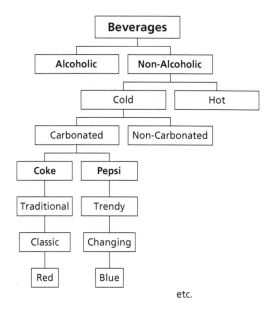

Figure 2.6. The Binary Structure of the Beverage Category

Brand Rhetoric

As stated in Chapter 1, Jakobson extends the binary structure of discourse to the realm of rhetoric, claiming that the substitution of one term for another, based on either similarity or contiguity, forms the basis of rhetorical discourse. Roman Jakobson (1956) linked rhetoric to innate cognitive processes that enable people to interpret and organize their worlds and communicate with others. Unlike the paradigmatic and syntagmatic axes of discourse, which are structured by codes, rhetorical figures play with the codes structuring the literal meaning of things and trace the speaker's or narrator's point of view in discourse. They contribute to brand discourse by interpreting and organizing the meaning of an experience into a brand world.

In typical Structuralist fashion, Jakobson reduced the dozens of rhetorical figures in Aristotle's *Rhetoric* (1984) to two broad, inclusive operations: metaphor and metonymy. Metaphors are formed by substituting one term for another based on their similarity, e.g., car > "my baby." Metonymies are formed by substituting one term for another based on their contiguity, e.g., smoke > fire.

Metaphor. Metaphorical figures are based on the replacement of one term for another, similar term. Metaphors expand the semantic field of a statement by linking apparently incompatible cultural categories, such as cars and people, in a single figure. For instance, when a consumer says of their car, "It's my baby," they evoke the rich emotional relationship between a parent and a baby in order to amplify the description of their relationship to their vehicle. In their Shox running shoe ad (Figure 1.9), Nike creates a visual metaphor between Shox and a turbo engine. The advertiser placed a Nike running shoe in place of the piston in a turbo engine to create a comparison between the engine and the runner, a comparison facilitated by the Nike shoe. I discuss the Nike ad in detail in Chapter 1.

Metonymy. Metonymy substitutes one term for another on the basis of their contiguity. For example, in the statement, "Dark sails broke the horizon," the speaker references the advancing enemy by means of a fragment of the whole idea—the sails on the enemy's ships. Metonymy creates suspense by suggesting an action that the reader or spectator must fill in for him or herself. It is a powerful figurative device in advertising and cinema because it engages the spectator actively in the construction of the story.

The cinematic style of Alfred Hitchcock emphasizes metonymy as a way of suggesting something happening off-screen by showing only a part, such as a bleeding hand, or a close-up on a screaming face. To build suspense, Hitchcock would show just enough of the murder scene to make the spectator imagine the worst—perhaps a dead body belonging to the bleeding hand or a crime scene being viewed by the screaming face.

In the Nike Shox advertisement, metonymy creates the logical links between the piston and the engine, on the one hand, and the shoe and the runner, on the other, which motivate the metaphorical leap joining the engine and the runner in a very creative use of visual metaphor.

The Brand Persona

Jakobson also claimed that individuals and even social groups are innately predisposed to interpret the world either metaphorically or metonymically. He discovered this phenomenon by studying the free associations of aphasics, people who have lost speech functions. He also discovered that favoring either association by similarity (metaphor) or association by contiguity (metonymy) contributed to the unique poetic style of authors. Shakespeare interprets the world metaphorically, while twentieth-century author Ernest Hemingway views the world metonymically.

Metaphor may enrich the creative dimension of a brand that promises self-indulgence, escape, or fantasy, such as a luxury perfume. Metonymy might more accurately represent a brand positioned to deliver rational benefits, such as medical or financial services, where the message connects a cause to an effect.

Furthermore, just as the rhetorical style of an author contributes to the narrative persona of a novel, so the rhetorical style of a brand discourse contributes to the brand persona. Some brands incline more toward the linear and rational style of metonymy, others toward the polyvalent and emotional style of metaphor. They "speak" to the brand philosophy, personality, and relationship to consumers, in the same way that they communicate the personality and point of view of the narrator in a novel. The brand's rhetorical style is sacrosanct. Just as Melville would not suddenly change the personal style of Ishmael narrating *Moby Dick*, so IBM cannot suddenly communicate in colorful metaphors without compromising the identity and persona of the IBM brand itself. A close look at the cultural paradigm associated with the IBM brand, structured by the relationship of man, illustrates this point.

Man and Machine: Positioning the Personal Computer

The binary relationship of Man and Machine consistently structured the representation of technology for consumers in advertising for the personal computer category in the late 1990s. In comparing brand communication for IBM and Apple over a five-year period from 1995 to 2000, two contrasting positioning strategies emerge—high tech and user-friendly. These brand positions are traced in advertisements in nonverbal markers such as camera angle, subject-address, color tones, and mood.

IBM focuses on high-tech expertise and professionalism. This positioning is expressed in a serious and distant relationship between Man and Machine; the use of white, gray, and blue instead of a full spectrum of colors; and medium shot camera angles that keep the spectator at a distance from the computer as an observer.

Apple, on the other hand, uses a full spectrum of colors; communicates a friendly, accessible personality that is accessible to the average consumer; and uses close-up camera angles, which place the consumer close to the computer. Such visual cues communicate a user-friendly brand personality and an intimate relationship between Man and Machine.

Brand Mythology

Over time, the logo signifies more than the company itself and stands for the broader cultural myth consumers associate with the brand, especially iconic, universally recognized brands. Take for example the association of Coca-Cola with truth and reality, that is, "The Real Thing." Iconic brands are so powerful that the logo might dispense with the company name altogether and stand for the brand by means of a famous logotype. Nike, for example, no longer needs to use the Nike name, because the swoosh symbol communicates the brand mythology on its own.

Brand mythology draws upon all of the semiotic structures, operations, and figurative dimensions examined in this chapter. Brand myths communicate a larger than life story about consumers that mitigates, in symbolic terms, social tensions and cultural paradoxes that cannot be settled by society or individuals in everyday life. For example, the Nike brand resolves, in consumer's imaginary, the tension they experience between their dreams of physical achievement and their sedentary office jobs, inspiring them to "Just do it," if only on weekends.

Case Study: What is Woman?

I began this chapter with an overview of an advertising campaign that misfired. Although the new "Woman" campaign seemed to have all the ingredients for a successful product launch—a new scent, innovative packaging, and the popular supermodel Cindy Crawford, the campaign failed in prelaunch testing with consumers. As noted previously, ambiguities in the representation of women in the new ad campaign signaled deeper uncertainties in the strategic positioning of the brand and the role of the new perfume in the lives of the target market.

In this section, I demonstrate how semiotic analysis was used to diagnose the problem and develop a new positioning and creative strategy for the brand. I deliberately chose a case that did not involve extensive secondary research or qualitative research with consumers in order to present the basics of this analytical process. This study involved:

- A brand audit of advertising for the category;
- A binary analysis of the dominant cultural myths represented in the advertising;
- A strategic positioning grid mapping research findings;
- Creation of a unique, innovative positioning for the brand; and
- Recommendations for creative strategy.

THE BRAND AUDIT

Advertising is a window onto the soul of the brand, so an audit of competitive advertising is usually a quick and easy way to diagnose strategic problems. Furthermore, I came to the project at the point of advertising testing, so I began with the advertising and worked back toward an understanding of the unmet needs of consumers that the brand could resolve.

Methodologies

This stage of research began with the collection of over 100 print advertisements for women's colognes and perfumes. Magazines ranged from high fashion, such as *Vogue, Elle,* and *Marie Claire,* to women's specialty magazines, such as *Cosmopolitan* and *Glamour.* To make the data set more manageable, I first sorted the ads in terms of their inclusion or exclusion in the luxury perfume category. By omitting mass brands such as Revlon, Max Factor, and Cover Girl, I reduced the original stack of ads down to the manageable size of thirty ads for brands including Calvin Klein, Chanel, Clarins, Clinique, Dior, Elizabeth Arden, Estée Lauder, Lancôme, Paloma Picasso, Ralph Lauren, and Yves St. Laurent.

Next, I distinguished oppositions between the luxury and mass categories of perfume brands in terms of price points and distribution. The luxury brands are sold only at high-end department stores or boutiques, and their prices are three to four times higher than mass brands of perfumes and cosmetics. Furthermore, the luxury brand advertisements steer clear of sales promotions, new product announcements, or sponsored endorsements that reflect upon the commercial functions of the ad. Luxury advertising contributes to the brand mythology and provides an escape from the mundane realities of shopping.

Like works of art, luxury brands promise the consumer access to transcendent experiences such as beauty, limitless wealth, and immortality. Since perfume itself is ephemeral and impermanent, the brand benefits of the luxury perfume category are entirely based on the delivery of intangible aesthetic associations of the brands with idealized representations of women at personal, social, and existential levels of discourse. The strategic question, then, for the "Woman" brand, was how to distinguish the brand from competitors by exploring the question, "What is Woman?"

The Gender Paradigm

A semiotic analysis of luxury advertising produced two sets of images characterized by the binary opposition of two rhetorical styles and two cultural interpretations of women. One set used only black-and-white photography; the other set used only color photography. The black-and-white ads employed metonymy to engage the spectator in the narrative depicted in the image—we see a part of a story and must fill in the details; the color ads employed metaphor to make comparisons between the perfume and the feminine icon in the image. The metaphorical ads communicated poetry, fantasy, and complexity; the metonymical ads communicated prose, reality, and simplicity. Further analysis revealed that the opposition of metaphorical and metonymical styles formed a paradigmatic set of binary pairs contrasting the personalities, the subjectivities, the camera angles, and other aesthetic differences of one set from the other. In line with Jakobson's theory (1956) that individuals and even cultural movements show a propensity toward either metaphor or metonymy, analysis showed that the contrast of metaphorical and metonymical styles in the ads also betrayed cultural conflicts between two archetypes and two interpretations of the feminine within the luxury category: the Goddess and the Girl Next Door.

The Girl Next Door. Black-and-white photography is a code for expressing realism in cinema. Hence, Steven Spielberg shot sections of *Schindler's List* in black and white in order to drive home the reality of the events depicted in the film. The black-and-white photography made the scenes look as if they were taken from old, black-and-white documentary footage. In the perfume study, the black-and-white ads present a "slice of life" of real women. Although the characters are supermodels, their understated luxury and social interactions bring them down to the level of mere mortals, or everyday "women." They wear little makeup and jewelry and are dressed in simple, classic styles. The images tell a story that we must complete: a man and woman embrace, a couple looks into each other's eyes, a mother interacts with a child (see Figure 2.7).

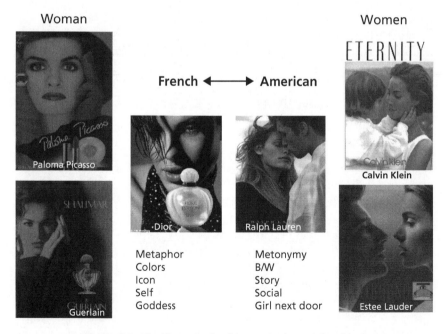

Figure 2.7. The Binary Audit of Luxury Perfume Advertising

In addition to the black-and-white photography, codes for camera angle and character point of view reinforce the realism and narrative style of the ads. The scenes are shot in medium or medium close-up, and the characters look at other people within the image, rather than out at the camera. This positions the consumer/spectator as a voyeur looking in on a scene, the vicarious participants in the brand story (Metz, [1977] 1981).

This style of advertising communicates accessibility and reflects an emerging trend toward "accessible luxury" that is open to both high-end and middle-market, "masstige" (i.e., between mass and prestige) consumers. Ralph Lauren perfected the lifestyle approach to luxury branding, focusing not so much on product benefits but on the consumer's ability to participate in the lifestyle and "stories" of the beautiful people in his ads. Interestingly, all of the images in the black-and-white set represent American brands, such as Ralph Lauren, Calvin Klein, DKNY, and Estée Lauder.

The Goddess. In contrast to black-and-white photography, the color photography in the luxury ads highlights the rich sensuality of intense colors and textures and the artificial and artful nature of the image. The women wear makeup and jewelry, rich fabrics, and couture styles. Instead of realism, the images suggest a timeless, mythical dimension in which the woman is associated with the universal Goddess. In addition to the color photography, the camera angle, background, and character point of view locate the models in a timeless, dream-like space void of human relationships.

In advertising for brands such as Chanel, Dior, Givenchy, and Yves St. Laurent, women are shot in extreme close-up, which emphasizes the iconic dimension of their faces rather than referring to a story out of frame. The visual metaphor does not invite the consumer into the character's world as much as it creates an icon to be admired from a distance. The models look directly into the camera, foreclosing the spectator's participation in the image as a voyeur by recognizing and demystifying the gaze of the camera. Such stylistic cues reflect an approach to luxury branding that builds equity on fantasy, inaccessibility, and rarity. Interestingly, the ads in the color set all represent French brands.

A Positioning "Woman"

We began our discussion of semiotics and brand strategy with an analysis of an ambiguous two-page advertisement for the new "Woman" brand perfume (Figure 2.1). Findings from a semiotic analysis of advertising for the category suggest that this ambiguity was particularly strident because it reflected deep cultural conflicts within the category. Analysis began by sorting dozens of print ads into binary categories, starting with the most obvious contrast between the ads, the use of black-and-white versus color images. The black-and-white/color binary led to the identification of a paradigmatic series of formal contrasts

between the two sets of ads, including the binaries self/social, looking out/
looking toward others, formal/casual clothing. Each side of the binary represented two styles of representation and two feminine archetypes: the Goddess
(woman) and the Girl Next Door (women) (see Figure 2.8).

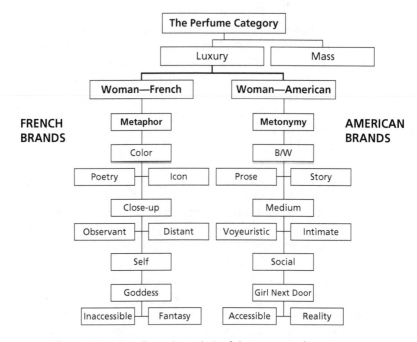

Figure 2.8. A Paradigmatic Analysis of the Luxury Perfume Category

The woman/women paradigm was supported by other stylistic binaries.
The rhetorical style of the ads in color was metaphorical and iconic, while the
rhetorical style of the ads in black and white was metonymical and narrative.
Closer analysis showed that these two types of women and two styles of
representation were based on the two national cultures where the brands
were manufactured: French and American. American brands such as Estée
Lauder, Ralph Lauren, and Calvin Klein employed codes for visual realism,
such as the black-and-white photography, casual dress, and prose narrative.
French brands such as Guerlain, Paloma Picasso, and Dior employed codes
for visual fantasy, such as color photography, formal dress, and poetry.

The "Woman" campaign failed because the brand strategy did not take into
account the deep cultural tensions structuring the feminine in the category.
Not only did the "Woman" campaign represent conflicting cultural archetypes for women, it also combined in one campaign two distinct positionings
for the brand, leaving consumers with the question, is "Woman" the Goddess
or the Girl Next Door? (see Figure 2.9).

Goddess or Girl Next Door?

Figure 2.9. Two Feminine Archetypes, Two Styles of Advertising

STRATEGIC ANALYSIS

The binary analysis of the category provided means for mapping the paradigmatic dimensions of the category on strategic grids, summarized in Figure 2.10. The upper-left quadrant includes French brands with codes for attributes for the Goddess, such as metaphorical, iconic, poetry, distant, and inaccessible; the lower-right quadrant includes American brands with codes for attributes for the Girl Next Door, such as metonymical, narrative, prose, intimate, and accessible.

The strategic grid graphically demonstrates how aesthetic codes are embedded in distinct cultural systems and ideologies, such as French and American, and how mixing aesthetic styles entails a conflict between two cultures and two interpretations of the notions of women and luxury. Failure to understand the underlying structure of meaning in the category led to an unclear positioning for the new "Woman" brand and accounted for the failure of the ad campaign in prelaunch testing.

This much said, to be competitive, brands must break away from the pack and carve out a unique space in the category. By mapping brands on a strategic map, it is simpler to identify spaces that have not yet been occupied by competitors. Looking at Figure 2.10 again, one notices that most brands at that time of this study occupied either the French or American quadrants. The "Woman" brand would have to move outside of the box defining American

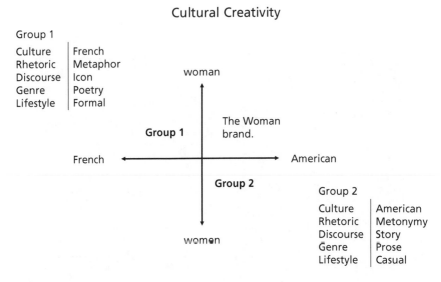

Figure 2.10. Positioning Against the Grain

luxury in order to be distinct from competitors. The brand's legacy and style determined where the "Woman" brand should fall on the grid.

Cultural Creativity

Iconic brands not only reflect cultural myths, such as the eternal feminine, they reinterpret these myths in the light of contemporary consumer needs for meaning and identity (Holt, 2003). In the next phase of analysis, I analyze findings from the brand audit to steer the "Woman" brand into a new direction and a new cultural paradigm—the "Woman" brand spokesperson as an American legend.

We began our strategic analysis with the assumption that Halston, the creator of the "Woman" brand, was rooted in an American worldview. However, taking a closer look at the Halston's legacy, we found that he described himself as a neoclassical designer with European roots. He translated European aesthetics into a new, American vocabulary. He also hired a famous Italian designer to create packaging for the brand. We therefore decided to move the "Woman" brand from the lower-right quadrant to the unoccupied upper-right quadrant, positioning the brand between the classical ideal of woman, the Goddess, and the American cultural context. This positioning distinguished the brand from competitors in the American luxury perfume category, while remaining distinct from French brands. It also created a new cultural space for the brand consistent with the Halston's cosmopolitan origins and an emergent archetype, an American Legend, casual and realistic, but also worldly and sophisticated.

An American Legend

The "Woman" brand would be positioned midway between the Goddess and the Girl Next Door, and would be associated with an iconic American woman who had become a legend in her own time. This feminine archetype would be timeless but not dwelling with the gods. The advertising campaign would merge elements from both representations of the feminine. The "Woman" brand would be anchored in realism rather than fantasy, so the image would be rendered in black and white, and the model's dress and makeup would communicate the simplicity and informality associated with the American feminine archetype. The brand, however, would communicate the sophistication and iconic power associated with the European Goddess. The model would be shown alone in close-up on an undefined, timeless background. We even suggested the tagline, "Woman—an American Legend."

In this example, I showed how the semiotic analysis of advertising uncovers deep cultural tensions within a category that influence the way consumers read advertisements. However, the power of semiotic analysis extends beyond advertising research and has broad applications in the realms of cultural analysis, consumer behavior, and strategic planning.

In the marketing research literature, semiotics tends to be narrowly associated with the organization of meanings in advertising (Sherry, 1987; Mick and Buhl, 1992; Scott, 1994a, 1994b). However, the field of inquiry of marketing semiotics is as broad as the consumer's world. It includes not only the mass media but consumer rituals and gestures, social relationships, and the organization of their domestic space. Semiotics links design to the cultural priorities of the consumer for a range of marketing activities, such as product and packaging design, retail architectonics, and advertising execution. Semiotics can be applied to the analysis of all kinds of media and across various levels of analysis from the smallest unit (such as the color of the logo) to the broadest (such as the corporate culture or the retail environment). Semiotic analysis also provides a means of aligning consumer research, the cultural environment, and brand communication by articulating the underlying system of codes that they all share.

In Chapter 3, I will show how semiotics can be used upstream in the planning process to ground positioning and creative strategy in a deep understanding of the Consumer Brandscape.

3 Mining the Consumer Brandscape

"No brand is an island."

While the casual observer may think of the brand as a product, a logo, or even a jingle, the brand actually forms a complex ecosystem of commercial, cultural, and social forces. Brands draw energy not just from their own heritage or essence but from a multitude of intersecting influences shaping the physical, virtual, and symbolic terrain in which the brand lives. I call this terrain the Consumer Brandscape, and it is constructed by means of an ongoing give-and-take between the brand, the consumer, and the cultural environment. Like a mental landscape, the Brandscape frames the scope and depth of the brand context and engages consumers in the brand world.

The Consumer Brandscape

The Consumer Brandscape is both a process for integrating brand meanings across business functions and markets and a blueprint illustrating the network of intersecting codes and meanings that contribute to consumers' perceptions of a brand. The meanings that form the Brandscape are derived from all aspects of brand management—from the corporate culture to the product line and pricing strategy—not just advertising.

The word "brandscape" has been used elsewhere to describe the branded corporate environment (Sherry, 1998), the constellation of meanings consumers associate with brands (Thompson and Arsel, 2004), and branded urban architecture (Klingman, 2007). I use the term to define a symbolic system that integrates the social, cultural, and semiotic dimensions of brands in a coherent yet flexible whole. The Brandscape system includes several dimensions of meaning: the codes structuring the cultural category, the emotional territories associated with the category, and the material signifiers used to communicate these meanings in representations such as packaging and advertising (see Figure 3.1).

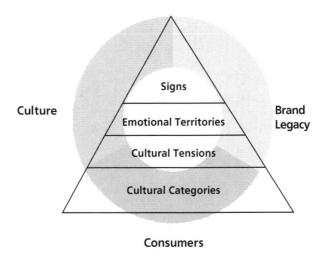

Figure 3.1. The Consumer Brandscape

THE BRAND SYSTEM

The concept of an integrated Consumer Brandscape draws upon Aaker's analysis (1996) of the "brand system," inasmuch as it emphasizes the alignment of all brand functions around a core brand identity or message. Aaker develops a management process for assuring that the brand essence is preserved over time and across markets. He analyzes the brand system in terms of four elements, including the brand-as-product, the brand-as-organization, the brand-as-person, and the brand-as-symbol. Brands lose equity if any one of these elements fails to support the overall message and mission of the brand. For example, a hierarchical organization in which decisions about the brand are made from the top down would destroy a brand that relies on creativity and rapid change, as in the world of Internet marketing.

It has been my experience that brand managers resort to semiotic research to revive a brand that is losing market share or to create advertising at the end of a strategic planning process. However, this is a very limited use of the semiotic tool kit. Since semiotics aligns consumer research with the brand legacy and the competitive environment, it should be integrated into the strategic positioning process, upstream in the planning cycle. Semiotics can be used to anticipate changes in the culture of the target market and the category, and calibrate the brand to emergent codes in the business and cultural environments.

Instead of simply managing the Consumer Brandscape, this process provides ways of mining the Consumer Brandscape, reaching deep into its symbolic terrain to find sources of innovation and cultural creativity. Just as miners make many trips down the shaft, management must routinely seek new veins of information, new directions for exploration, and new gems to bring to the surface.

THE SEMIOTIC DIMENSION

The current semiotic approach to brand management also extends Aaker's model by focusing on the social and cultural codes that structure brand meanings and relate them to the culture of consumers over time and throughout the world. This perspective builds on Grant McCracken's account (1986) of symbolic consumption in terms of "meaning transfers" originating in the minds of consumers. The mental transfer of meaning from one cultural category, such as pleasure, to another, such as soft drinks, forms the basis of brand identity and the semiotic value of goods. The marketing semiotics approach begins with the premise that semiotic codes structure the meaning of the product category, the organizational culture, the brand personality, and the symbolism used to represent these meanings in the marketplace. Semiotic codes are responsible for consistently integrating brand meanings throughout the marketing mix, across markets, and over time.

The Consumer Brandscape forms a network of meanings derived from multiple cultural contexts. For consumers to integrate these cultural contexts at all, they merge meanings from one context to another by means of symbols. Humans are innately capable of making symbolic connections among far-flung meaning systems from advertisements and brand logos to celebrity icons, legends, and personal history. This cognitive ability was theorized by Freud to explain dream formations and free association in psychoanalysis (1976). Linguists call these "meaning transfers" (Nunberg, 1995).

Advertising and marketing communication mediate the transfer of meaning between cultural categories as diverse as product attributes, masculinity, freedom, and consumption, and then attach them to brands (McCracken, 1986). Over time such meaning transfers become embedded in popular culture, so that icons such as the Marlboro Man transcend the brand per se and become symbols for cultural ideals and myths. Thus, consumers and the goods they consume become "way stations" of meaning (McCracken, 1986) in the construction of consumer culture, rather than the passive recipients of meanings assigned by marketers.

For example, an advertisement associating the Coke brand with Santa Claus can be linked to cultural texts about families, tradition, and the "sacred," which consumers internalize with personal memories, emotional states, and people. By mapping these kinds of associations into networks of meaning, the researcher can track the kind of meaning transfers consumers make between the brand and their world. Furthermore, rather than simply interpret meanings in current brand communication, semiotics research builds Brandscapes by constructing links between consumer research, the brand legacy, and developments in the category.

Brand equity is built upon meaning transfers of this kind, which impact the perception of quality, the brand's relevance for the consumer, and its ability to create culture. For example, the Coca-Cola Company created advertising early in its history that embedded the Coke legacy in American rituals, traditions, and values. The company even claims responsibility for our current interpretation of the Santa Claus character.[1] Like a snowball, the brand acquired a growing depth and scope of associations, since the cultural symbolism of the ads—from Mom and apple pie to the family Christmas—traces paths between the brand and a broad network of consumer beliefs, values, and emotions. When brand strategy draws upon the semiotic networks linking the brand with the consumer's world, rather than relying only on their heritage, the brand will not only "make sense" but will enter consumer culture where it resonates with consumer needs and wants.

Even iconic brands (Holt, 2004) grow or decline in direct proportion to the coherence and relevance of the brand message for consumers across business functions and over time. I illustrate this principle with reference to two blue-chip brands, Kodak and Blue Cross, and two very different approaches to strategic brand management. Both companies struggled with change in their respective industries, but only one emerged a winner, because the company proactively researched the culture of consumers, aligned this culture with their brand legacy and promise, and used this information to develop new products and a relevant communication strategy.

KODAK: THE PERILS OF CATEGORY LEADERSHIP

In a twelve-month period beginning at the end of 2000, the Eastman Kodak Company lost 75 percent of its stock value and surrendered substantial market share to competitors. This dramatic fall came as the result of many years of corporate complacency about changes in the imaging industry. Management had failed to align the brand with emerging trends in digital technology and the changing needs and wants of their target market. It is an established marketing principle that "marketing myopia" (Levitt, 1960) of this kind is a major cause for brands to fail. In the case of Kodak, it prompted a downward spiral in 2000 that continues to this day and threatens the company's very existence (Lentini, 2008).

For over 100 years, beginning in 1880, the Kodak brand was synonymous with technological innovation in the service of consumers. The brand message says it all: "You push the button, we do the rest." Kodak did not so much invent modern photography as invent consumer photography at a time when photographic "moments" were limited to periodic visits to a professional photographer. With the invention of the inexpensive Brownie camera in 1900, consumer photography became accessible on a mass scale and changed the very nature of photography from a professional practice to a popular pastime. Moreover, Kodak had all the attributes associated with strong brand equity, including universal awareness, customer loyalty, superior perception of quality, and a broad range of positive brand associations (Aaker, 2007). The "Kodak Moment" is embedded in popular culture as the symbol for family, memories, and the American way. By century's end, Kodak had become the undisputed leader in the 35mm photo category.

Kodak's fall from grace began, ironically, at the peak of the company's market performance in the late 1990s. Brimming with confidence, management paid over $75 a share in dividends to investors rather than invest in R&D. However, Kodak had insulated itself from the sea change that was transforming the photo-imaging industry and consumer culture since the 1980s. Tucked away in their vintage headquarters building in Rochester, New York, Kodak chose to cash in on its current equities in a declining technology.

Signs of Complacency

Like the "Kodak Moment" that propelled the brand to global iconic status, Kodak became frozen in time and rested on its laurels. A corporate culture of nostalgia and tradition formed a barrier to innovation that is communicated at the levels of new product development, pricing strategy, advertising, and organization itself.

Kodak's rigid hierarchical organization, modeled after the original family business, combined with limited input from younger managers, kept management on a status quo course. Next, at a time when competitor Fuji Film was giving away 35mm film to bring consumers to their brand, Kodak continued a premium pricing strategy that was no longer justified by the declining demand in 35mm film. Finally, the visual semiotics of corporate headquarters reflected a culture of complacency. Housed in a drab, 1930's style building, the architecture of the Art Deco tower and the old fashioned interior decor communicated nostalgia for better times rather than a vision for the future. As the architectural "face" of the company, the visual semiotics of Kodak headquarters makes a strong statement about Kodak's deeply entrenched resistance to change in the 1990s, when it was struggling with the advancing threat of the digital imaging industry.

It was not for lack of technological expertise that the Kodak misfired in the digital imaging industry. The digital camera was invented by Kodak engineer, Steven Sasson. Furthermore, Kodak had been developing state-of-the-art photo-imaging technology for industries for many years. The problem stemmed rather from the management's failure to understand the behavioral implications of digital technology for consumers entering the category in a post-Internet world.

A Semiotic Strategy

When companies commit themselves to aligning brands to changes in the marketplace, semiotics can provide a compass. The semiotics compass integrates secondary, "trend" research, competitive analysis, and primary research with consumers into a Brandscape of the environment. Semiotic analysis of the data would highlight the essence of the brand that transcends the culture and the competitive environment, then "translate" this essence into terms that relate to these contexts.

The brand essence may draw upon unique product technologies and benefits, but it also transcends the product. When companies identify their brands with product attributes, they can become bogged down by identification with outdated technologies and product benefits that no longer satisfy consumer needs.

For example, Kodak is the standard bearer for low price and ease of use. The company built an industry and a photo-imaging culture upon these two simple concepts. However, the company failed to adapt these core equities to the digital market—not because they lacked the technology—but because they lacked understanding of the social and cultural factors that integrate digital technologies into consumers' lives in the Internet age. Shooting, printing, and storing pictures have been redefined by dramatic changes in the way information is copied and disseminated in digital consumer culture. Digital photography did not revolutionize consumer behavior; the Internet revolutionized consumer behavior and changed consumer expectations and needs associated with making and sharing pictures.

The Kodak Brandscape

A cursory analysis of the brand legacy, the category, and the culture of consumers in the imaging industry highlights the tensions between Kodak's strategy and their competitive environment at the edge of the digital consumer revolution. The rudimentary Brandscape serves to visualize this analysis (see Figure 3.2).

A binary comparison between the cultures associated 35mm and digital imaging draws attention to the conflicting meanings consumers associate with these two technologies and their implications for brand identity.

Photography. Photography is an imaging technology based on the impression of of light on a chemically treated surface. 35mm photography is inscribed with the passage of time. As soon as the camera seizes a scene on film, the moment has

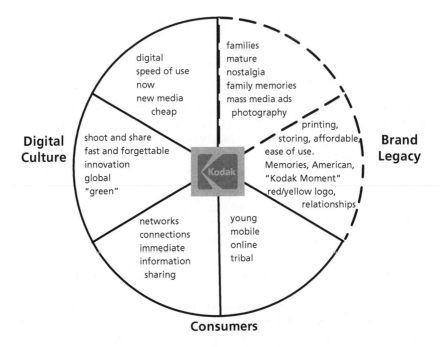

Figure 3.2. Tensions in the Kodak Brandscape

already passed. Kodak built a brand on this simple idea. The famous "Kodak Moment" is always and already a moment in the past, imbued with nostalgia over times past. The brand transcended the practical benefits of ease of use and low price, and became the brand that delivered memories. Kodak pictures preserved family stories, to be displayed in frames or collected in albums—like heirlooms to be stored away for posterity. As a result, Kodak emphasized technologies associated with the end product—high-resolution film, sharp colors, beautiful prints, and superior quality paper.

Digital Imaging. By contrast, digital imaging is a form of electronic information collection and is inscribed with immediacy, experience, and instant gratification. Consumers expect different things from digitalized data than they do from "hard copy" products. A picture in electronic format lacks the feel and beauty of photo print, but satisfies consumer expectations of Internet culture, defined by instant access, convenience, ease of transmission, and storage. Furthermore, as Internet culture evolved, digital imaging serves the social networking function, keeping friends and family abreast of daily events. The "moments" are not necessarily memorable nor are they usually preserved on paper. The end product is not as important as the process involved with shooting, capturing, sending, and receiving images online.

Kodak failed to adapt their core equities—low price and ease—to the digital market because they lacked insight about the ways digital technology transformed the way consumers behave with cameras. The Internet changed expectations about the role of imaging in consumers' lives. These expectations determine consumer needs and wants before, during, and after seizing a picture. Digital photography serves the social networking needs of consumers on the Internet. "Click and share" took precedence over "print and store." Kodak was blinded by a brand heritage of memories and beautiful pictures while the environment was morphing into a culture of impermanence and social networking.

Brand Semiotics

Managers and scholars alike traditionally assign semiotic research to down-stream marketing activities such as copywriting, retail design, and naming (see Sherry and Camargo, 1987; McQuarrie and Mick, 1992; Scott, 1994*a*, 1994*b*; Beasley and Danesi, 2002; Aaker, 2007). This practice is based on the assumption that brand meaning begins and ends with the marketing communication function.

However, brands are entirely semiotic, and even the most practical business functions, such as pricing, enter the Brandscape as signs. Semiotic analysis can play a strategic role early in the strategic planning process to align the brand with the movement of meanings associated with the product category, the consumer target, and the cultural environment.

The decision to discount, for instance, is inseparable from the perceived value, identity, and positioning of the brand in the consumer's mind. For example, luxury brands are associated with rarity and elitism. To maintain brand equity, luxury companies such as Hermès would rather destroy surplus merchandise than to sell it at discount. In other words, the production of brand meaning and value begins upstream with the interface of economics, culture, and consumption.

CODE THEORY

The decisions that consumers make throughout the day are shaped by codes governing a range of sign systems including language, gestures, colors, rituals, social behavior, and the organization of space and time. Some codes are conscious and formal, such as the *Rules of the Road*, some are unconscious and unspoken, such as the cultural stereotypes we associate with people. They operate on multiple levels of experience from the personal to the interpersonal, from the public arenas associated with social organization, such as traffic control, to the personal arenas associated with brand preferences and emotions.

Codes and Culture

Codes are conventions that dictate the way social groups articulate the muddy world of phenomena into shared cultural categories, the building blocks of meaning. In the terms of Italian semiotician Umberto Eco (1979: 61), "The codes, insofar, as they are accepted by a society, set up a 'cultural' world linked to a cultural order [for] the way in which a society thinks, speaks, and, while speaking, explains the 'purport' of its thought through other thoughts."

In his discussion of culture and consumption, McCracken (1986) states that cultural categories create the distinctions that lead to meaning but may underestimate the role of semiotic codes in the construction of these categories. Since codes are conventions, they ensure consensus and communication among members of social groups. For example, there are both universal and local codes determining the foods consumed at Thanksgiving in the United States. Serving turkey is the national code, but the preparation of the turkey may be codified by family traditions or ethnic codes. I once interviewed a Caribbean family that made a Thanksgiving casserole that mixed the traditional Caribbean ingredients of beans and rice with the traditional American turkey.

Some code systems are formal and institutionalized, such as traffic signs and passwords, while other codes define abstract ideals and values that prevail in a culture and can be manipulated or performed by individuals and groups in the course of daily life. In patriarchal cultures, for example, masculine and feminine archetypes are defined in terms of body type (muscular/soft), cognition (one dimensional/multidimensional), and personality (rational/emotional). The semiotician identifies these broad oppositions in the data set, then looks for ways individuals and discourses digress from these types, when, for example, women are shown to be muscular, one-dimensional, and rational. I used this approach in Chapter 2, for example, to map the perfume category in terms of broad oppositions between the Goddess and Girl Next Door. By means of consumer research I then identified a new cultural space and new positioning for a luxury perfume brand that embraced tensions between these two archetypes.

The Binary Structure of Codes

Codes structure meaning in terms of binary pairs that correlate with cognitive processes of differentiating and distinguishing one sign unit from another in language (Saussure, [1916] 2000). First of all there is the binary structure of signs themselves. The Signifier/signified relationship is structured by codes associating a material signifier (word, image, gesture, etc.) with a "signified" or concept. It is important to remember that since the S/s association is ruled by social convention and perpetuated by habit, this relationship is dynamic. The American flag, for instance, connotes different meanings in the United States than it does in enemy territories.

Binary analysis has obvious advantages for positioning brands and differentiating them from competitors. A cursory analysis of the binary distinctions between the Coke and Pepsi brands bears this out. Coke is traditional and classic; Pepsi is trendy and modern. Companies can maintain their competitive advantage in the marketplace by monitoring the ongoing clarity of such binary distinctions over time.

Codes structure the production of meaning in an array of media. In advertising imagery, for instance, spatial codes such as top/down, depth/surface, left/right, foreground/background structure relationships among elements in an image. The message may be structured by social and cultural codes for gender (male/female), social class (high/low), and rank. And, as we discussed in Chapter 1, codes structure the association of brand signifiers, such as the logo and color scheme, with signifieds, such as the company identity or brand personality. The meaning of these binaries is dictated by cultural convention. For example, the practice of reading verbal texts from left to right among speakers of European languages influences the way they read images. The meanings associated with male and female are also dictated by the cultural context.

The binary structure of meaning production is due to universal cognitive processes that structure logic as dialectic—thesis, antithesis, synthesis. In linguistics, binary oppositions between phonemes or sounds dictate the meanings of words. Take the word "pet" for example. The binary opposition between the vocalized /b/ sound and the unvocalized /p/ sound entails changes in the meaning of the word, so "pet" would become "bet."

In semiotic systems other than language, similar oppositions structure the meaning of representations. For example, the opposition short hair/long hair marks the opposition of male style/female style in American culture. To identify the codes structuring a cultural category such as gender, the semiotician organizes the signifiers associated with that topic, such as hairstyle, facial expression, and body type, into a binary system or paradigm of meanings. For example, in a given context, the opposition male/female may entail other oppositions such as muscular/soft, rational/emotional, one dimensional/multidimensional.

Codes in Diachronic Perspective

So far I have discussed the formal aspects of codes structuring semiotic systems. This level of analysis accounts for the synchronic or timeless structure of codes. In everyday consumer behavior, these formal codes are susceptible to modification by changes in the environment over time, which defines the diachronic evolution of codes.

The Consumer Brandscape is an organic system in which multiple codes work together to create meaning. This means that change in any single cultural category, such as the evolution of fashion, ideology, or technology, will naturally create change in the other categories. Take the innovative fashion designer who makes news by mixing colors that run counter to the fashion code. Over time, counter-code behavior becomes codified as a new, acceptable way of putting together an outfit.

As an organic system embedded in consumer culture, the Brandscape changes over time, as some codes recede into the background and others emerge over the horizon. Historical analysis of the codes structuring brand perceptions and consumer behavior is crucial for keeping the brand relevant (see Harvey and Evans, 2001). The process differentiates three types of codes, including:

- *Residual codes.* Residual codes have lost their luster and are clearly unfashionable. For example, the dress code for proper young women once included high collars and long skirts.

- *Dominant codes.* Dominant codes have widespread acceptance in the culture at a given time; but as soon as they reach dominance, they have lost their originality and "edge" for trendsetters in a category. For example, the SUV was the best-selling vehicle in America until the current "green" movement tarnished its reputation.

- *Emergent codes.* Emergent codes evolve in response to social and cultural transitions associated with life-stage, migration, and technological in-novation. For example, when Toyota launched their hybrid car, the Prius, in the US market in 2003, it appealed to a small group of conscientious and rebellious consumers who were willing to put their money behind their values.

THE FASHION SYSTEM

The system of codes organizing the Consumer Brandscape is diverse and multilayered. The following example demonstrates how consumers negotiate multiple systems of meaning in order to make decisions related to clothing fashion, including color codification, branding codes, and cultural codes. They also adjust to changes in these codes over time.

Fashion is a semiotic system codified by culture leaders in a society, such as artists, designers, and marketers, who anticipate changes in the social and cultural priorities that confer legitimacy on the tastes, styles, and behaviors of consumers "in the know" (Barthes, [1967] 1983). For this reason the fashion system has been called a medium for meaning transfer between cultural categories and brands

(McCracken, 1986). Fashion transcends traditional status markers such as wealth and social class by anointing innovators and culture bashers who challenge the status quo. Fashion is also a showcase for the consumer's self-construction and their cultural and ideological identities and positions, and a vehicle for mediating social relationships. It can be seen as a system of interpretive frames for structuring personal identity (Thompson and Haytko, 1997).

Consumers confront a series of fashion decisions in order to put together an outfit. For example, to match a pair of navy blue slacks with a jacket and a shirt, they make decisions about color, design, and the personal statement of the jacket that is chosen. Fashion-conscious consumers internalize unspoken rules about coordinating colors, adding accessories, and mixing and matching styles and brands in a given outfit.

Codes operate within a specified cultural category, such as a subculture, a product category, or a fashion trend. Codes evolve by means of social consensus and organize the consumer's range of options in a series of binary pairs, such as color matching/mismatching, business/casual, and conservative/trendy.

Color Codes

Ethno-linguist Benjamin Lee Whorf ([1956] 1964) discovered that phenomena like colors are entirely dictated by the cultural conventions, including the words each language provides for describing them. Whorf called this "linguistic determinism." Thus, one language may include half a dozen terms for "blue" because blue has a complex function in the cultural life of the social group; in another language, one term for blue may suffice. These kinds of cultural codes also find expression in fashion. In a given cultural context, fashion may dictate that navy blue matches red, white, pastels, and khaki, but mismatches with black, brown, and darker shades of green and other shades of navy blue. Fashion may also dictate when, why, and if navy blue is appropriate at all.

Consumers make a series of choices along a paradigmatic set of possible matches with a color, such as blue. The grid provides a rudimentary analysis of the binary construction of meaning in a product category that guides consumer perceptions and choices (see Figure 3.3).

Brand Codes

In addition to the decision regarding formal or casual dress codes, consumers face additional choices in terms of the brand of clothing they choose. They may want to express their personal taste and choose a brand of business dress that mixes and matches colors in ways that run counter to the dominant code. At this level, they are invited to sort through an array of decisions associated with brand image that are communicated in the price category, advertising, and style, and include brand personality, status, originality, age group, reputation, and so on.

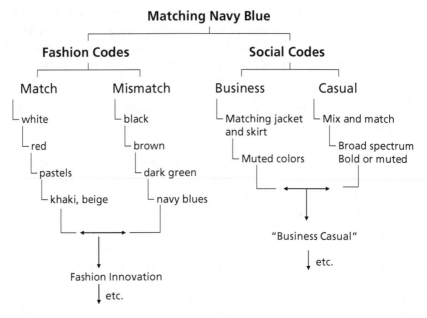

Figure 3.3. The Dynamic of Consumer Decision-Making

Fashion Codes

Avoiding mismatches is just one level of the decision-making process, however. In addition to following aesthetic codes, the consumer must negotiate the dress codes associated with the social occasion. The codes for business or casual dress are also dictated by the industry in which the consumer works. If the consumer is choosing an outfit to wear for a business presentation at a conservative company, he or she would likely follow the codes for business attire on the grid. Of course, there exist a broad range of social codes at work in consumer culture from the codes ruling appropriate attire to the organization of social space at an event, the structure of rituals such as fine dining, and the interpretation of elite or popular taste (Bourdieu, [1979] 1984; Lévi-Strauss, [1963] 1967).

Building the Consumer Brandscape

Successful brands not only mirror culture; they create culture, in the form of trends, icons, and meanings that produce culture. Although MP-3 players had been around for some time before Apple launched the iPod, the iPod brand created a brand culture that integrated mobile technology into the personal identity and daily functions of consumers. In this section, I demonstrate how semiotics can contribute to brand innovation by tracking the evolution of social and cultural trends, anticipating emergent trends, and moving brands into that new space. I begin with an overview of the research process, discuss the role of advertising for brand repositioning, and present a business case for the Blue Cross brand.

THE RESEARCH PROCESS

The semiotics process begins with primary and secondary research. The research is designed and implemented with a semiotic perspective that exposes the deep symbolic structures organizing meanings in the culture of consumers and the brand category.

Step One: Data Collection

The semiotics process begins with selecting and analyzing a data set consisting of texts associated with (*a*) the brand heritage, (*b*) consumer insights, and (*c*) the target culture. The text is the minimal unit of semiotic analysis, a sign system comprising words, images, physical spaces, or other signifiers. The text concept even extends to consumer behavior (Hirschman and Holbrook, 1992). As an object of analysis, the text has clearly defined boundaries, such as the frame around a print advertisement, the beginning and end of a consumer interview, or the dimensions of a product package. Data collection can be organized around three main activities, including (*a*) an audit of the competitive set, (*b*) an overview of cultural trends, and (*c*) primary, in-depth research with consumers.

The Brand Audit. The brand audit includes the positioning strategy and target market, brand image, and competitive environment. Texts include historical communications and advertisements for the brand and competitors, and retail design and layout, and an overview of secondary research on the target market or preexisting consumer data for the target.

The Culture Sweep. The culture sweep, as the term implies, scans the brand environment for trends in the product category, popular culture, and the broader world as they relate to the target market. Texts include books, movies, Internet sites, retailing trends, advertising trends, talk shows, cultural icons, movies, and magazines.

In-depth Research with Consumers. To probe the emotional depth of consumers' lifestyles and brand preferences, semiotic research relies on in-depth interviewing techniques, including ethnographic observations and discussions in consumers' homes. In-depth consumer research explores lifestyle and relationship factors, domestic space, brand perceptions, consumer behavior related to shopping, purchase process, brand loyalty, product usage, and other market behaviors.

Step Two: Decoding the Data

At this stage, coders sort the data into sets, moving from general cultural categories such as gender and mythology to the overriding message, to emotional territories associated with the brand. Emotional territories are usually communicated in semiotic cues ranging from product attributes to consumer experiences and advertising messages. Sidney Levy (1981), a pioneer in brand semiotics, identifies three main clusters of meaning that could be associated with a product, including (*a*) product attributes, (*b*) experiential qualities, and (*c*) people and places.

A rudimentary outline of the decoding process is outlined in Table 3.1 For example, the SUV was the most profitable category of vehicle in the United States for over a decade in the 1990s because it satisfied consumer needs for freedom, self-reliance, and power associated with the all-American pickup truck.

These emotional needs were communicated in advertising cues that emphasized off-road experiences and in product dimensions such as the high ground clearance, strong towing and hauling capacity, 4×4 handling, the big tires, and strong chrome trim. It was a station wagon on steroids. The growing need for this type of emotional statement could be explained by cultural trends in the 1990s, such as the ever-shrinking American frontier, the

Table 3.1. Decoding the SUV Category

		The SUV category	
Cultural category	*Tensions*	*Emotional territories*	*Semiotic cues*
Gender	Masculinity/ femininity	Power, control, bold	Torque control, big payload, truck chassis, chrome trim, "tough"
Myth	Freedom/ boundaries	Rugged, discovery, man against nature, the road less traveled	4×4, off-road capability, terrain, mountains and valleys, no frills, rough ride, cowboys
Ideology	Individualism/ conformity	Limitless space, independence, movement, self-actualization goals	Unpaved terrain, solo driver, unique style
Personal space	Big/small	Super-man or woman, impactful, room to move	High ride, big wheels, wide natural vistas, wide frame, "no boundaries"
Brand benefits	Utilitarian/ existential	Gas guzzler, unsafe, polluting vs emotional benefits	Colors, tag line, claims, imagery

increasing mechanization of American life, and the new, more independent image of soccer moms.

Step 3: Strategic Analysis

Strategic positioning can be defined in terms of the brand's relative conformity to the overarching paradigms associated with a product category. For example, not all SUV brands are created equal—they will conform more or less to the broad category dimensions outlined above. It is this "more or less" that defines the positioning of a brand in relation to other brands in a category.

Mapping the Category. In order to map these relationships, we first have to identify the binary logic that structures the meaning of the cultural categories themselves. In semiotic perspective, masculinity is a relative concept; it is meaningful only in relation to its opposite, femininity. Similarly, some SUV brands are more independent and rugged than others. To identify the positioning of brands in relation to these extremes, we break down the cultural categories into a paradigmatic series of binary pairs, such as *Gender* > masculine/feminine, *Myth* > freedom/boundaries, *Ideology* > individualism/conformity, *Space* > big/small, and *Experience* > rugged/comfortable. These oppositions are mapped on binary grids, creating four quadrants in which brands can be positioned. The traditional SUV is positioned as masculine and rugged. To occupy a new space in the category, an SUV brand such as the Lexus could combine urban adventure with traditionally feminine attributes such as comfort and aesthetics. This positioning would be located in the lower right quadrant of the strategic grid shown in Figure 3.4.

Balancing Cultural Tensions. Mapping the paradigmatic structures of the brand category has the additional benefit of foregrounding tensions within culture in which most brands operate. While the binary pairs themselves structure polarities within cultural categories, these cultural tensions often occur between cultural categories. For instance, the binary opposition safety/risky structures a utilitarian category of consumer security. The binary opposition conservative/adventurous structures an existential category of consumer identity.

These kinds of binary tensions structure the semiotic parameters of all product categories. Consumers constantly make trade-offs within these tensions when they choose brands. For example, if they are looking for an exciting vehicle but worry about their child's safety, they look for brands to negotiate tensions between the utilitarian and existential benefits of a vehicle, allowing them to "have their cake and eat it too."

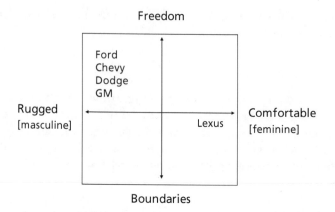

Figure 3.4. Strategic Dimensions of the SUV Category

A case in point is the emerging issue of the questionable safety and gas mileage of SUVs built on a truck frame. In the late 1990s the public became aware of the SUV's tendency to roll over in accidents and the rising cost of filling the gas tank. Prompted by lawsuits and a decline in sales, automakers developed the Cross-over Utility Vehicle (the CUV), an SUV on a car frame. Although the CUV has better stability and fuel efficiency than the truck-based SUV, its association with a car undermined the traditional muscle and sex appeal of the truck-based SUV. Here is a clear example of a tension between the utilitarian needs for safety and economy and the existential needs for freedom and power associated with the truck.

This posed a positioning challenge to automakers that sought to appease concerns about the SUV but did not want to lose the emotional equity consumers associated with trucks. Current advertising for the CUV category reveals tensions between utilitarian and existential consumer needs and has created chaos in the CUV category, which lacks a single overriding message, myth, or consumer target. Is it a car or a truck? Is it masculine or feminine? Some companies, including Ford, Honda, and GM, minimize the car-frame message and position their CUVs like traditional, truck-like SUVs. Still other brands highlight the safety and economic features of the CUV and appeal to existential needs for romance and humor. Some brands swing between these positions from one campaign to another.

Tensions of this nature often accompany changes in technology, consumer culture, and ideology, and present unique challenges to marketers. Rather than ignore these tensions, marketers can build upon cultural tensions to create innovative brand positioning. Teasing out tensions in the marketplace is the first step in this process. The next step is to provide consumers with a rationale for changing their perceptions of the new product or technology.

THE ROLE OF ADVERTISING

Advertising plays a key role here. In the symbolic–imaginary realm of word and image, advertising can draw upon cultural tensions to create nuanced and multilayered meanings that are hard to communicate in a positioning statement alone. Rhetoric and montage are only two of the devices at the disposal of advertisers for overlapping two or more meanings in a single figure.

Brands gain depth by mining the tensions within a category or market, such as conflicts between utilitarian and existential needs (see Holt, 2004). Advertising is an important marketing function that can play with, if not resolve, these tensions in the imaginary–symbolic realm. Rather than simply showing a straightforward appeal to product benefits, advertising for iconic brands such as the Marlboro Man negotiate conflicts between deep, universal human needs, such as freedom and justice, and reality, where most of us are constrained by limitations in the environment.

Michelin makes forceful use of this principle to negotiate tensions between utilitarian and existential appeals in the automotive category. In an early "baby Michelin" ad, we see the black-and-white checked fabric of a race flag and hear the sound of race cars in the background. As the camera pulls away from the checked pattern, we realize that we have not been looking at a racing flag but a baby's diaper in black-and-white check. As the baby walks a Michelin tire, the voice over says, "Because there are races that last 24 hours; because there are rallies that last 4 days, there are high performance tires called Michelin."

The tensions within the automotive category between rational, utilitarian appeals and fun and adventure appeals are not resolved as much as they are negotiated by the superimposition of the soundtrack about racing over the image of the baby. The ad ends with the tagline written over the image of the baby—"Because so much is riding on your tires." By superimposing the sounds and voice-over narrative about the race with the visuals of the baby in a diaper and the tagline about safety, the ad campaign draws energy from the utilitarian/existential binary and positions Michelin as the brand that enhances performance and pleasure without sacrificing safety.

Mining the Baby Boomer Brandscape: The Blue Cross Case

In the previous discussions, I presented some rudimentary tools for building brand value by mapping, mining, and managing the Consumer Brandscape. I also presented the example of Kodak, a brand that lost value because management lost touch with the culture of consumers and the competitive environment, complacent with the brand's past performance. I now turn to a business case that illustrates how semiotics research enabled Blue Cross to successfully develop a line of products targeted to Baby Boomers.

CASE SUMMARY

Decades of corporate downsizing have forced many individuals out of the traditional retirement timeline. As consumers over age 50 retire early, they are often left in a health insurance limbo between the time they retire and the time they achieve the age of 65 and the onset of Social Security coverage (Lohr, 2004; Schultz, 2004; Moos, 2008; Collins et al., 2006). Consumers who actually choose early retirement face daunting trade-offs between the scope and quality of coverage and the costs associated with them.

One of the Blue Cross companies decided to turn this consumer problem into a business opportunity by anticipating the growing need for insurance tailored specifically to early retirees. The company had already identified a clear and profitable opportunity in this segment, as reflected in the sheer numbers of individuals entering the preretirement life stage in the early 2000s. Consumers reaching retirement form the fastest-growing consumer segment in the United States. At the time of the study in the early 2000s, the preretirement group, aged 51–64, was projected to grow 35–50 percent in each of the next five years. Furthermore, since Baby Boomers will live on average twenty years longer than their parents' generation, businesses will have to consider retirement as a full life stage that could last as long as consumers' work lives.

Management realized that they needed to put a face on this emerging market and develop strategy that would address not only financial and demographic factors but also relate to the emotions, values, and lifestyle needs of consumers of this generation. For this reason, the research department scheduled semiotics research upstream in their planning process, followed by concept development, testing, launch, and early assessment. By this means, the Blue Cross achieved "first entry" leadership in the early retirement consumer market as a consumer-centered health care brand.

The Marketing Challenge

Traditionally, health insurance companies have targeted business-to-business agents, not end users. Moreover, they tailored products and services according to demographic variables of consumers, such as age, income, marital status, and family size, rather than qualitative factors such as values and lifestyle. However, since consumers have become increasingly proactive in the purchase process, shopping online to compare and contrast plans, companies are turning to qualitative research to identify lifestyle segments and unmet emotional needs of consumers to develop new products. This was particularly true for the current case because there was no historical precedent for targeting this emerging segment, early retirement Baby Boomers.

The Research Process

The research process involved constructing a Brandscape of the Baby Boomer culture based on data from secondary research, an audit of the Blue Cross brand, and primary research with over 100 consumers in focus groups and at home.

FINDINGS

Earlier in the chapter, I illustrated how consumers make a series of binary trade-offs to create an outfit in navy blue. Consumers make similar trade-offs on a broader scale to negotiate the tensions and contradictions inherent in human behavior and culture, such as the need to feel young and the reality of aging. To make sense of the health care category, semiotics research analyzed the tensions structuring consumer behavior at the preretirement stage, as reflected in cultural texts and primary research. Consumers in the study were experiencing life-stage transitions between working and retirement, and were also challenging, as a cohort group, previous generations' myths and stereotypes of maturity and retirement. These findings are summarized in Table 3.2.

Cohort Group

Cohort group factors are expressed as lifestyle choices and attitudes formed by the culture of the particular time period in which consumers live, in this case, the postwar, Baby Boomer generation. Although aging may contribute to biological and psychological changes shared by all, external, historical factors dictate the ways these changes are manifested in lifestyle decisions and consumer behavior over time.

The Boomer generation is distinguished by its sheer size, its impact on social, economic, and cultural change throughout its lifetime, and its history of transforming the expectations of each life stage this group enters. Teethed on high expectations, widespread postwar affluence, and a sense of entitlement due to their sheer size and impact, Baby Boomers experienced dramatic social changes in American society in their lifetime, including the expansion of civil rights, the deconstruction of gender roles, and changes in family structure. They were shaped by innovations such as the Pill, the personal computer, and rock "n" roll.

Table 3.2. The Preretirement Brandscape

The Preretirement Brandscape			
Cultural category	Tensions	Emotional territories	Symbols
Cohort group	Boomer generation	Engaged, energy, sexuality, courage, innovation, risk, rebellion, no boundaries, protests, break the rules, set the rules, mobility, choice, no roadmap	Associate maturity with athletics, romance, partners, adventure vacations, cosmetic surgeries, vintage rock, RV travel, the open road
	Retirement stereotypes	Boomers resist stereotypes: engage with life, keep moving, stay radical, plan a new career, not the funeral	Boomer's reject these messages: terminal illness warnings, the rocking chair and walker, religious messages, couples cruising quietly into the sunset
Life stage	Work life	Younger: ego centered. Left brain > quantity, logic, idealism, difference from others, competition, power-driven, a win–lose mentality	Signs of success, self-promotion, trendy, acquisition, big houses, cars, etc. Energetic, dynamic goals
	Retirement	Older: transcendence centered. Right brain > quality, creativity, realism, sharing, cooperation, influence, win–win	Boomers plan the next phase of an active life, like a second career. Seek balance between ego and altruism. Boomers reject complacent, cheery images of retirees, gray hair, golf, doting grandmas, and small, slow cars
VALS segment	Pragmatists	Prioritize financial security, protecting assets and protecting health. Plan their financial futures early in life	This segment seeks a premium plan to offset the potential cost of long-term illness, and to pay for preventive care
	Idealists	Prioritize personal control, meaning, living a full life, enjoying the moment, and freedom over protecting assets	This segment seeks a basic, less costly plan through the Internet or agents, and will reduce their lifestyles to pay for a long-term illness
		Extreme idealists were risk takers	Risk takers had no stable insurance
Blue Cross brand	Professional medical	Company: reputation, product benefits, choice of plans, price	Blue Cross = Red Cross—to the rescue! Fear-based health warnings
	The human factor		Ads center on doctors and plans, not the emotional needs of consumers

A male respondent reported how these changes have affected his own family life. "[The previous generation] was regimented. There was mom, dad....Everyone had a role. Now everyone comes in and we talk about what we're going to do to make things better."

Baby Boomers have redefined maturity and retirement as they have redefined all of the life stages that preceded these. They value energy, sexuality, courage, innovation, risk, rebellion, and breaking boundaries. Whether or not respondents actually traveled cross-country in the recreation vehicle, the RV symbolizes their need to travel the open road of their retirement without a fixed roadmap. In contrast to their parents' generation, Boomers tend to postpone preparing for retirement and death. Many respondents avoided answering direct questions about the inevitable consequences of aging and serious illness. They referred to retirees as "those people," not themselves. They had trouble answering the "worst-case scenario" questions about what they would do if they came down with a serious illness.

Life Stage

Consumers contemplating retirement inhabit a transitional life stage, straddling the world of work and the world of retirement. These two life stages are associated not only with lifestyle changes but with specific cognitive states and attitudes (Wolfe, 2008). Life-stage factors are associated with developmental factors that transcend to some extent the unique culture of a specific generation. Human beings undergo biological and cognitive changes as they age, which accounts for changes in outlook, behavior, and self-perception, that are universal to humans at specific ages of life, regardless of the era in which they live.

Work. During their work lives, younger consumers are driven more by ego-centered values such as success and self-actualization associated with their career achievements. They tend to be driven more by left-brain, logical, and quantitative thinking that emphasizes logic, idealism, their difference from others, and competition. They view work relationships in terms of a win–lose situation. Quantity takes precedence over quality in areas such as finances, professional relationships, and possessions. At this stage, they associate personal success with professional promotions, keeping up with styles and trends, owning bigger houses and cars, and acquiring more goods.

Retirement. Carl G. Jung (1969) defines seven tasks of aging in terms of the gradual surrender to the inevitable advance of time, a harsh, realistic look at aging and death, and the letting go of the illusions associated with youth. Aging brings out transcendence needs in the individual, such as altruism, personal growth, and cooperation, and emphasizes right-brain functions such as creativity, feeling, influence, and cooperation. Setting the ego aside, aging consumers emphasize their common ground with others, cooperation rather than competition, influence rather than power, quality rather than quantity.

Consumers in the current study still viewed retirement from the perspectives of their work lives. This perspective reflected the tensions they experienced between the ego needs associated with work and the transcendence needs associated with retirement. Respondents in the study did not think of retirement as an end of anything: "Retirement doesn't mean you have to quit." They often replaced the term "retirement" with words such as "the next stage," "a time for me," and "my next career." One respondent said, "I've always thought of retirement as a career change—leaving the job I had and finding a new one." They demand more of retirement than a retreat from life, hoping that they can "stay in the race" and pursue vocations they postponed. A male respondent voiced the opinions of many respondents when he said, "Don't work at something you hate for 30 years, retire, then die." Respondents plan to leave the "rat race" of competitive, high-pressure jobs and work at jobs that fulfill their needs to express their creativity, give back to society, and also enhance their material lives.

Consumer Ideology: Utopian or Pragmatic?

The Baby Boomer generation is characterized by high ideals and utopian visions for society. They refuse to admit defeat and seem to be in denial about their inevitable mortality. When they consider decisions about health insurance, they negotiate tensions between their utopian ideology and the realities that they must face as they prepare for retirement, such as health risks and financial readiness.

Findings from the primary research reminded us that not all members of a cohort group are alike. To some extent, retirement readiness is related to age—respondents over age 60 were obviously more willing than those just over 50 to consider the realities of aging and retirement. However, innate disposition and life experiences created ideological variations among consumers in this category, regardless of age. Respondents could be segmented into Planners, Idealists, and Gamblers, based on the relative strength of their utopian or pragmatic ideologies and their perceived need for health insurance. Planners had been planning for retirement since entering the workforce, and they will pay high insurance premiums to protect their acquisitions. Gamblers prefer financial risk to a boring lifestyle and are unprepared for retirement. Tethered neither to a long-term job, marriage, or possessions, they often went uninsured and trusted Fate to come to the rescue in the event of serious illness. Idealists put greater value on personal growth, service to others, and peace of mind than on material possessions. Unlike Gamblers, they nonetheless chose less expensive health care plans and would rather reduce their lifestyles, even sell their homes, to meet medical emergencies than to pay high insurance premiums.

The Blue Cross Brand

Blue Cross had established health insurance as an extension of health care and traditionally emphasized their association with medical professionals and hospitals, rather than end users. Their core business was targeted to medical professionals and agents. As the result of the current study, they developed a health insurance brand targeted to the end user, men and women planning to retire before they were eligible for Medicare. Management repositioned the brand extension to communicate emotional benefits to consumers, rather than medical professionals.

Brand Positioning. At the time of the study, the Blue Cross brand, like most financial companies, centered on functional attributes such as costs and benefits. They identified consumers by demographic characteristics such as age and family status, rather than lifestyle or cohort group, since their communications strategies were aimed at health care providers, not patients. They emphasized the medical and financial benefits of health insurance and neglected the emotional factors associated with consumers at various life stages. Since companies did not tend to segment consumers by values and lifestyles, they knew very little about consumers' personal motivations for purchasing insurance. As a result, they could not communicate clearly to consumers about the emotional benefits associated with their brand or relate to the particular social and psychological needs of the target market. Furthermore, both their positioning and their brand symbolism were at odds with the values and lifestyles of the Baby Boomer generation and would have to be revised for the company to succeed in the preretirement markets.

Brand Symbolism. At the time of the study, Blue Cross brand communication focused more on company expertise and product benefits than on building relationships with customers. The use of blue in the Blue Cross logo and website reinforced the brands' association with medical professionals and hospitals, since blue has become the dominant color code for marketing the health care industry. Blue Cross web sites highlighted doctors, hospitals, and plan information, rather than the emotional needs of consumers. The human figures in company advertisements were sick patients and caring doctors and nurses. The implicit association of the Blue Cross with the American Red Cross suggested crisis and fear rather than hope, and could create a barrier to acceptance with Baby Boomers, who view retirement as the beginning of a new life rather than a medical emergency.

Our research revealed that Baby Boomers reject messages that addressed aging and end-of-life fears, so the current positioning of the brand would deter Baby Boomers from accepting an insurance plan from Blue Cross. Boomers, we found, view retirement as the beginning of a new life rather than a medical emergency. Boomers reject messages about retirement and old age that focus on end-of-life situations, such as long-term care and terminal illness. They rejected traditional symbols of aging such as the rocking chair and walker, religious messages, and couples cruising passively into the sunset. They also shunned complacent, cheery images of retirees with gray hair playing golf, of grand-mothers doting on children, and driving small, slow cars.

Boomers associated maturity with athletics, romance, adventure vacations, cosmetic surgeries, vintage rock, RV travel, and the open road. They also hoped that they will be able to share retirement with partners. They sought health insurance programs that promised to enhance life and happiness, not ward against their inevitable physical decline.

STRATEGIC IMPLICATIONS

As social science discipline, semiotics anchors brand strategy in the culture of consumers, foregrounding tensions within a product category and consumer segment, and tracking changes in the codes structuring meaning in the category or segment over time. A diachronic analysis of the meaning of retirement over the years casts in relief the challenges facing the Blue Cross brand as it enters the preretirement insurance market.

An Emergent Paradigm

The meaning of retirement has changed over time. The semiotician tracks these changes in the popular culture, separating old-fashioned or "recessive" codes communicated in old movies and books, from the dominant, stereo-typical codes that structure the meaning of retirement today. Furthermore, by conducting consumer research, the semiotician can identify emergent codes that have not been solidified in the popular culture, but will eventually replace the current, dominant codes structuring meaning in a cultural category[2] (Table 3.3).

Recessive codes associate retirement with old age and medical disability, symbolized in the Clinic and the Red Cross in the upper-right quadrant. The dominant cultural codes associate retirement with one long holiday,

Table 3.3. The Evolving Meaning of Retirement

Residual codes	Dominant codes	Emergent codes
"The Clinic"	"The Cruise"	"The Road Trip"
The end of the road, regimented, resignation, immobility, surrender. The medical or financial discourse. A realistic look at the end of life. Emotional needs to satisfy fear and apprehension	A closed circuit, controlled and directed, gazing into the sunset, spectating, anchored, transcendence. Emotional needs for caring, security, relationship	The open road, control, self-directed, discovery, mobility, freedom, living the dream, staying in the game. Emotional needs for freedom, impact, control, discovery, fun
The Blue Cross Brand	*The Dominant Culture*	*The Boomer Segment*

symbolized by the cruise boat that moves passive, elderly consumers off into the horizon in the lower-right quadrant. The emergent codes, as we identified in the ethnography, associate retirement with active consumers taking charge of this new phase of life. They have left the "rat race" and take on retirement as an adventure, and are represented in the lower-left quadrant. Though not all respondents took road trips, the mobile home and the open road symbolize the emerging ideal of retirement as an opportunity rather than a dead end. It was our challenge to find a positioning for the Blue Cross Pre-Retirement plan that would draw upon their traditional legacy and tap into emerging codes in the Baby Boomer culture.

Strategic Analysis

In order to underscore the parallels between these cultural codes and potential brand positionings for Blue Cross, researchers mapped the alternative life-styles, values, and aspirations of consumers in the segment on a double-axis grid structured by the binary opposition ego/transcendence associated with the transition from work to retirement, and the binary opposition pragmatic/utopian associated with the relative values consumers attach to practical or lifestyle priorities when they make health insurance decisions (see Figure 3.5).

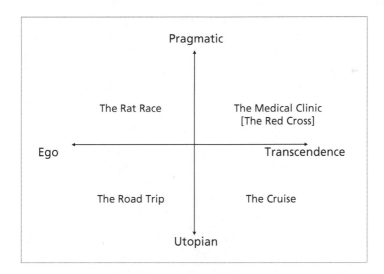

Figure 3.5. Strategic Dimensions of the Preretirement Category

The Clinic is an apt metaphor for the health insurance discourse on aging and retirement and falls in the upper-right quadrant of the grid between utilitarian and transcendence. The health insurance messages in this category focus on medicine, financial security, and health risks. While the Cruise discourse holds the retiree in a closed circuit of movement and the Road Trip discourse places the retiree on the open road, the Clinic discourse represents the end of the road—illness, stagnation, and ultimate demise.

The Cruise symbolizes the dominant paradigm of retirement. The couple looks off into the horizon, the sun setting on their lives. They have left their ego needs behind and have transcended the worries and ambitions of work life. Rather than take initiative, they are moved along by a ship in the closed circuit of an itinerary planned by others. Voyagers on a cruise are spectators, not actors; they are cared for and entertained, but have handed over control to someone else.

The Road Trip symbolizes an emerging ideal of retirement. Baby Boomers have left the rat race but have not abandoned the ego needs related to work and self-actualization. They plan to do more at retirement than cruise out to sea. Not only did many respondents plan to take long road trips; the road trip also symbolizes their desire for spontaneity, freedom, and control. On the road trip the driver can pick up and go at will, leave behind the daily routine, and discover new things. The road trip also means leaving lots of baggage behind, especially material possessions that may limit their movements and choices.

In order to succeed, Blue Cross would have to reposition the brand in line with the consumer-centric values associated with the dominant and emergent codes operative in the category, including the emotional needs for care, security, and relationship associated with aging, and the utopian needs for freedom, impact, control, discovery, and fun associated with the Boomer generation. The positioning strategy outlined in Figure 3.6 highlights the consumer-centered focus of the preretirement brand extension and suggests direction for creative strategy focused on consumer lifestyle rather than

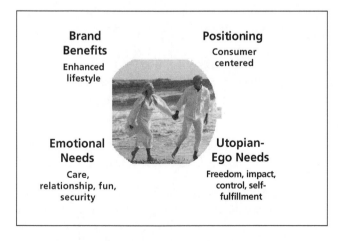

Figure 3.6. A Consumer-Centered Positioning

medicine. Brand communication shifted focus from the imminent threat of illness and death to the lifestyle benefits associated with a secure, reliable health care brand.

The positioning grid condenses findings from the research process that began with an audit of the brand and the competitive set, an overview of secondary sources, and primary research. The company adopted a consumer-centered repositioning strategy that both responded to the life stage and cohort group needs and wants of consumers in the preretirement segment and also tailored plans and benefits to the unique needs of consumer subsegments such as Planners, Idealists, and Gamblers. These needs would include product and pricing factors such as choice and flexibility and consumer service committed to building a long-term relationship with the customer. The repositioning plan included an advertising strategy that communicates fun, humor, and the lifestyle benefits of a good insurance plan, not just the fear-based benefits associated with the worst-case scenarios consumers associate with the Red Cross.

CONCLUSION

The Blue Cross case illustrates the importance of building brand strategy on the foundation of a Consumer Brandscape that integrates a study of popular culture, the product category, and the culture and lifestyles of consumers. Blue Cross not only avoided the pitfalls of complacency but created brand value by means of a research process that integrates consumer knowledge, cultural insights, and brand heritage in a coherent system of meanings, and identifies the underlying semiotic structures that contribute to movement and excitement in a product category. In the following chapters, I expand this kind of analysis to retail design, advertising strategy, ethnographic research, and brand extensions.

▓ ENDNOTES

1. Please visit <http://www.thecoca-colacompany.com/heritage/ourheritage.html>.
2. The notions of recessive, dominant, and emergent codes were developed by Lévi-Strauss (1962).

4 Brand Discourse

"Are you targeting extraterrestrials?"

In 1972, the US National Aeronautics and Space Administration (NASA) launched the Pioneer 10 satellite, the first spacecraft to fly to Jupiter, Saturn, the Milky Way Galaxy, and stars (NASA, 2007). Attached to the exterior surface of the satellite was a gold, 8×10 inch plaque inscribed with the time and location of the launch, a sketch of the spacecraft, and two human figures, male and female (see Figure 4.1).

Pioneer project manager, Larry Lasher, had the plaque installed to communicate information about the mission and people on earth to extraterrestrials who may encounter the satellite on its voyage through outer space. The Pioneer 10 was tracked closely by the Search for Extra-Terrestrials Institute, funded by NASA, hoping for signs that the Pioneer had encountered extraterrestrial life. As recently as 1999, Lasher waxed hopeful of the chance that somehow, somewhere, life in outer space might receive this communication.

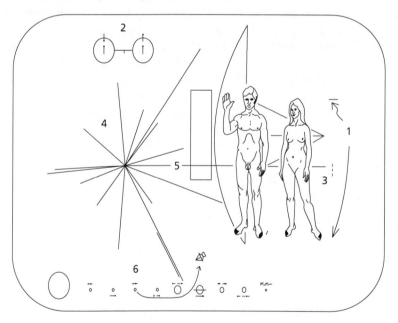

Figure 4.1. The Plaque on Pioneer 10

And even if Pioneer 10 does lose touch with Earth, its usefulness may not be at an end. The probe carries a gold plaque containing information for possible extraterrestrial readers in the distant future. Included are drawings of a human male and female, and diagrams indicating the time and place of present-day Earth. If the plaque is ever found—science fiction, perhaps—it would tell whatever found it where we are, when we are and who we are. (Lasher, quoted in Silber, 1999)

A cursory analysis of the representation of human figures in the Pioneer 10 plaque demonstrates the futility of Lasher's project for intergalactic communication. The first problem is that extraterrestrials probably do not share the same cultural categories structuring the meaning of this image in Western culture, from spatial codes and sign language to gender codes. Furthermore, even if they possessed the conceptual tools necessary for reading images in the first place, extraterrestrials would still not obtain an innocent representation of "who we are," since the plaque itself does not represent an objective view of mankind. Like all visual representations, it betrays a culturally coded interpretation of men and women in the West near the end of the millennium.

This example has important implications for marketers, since it highlights the misunderstandings that occur when brand communication harbors a cultural or ideological subtext that may misfire with consumers. Marketers might as well be targeting Martians if they overlook the mutual dependency of formal and cultural codes structuring the brand discourse. Of particular interest are the human forms on the plaque, which, according to Lasher, display "who we are" on earth. The plaque shows a male figure and female figure without the trappings normally associated with personal identity, such as costume, body markings, or colorings. The idea was presumably to represent humans in their natural state, thus sending a "universal" message about earthlings to our neighbors in outer space, even after the satellite lost contact with the earth. Although the figures may represent "what we are," biologically, the figures fall short of representing "who we are" as humankind, since they portray a limited cultural viewpoint of men and women. Both of the human figures are white, their hairstyles reference European culture, and their poses reflect Western gender stereotypes.

This example challenges the assumption that images present an unmediated, "natural" representation of reality. The Pioneer 10 image is not a mirror for humankind—it is a discourse, a statement about the world formed by the dialectical implication of the formal codes responsible for the structure of a message and semantic codes responsible for the content of a message. Before proceeding with the analysis of the Pioneer 10 image and its implications for advertising research, I will review the current literature on advertising communication, and introduce discourse theory as a way of deepening understanding of the codes structuring the text and subtext of advertising.

In the following sections, I present an overview of discourse theory, with increasingly complex levels of discourse analysis. These include every thing from the micro-discourses structuring meaning in a single image or logo, to the macro-discourses that communicate the positioning over multiple campaigns, time frames, and markets.

Discourse Theory

Discourse theory constitutes the single most important advance in semiotic inquiry since Saussure, because it takes into consideration the dialectical relation between the structure of sign systems and the social codes structuring *semiosis*, or meaning production, a process that engages a communicating agent (including but not limited to, a speaker) and a receiver (including but not limited to a single recipient) in a communication event. In order to understand how discourse theory can be applied to advertising, I will first trace its origins in linguistic theory, specifically in the work of French linguist Emile Benveniste. I will then discuss how philosophers expanded discourse theory beyond the statement to the analysis of cultural subtexts at the level of textual analysis.

BEYOND THE SIGN

Briefly defined, discourses are sites of communication that engage a speaker and receiver of a message in a communication event and reference a specific semantic context. Discourse analysis moves the focus of semiotics from the abstract system of codes structuring meaning production to the ways codes are deployed to structure propositions, judgments, and claims.

Discourse theory evolved from structural linguistics and the work of F. Saussure. Structural linguistics emphasized the dialectical structure of meaning.

Saussure's binary analysis of the sign was no mere theoretical exercise. It challenged the traditional, metaphysical interpretation of reality as "a given" or origin that signs are called upon to represent. By disengaging the signifier from the signified, Saussure emphasized that meaning was ruled by conventions and codes, rather than the inherent nature of things. Saussure's discovery emphasized that sign systems are not merely vehicles for representing the transcendental "real"; they influence the way we interpret reality. As Deeley puts it, "at the heart of semiotics is the realization that the whole of human experience, without exception, is an interpretive structure mediated and sustained by signs" (1990: 5).

Furthermore, though Saussure wrote about the implication of a phonetic *signifier* and a concept or *signified* in the linguistic sign, the structural analysis of signs can apply to symbols, such as logos, as well. [Figure 4.].

Saussure's binary analysis of the sign was not mere theoretical exercise. Though Saussure wrote about the implication of a phonetic *signifier* and a concept or *signified* in the linguistic sign, the binary structure of the sign provides a rudimentary model for poetic signs, e.g. the brand logo (Figure 4.2).

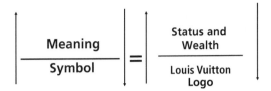

Figure 4.2. The Dual Structure of Signs

THE BINARY STRUCTURE OF DISCOURSE

Since Saussure, linguistic theory has expanded beyond the study of the sign per se to account for the ways signs are organized in socially and culturally constructed discourses. In the 1960s, Benveniste proposed changing the focus of structural linguistics from the sign as the minimal unit of analysis to the sentence. In order to account for nonlinguistic discourses such as images, Benveniste substituted the sentence form with the term "énonciation," roughly translated as "statement," which consists of the dialectical implication of the structure of signs—what Benveniste calls the "semiotic level" and the structure of meaning, or the "semantic level." By extending the study of semiotics from the sign to the statement, Benveniste accounted for the impact of the context on the precise meaning of a sign, and the intersubjective exchange of meaning between the creator and receiver of the message, its "subject address."

Meaning and Reference

Discourse involves an act of predication that links a single sign to other signs in a statement (Ricoeur, 1976) and anchors meaning in the reference to a context. The reference of discourse may add nuances and subtexts to a statement, the "meaning of meaning," as it were. These may include the speaker's intentions and the connotations suggested by the context. For example, the word /tree/ evokes the idea of a tree according to the semantic conventions of the English language. However even a simple statement such as "The tree is falling!" embeds the word /tree/ in a context shared by two or more interlocutors in a communication event. Furthermore, when the meaning and reference of a statement are in conflict, the statement either betrays a lie or the speaker's ironic tone. If someone exclaimed, "What a beautiful day!" in reference to a cold, stormy day, they communicate their own disgust with the weather by saying one thing and meaning something else (Figure 4.3).

Voice

Benveniste expanded the notion of subject-address beyond the linguistic codes for "I" and "you," and concluded that every manipulation of the structure of a

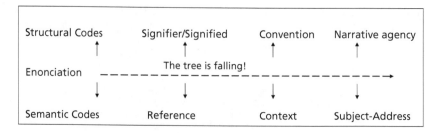

Figure 4.3. The Structure of Discourse

statement draws attention to the organizing agency or "voice" inscribed in discourse. In literature, for instance, metaphor, irony, adjectives, and adverbs betray the opinion and perspective of the narrator. For example, the metaphor, "there is a garden in her face," does not describe meanings inherent in the face of a woman, but the narrator's subjective opinion.

VISUAL DISCOURSE

Though Benveniste was a linguist, his theory of discourse has applications for nonverbal communication such as images and the mass media. Nonverbal discourse consists of the inscription of point of view and reference in the material of signs in any form. The theory of discourse accounts for the fact that visual representations are not innocent or "natural," but are inscribed with a particular ideological perspective, a point of view, and in sum, an interpretation of reality. The discursive structure of visual representation consists generally of any formal manipulation of the visual field—be it film, painting, photography, the Internet, or retail space. This kind of manipulation is exemplified in a close-up shot or the arrangement of goods on the retail shelf. Visual discourse also engages a recipient, that is, reader, speaker, spectator, or shopper, in the message, because these formal manipulations structure the spectator or shopper's engagement in the message. Furthermore, these traces of the organizing hand of the narrator or merchandiser in visual discourse can be analyzed because they conform to semiotic and cultural codes structuring meaning in representations.

Pioneer 10

To illustrate an analysis of visual discourse, I return to the Pioneer 10 image, drawing particular attention to the human forms on the plaque (Figure 4.4).

The two nude figures represent a man and woman, as suggested in the genitalia, size, and musculature associated with human males and females. Biological differences are paradigmatically related to gender roles in the image, which are

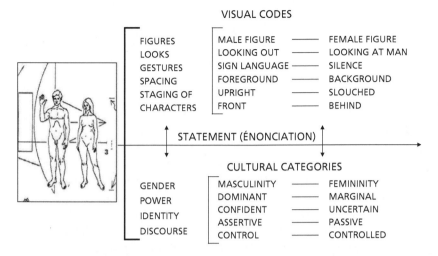

VISUAL CODES

FIGURES	MALE FIGURE	FEMALE FIGURE
LOOKS	LOOKING OUT	LOOKING AT MAN
GESTURES	SIGN LANGUAGE	SILENCE
SPACING	FOREGROUND	BACKGROUND
STAGING OF	UPRIGHT	SLOUCHED
CHARACTERS	FRONT	BEHIND

STATEMENT (ÉNONCIATION)

CULTURAL CATEGORIES

GENDER	MASCULINITY	FEMININITY
POWER	DOMINANT	MARGINAL
IDENTITY	CONFIDENT	UNCERTAIN
	ASSERTIVE	PASSIVE
DISCOURSE	CONTROL	CONTROLLED

Figure 4.4. Discourse Analysis: Form > Message > Culture

communicated through posture, gesture, and the direction of the characters' looks. The male is placed the foreground; the female stands behind him. The male stands straight; the female slouches down. Even more importantly, the male figure possesses "speech," as expressed in a kind of sign language. The male figure raises his hand in a sign of greeting and he also looks out in the direction of an imaginary interlocutor, addressing them with his gaze. The female's hands hang passively at her sides, and her eyes are looking in the direction of the male—as if he looks/speaks for her. The very absence of ethnic clothing or other markings on the bodies, such as hair or skin color, implies an equally oppositional relationship between the presence of the dominant ethnic ideal, that is, Caucasian, and the absence of ethnic "others" off-frame and out of sight.

The Ideology of Form

The formal organization of the image is thus inflected with an ideological perspective that is deeply engrained in the cultural context of the message. The postures and looks of the figures in the NASA plaque, their placement in the visual field, and their physical appearance communicate a gender subtext related to a specific place, the West, at a particular moment in time, mid-twentieth century. The male figure has the stronger position and looks out at the spectator, implicating him or her in his gaze. The female figure occupies the weaker position and looks off in the direction of the male. The paradigmatic association of the "look" with masculinity and dominance, and the "looked at" with femininity and submission, has structured gender representations since the emergence of the modern period in the seventeenth century.

It can be traced within the visual fields first of painting, then films and advertisements (see Mulvey, 1975; Oswald, 2010*a*). In other words, the formal codes organizing human figures in visual space are implicated in the cultural codes that structure gender and power.

Brand Discourse

Brands communicate with consumers in many forms from the design of product, packaging, or retail space to the cosmetic display at Bloomingdales or the menu board at McDonald's. For example, cosmetics displays in department stores used to be sacred areas of retailing, off-limits to customers. As marketing became more consumer-centric in the last century, the structure of the retailing environment changed to reflect a more empowered, self-directed consumer. Cosmetic retailers followed suit and moved products to self-service displays that enabled consumers to open, inspect, and sample products without the help of the sales person. Cosmetic trays filled with samples and make-up applicators were turned out toward the customer, as if to say, "Try me!" Thus, the retail brand "speaks" to consumers by means of design codes, such as the shape, location, and viewing angle of the product display (see Chapter 6 on retail semiotics).

Discourse analysis is particularly useful for evaluating how distinctive and consistent brand positioning is communicated in marketing communication over time and across media. Discourse analysis lays bare relationships between the literal meaning of marketing communication and the cultural subtexts that inevitably reference the codes structuring the values, beliefs, and cultural assumptions of consumers.

MCDONALD'S: A CASE IN POINT

A case in point is the representation of the female target in an annual report for the McDonald's corporation dating back to 1997. The annual report of a company forms a window onto the financial status of a company, its overall mission, and the soul of the brand. In fact, the advertising images in the report betray deeper, strategic problems that were brewing at McDonald's in the late 1990s (ElBoghdady, 2002; Martin, 2009). By means of structural analysis of the brand discourse in this set of images, I reveal an ideological subtext in McDonald's advertising that diminishes importance of women at a time when mothers with children were an important target segment. To say the least, the gender subtext suggests that management had indeed lost sight of its consumer base.

Figure 4.5. A Likeness of the Ad from McDonald's 1997 Annual Report

The Discourse Analysis

I begin with analysis of gender positions in a single advertisement and then show how this pattern is repeated throughout advertising in the report. Though the surface meaning of the advertisement above differs dramatically from the Pioneer 10 image, the organization bodies and looks in the McDonald's ad structures similar gender stereotypes to those inscribed in the Pioneer image. Two men are standing in the foreground of the image, shaking hands. In the background, a woman is seated, looking up at the men (Figure 4.5).

The men clearly possess the dominant "voice" in this ad, as reflected in their gestures, glances, and physical stance. They stand strongly and securely in the foreground of the image. They engage in a kind of male bonding ritual—shaking hands, looking directly into each other's eyes, and seem to be speaking to each other. The woman sits silently in the background, at a level below the men. Her gaze is focused on them; she is listening rather than speaking. The ideological subtext of this advertisement resembles that of the NASA image, because it places the female figure in a somewhat subservient role in relation to the male figures.

Were we to leave our review at the analysis of this single image, critics could say that the image was just an example of a bad ad, not a reflection of the brand positioning at that point in time. The ad is obviously targeted to a Hispanic audience, as reflected in the tag line, "*un momento asi solo en McDonalds*"— "A McDonald's moment." (Literally, "A moment like this only at McDonalds."). Defenders of the ad may claim that the image mirrors the role of women in Hispanic households, nothing more, nothing less. However, when I take into consideration the set of all images in the annual report in which this ad appeared, I discovered a pattern of meanings that contributed to a negative, if unintentional, subtext about women. All of the advertisements in the 1997 annual report show women in this light, forming a consistent subtext that dismisses women from the company's annual self-presentation. Another ad (#2) features two male NASCAR racers, and a third (#3) shows the back of Mom's head, her child looking toward the camera.

Women are hidden, absent, or marginalized in these pictures. This negative subtext about women not only suggests that the brand was out of step with the postfeminist culture of the 1990s. It also runs counter to the very important role of women with children in the overall positioning, identity, and revenue base of the McDonald's brand in the late 1990s.

Though management probably did not intend to move women to the background of their annual report to shareholders, the subtext of this communication reveals deeper strategic struggles at the company. The formal structure of this set of images suggests that the company had taken their eyes off the target market and lost touch with changes in the external culture, which probably contributed to the company's dramatic downturn at the century's end.

Managing the Cultural Subtext

Brands "speak" to consumers through marketing communication, from advertising and packaging to retail design, in the same way a speaker engages other speakers in conversation. Just as ambivalence and inconsistency raise doubts about the trustworthiness of speakers, so ambiguity, irrelevance, or inconsistency in brand communication threaten consumer trust and long-term value. To correct for ambiguity, management must begin with a clear understanding of the semiotic codes that structure text and subtext in brand communication, such as the direction of looks, body positions, and sign language in the McDonald's advertising. With this knowledge, management can then realign the form of the message with the culture of consumers. This is precisely how McDonald's made the correction.

A Repositioning

When the company repositioned the brand in 2003, they aligned the brand image with its global business initiatives, targeting a multicultural market of active women, children, and young singles, including men and women. The

Figure 4.6. A likeness of the cover of McDonald's 2003 Annual Report

new positioning is reinforced in the global, "I'm Lovin' It!" campaign, which signaled management's strategic response to the changing cultural environment. The new positioning was achieved precisely in terms of the ways advertising represented consumer empowerment by means of the "look" figure. For example, the covers of both booklets from the 2003 annual report feature ethnic females looking straight into the camera (Figure 4.6), and advertising for the new "I'm Lovin' It" campaign highlighted active women looking back at the camera.

A Shifting Cultural Paradigm

To summarize, advertising imagery in the 1997 annual report positions women in the background, in the margins, or out-of-view. It reflects an outdated stereotype of women as silent, passive figures in a man's world. In Figure 4.7, I have plotted this cultural stereotype on a semiotic square in order to show how management can deconstruct cultural stereotypes in the

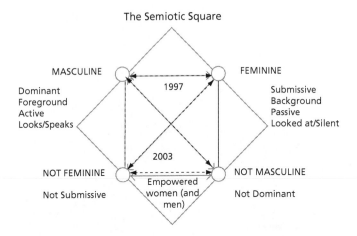

Figure 4.7. McDonald's 2003 Repositioning

repositioning process. Here, the cultural stereotype appears at the top of the square as the binary opposition between the dominant male and the submissive female. The lines drawn between these terms and their contrary terms, not masculine, not feminine, at the bottom of the square, represent the deconstruction of this gender stereotype, placing in question notions such as masculinity and femininity. This set of contraries—not masculine/not dominant, not feminine/not submissive—defines a new cultural space in which the new McDonald's image is positioned. It is the space of empowered consumers, female and male.

The new positioning is evident in the visual deconstruction of strict oppositions between masculine and feminine types and the emergence of the empowered female figure. The deconstruction of gender stereotypes was the tip of the iceberg of a more general movement of the brand toward a global, multicultural audience. This cultural positioning shaped creative strategy for the "I'm Lovin' It" campaign, as exemplified in a global advertisement for McDonald's in 2003 showing a young Asian woman smiling out at the consumer-spectator.

Though the analysis of a small set of advertising images may not provide exhaustive evidence of the company's financial strategy or the success of the brand at any point in time, it nonetheless provides evidence of the sensitivity to cultural change, unmet consumer needs, and the overall integrity of the brand—its consistency in communicating what it stands for and standing by what it communicates. In this case, we discovered that tensions within brand communication signaled deeper tensions at the company as management confronted changes in the marketplace. Furthermore, by focusing on gender stereotypes, this example shed light on only a narrow aspect of the positioning strategy of McDonald's for this period. The purpose of this analysis was to illustrate, in very simple terms, how the formal structure of an image, such as the organization of bodies and looks in advertisements, may communicate a cultural subtext (male/power, female/submission) that undermines, rather than supports, the brand positioning.

Managing the Brand Discourse

Discourse theory contributes not only to our understanding of the ways advertising makes meaning but also to the way brands sustain a positioning over time, remain distinctive in the competitive arena, relate to the culture of consumers, and engage the consumer-spectators in the brand world.

ANALYZING THE BRAND DISCOURSE

The previous examples shed light on the importance of differentiating the levels of analysis between the micro-discourse communicated in a single sign or image and the macro-discourse which accounts for the overall brand positioning and the broad cultural discourses which link the brand positioning to the evolving culture of consumers.

Levels of Analysis

In the following extended example, I lead the reader through three stages of analysis of communication for the Apple brand, including

- a synchronic analysis of the logotype used to symbolize the brand;
- a diachronic analysis of the logo in context of the brand history; and
- the cultural context of the brand; a strategic analysis of the brand in relation to the category.

Synchronic Analysis. Synchronic analysis focuses on the underlying structure of brand meaning that remains consistent at every point of contact between the consumer and the brand, from the logo to the packaging. Take logos for example. The logotype is a sign that condenses the brand message into an abstract symbol or icon. The logo is not just a metaphor for the brand, but a micro-discourse that references the brand positioning and the culture of the target market.

Diachronic Analysis. Just as verbal statements embed the single sign in the structure and reference of discourse, marketing communication too embeds individual signs, such as the logo, in the structure and reference of the underlying brand discourse and the culture of consumers. Though consumers respond in individual ways to brand messages, the effectiveness of brand communication relies upon the shared, not personal, perceptions of consumers, based on the codified associations between brand signs and the brand positioning. In this sense, the brand positioning forms a kind of "macro-discourse" that underlies creative strategy across media, markets, and time.

The Cultural Context. Brands are embedded in the broad cultural discourses that structure competitive difference and distinction in a competitive set, such as the existential relationship between Man and Machine in the personal computer category. To identify these paradigmatic structures in the culture, the semiotician does not rely on memory or intuition, but conducts secondary research to identify recurrences of the brand symbol in popular culture, corporate communications, and advertising. Researchers shift through popular films and novels, classical literature and pop music, historical and competitive advertising, and even the writings of experts such as psychologists and culture scholars, looking for recurrent meanings and organizing them into categories. For example, to determine the codes structuring gender stereotypes in consumer culture at a given moment in time, researchers draw evidence from dozens of sources in the mass media, popular culture, and the Internet.

Unpacking the Apple Logo

Logos transform natural signs into symbolic discourses by means of abstraction and condensation. For example, the Apple brand logo is more than a logotype referencing the company; it makes a statement about the brand. In the first place, the graphic design transforms the generic meaning of "apple"—a red fruit that grows on trees—into a symbol that communicates "apple-ness," freeing the image to suggest meanings that transcend apples per se and relate to the brand positioning. In the Apple logo, the apple is inscribed with a "bite," suggesting indulgence, tasting, and even the "bite" or sting associated with digging one's teeth into something.[1] (For an illustration of the Apple logo, see http://www.edibleapple.com/the-evolution-and-history-of-the-apple-logo).

The company website claims that the Apple logo references Eve's fateful bite from the apple in the Garden of Eden (Apple Corp., 2009). The logo also turns on end the association of the bitten apple with the Fall of mankind, by reframing the "bite" as a bold quest for knowledge. This reinterpretation of the original story of Eve traces brand "voice" in the logo, in the same way that metaphors trace the narrator's voice in the novel, or editing traces narrating

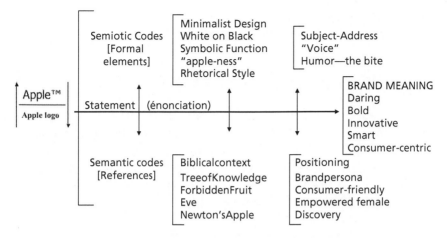

Figure 4.8. The Apple Brand Discourse: A Synchronic Perspective

presence in cinema (Barthes, 1977*b*). In the same way that "I" implies reference to an addressee or "you," in speech, the instance of "voice" in visual discourse implicates the consumer/reader in the brand story. Figure 4.8 demonstrates the complexity of the logo as a semiotic system that condenses the brand positioning in the formal design and cultural reference of an apple and addresses the consumer by means of the ironic "voice" of the brand.

A cursory examination of apple symbolism in the data reveals patterns of culturally coded meanings that have evolved in Western culture over the centuries. Even if consumers do not immediately think of Eve when exposed to the logo, secondary associations of apple symbols with knowledge, discovery, and transgression have been overdetermined in legend and popular culture, from the apple that fell on Isaac Newton's head, to the "Big Apple"—New York City. The "apple with a bite" may convey risk-taking or defiance of authority, and also a quest for learning, since Eve plucked the apple from the Tree of Knowledge. From the beginning, MacIntosh targeted schools and students, and chose the apple because of its habitual association with knowledge and school. The Apple logo thus condenses cultural meanings and Apple brand equities, including education, innovation, and breaking the rules.

Founders Jobs and Wayne designed the original logo, a drawing that shows Isaac Newton sitting under an apple tree reading a book. An apple hangs above his head, presumably ready to fall on his head, whereupon he discovered gravity, as the story goes. The visual design resembles a Victorian etching, trimmed with a banner inscribed with the company name, the "Apple Computer Company." A few years later, the company replaced the drawing with a modern, rainbow-colored silhouette of an apple with a bite in it, designed by Janoff. The stylized apple design has become a global icon for technological innovation, modernism, and style. The consumer target has evolved from schools and students to all forward-thinking, style-conscious consumers.

IMPLICATIONS FOR BRAND STRATEGY

A discourse analysis of brand communication shows how a single communication vehicle, such as a logo or advertisement, is implicated in a broader system of meanings related to the historical positioning and cultural context of the brand, which I call the macro-brand discourse. In the current section, I extend the scope of analysis and examine the broad cultural paradigms that structure meaning across a product category.

The Meaning of Personal Computers

In the 1980s and 1990s, Apple and IBM defined the strategic parameters of the personal computer (PC) category in terms of a broad cultural discourse defining the relationship between Man and Machine. Apple was consumer friendly, IBM was aloof and professional. Competitors, such as Compaq, were challenged to find a distinctive space in this competitive arena. The following case examines how the Compaq brand floundered to find a unique positioning in the category, leading to the brand's demise.

In 1990, Compaq was a rising star in the PC market, positioned as a low-cost, high-quality alternative to IBM. By the late 1990s, the company was rapidly losing market share, and the brand was increasingly identified with a low-cost commodity. In a famous takeover in 2003, the company was acquired by Hewlett Packard. Our analysis of competitive advertising in the PC market between 1992 and 1997 suggests that Compaq failed because it did not stake out a unique and consistent positioning in a category defined by the existential question of how consumers interface with machines.

The IBM and Apple brands defined the emotional dimensions of this interface of Man and Machine. Distinctions between the brand positionings of IBM and Apple form a paradigm of binary oppositions, beginning with the brand names themselves. The International Business Machines name is straightforward; it references the product and emphasizes technology. The Apple name is poetic; it symbolizes creativity and emphasizes the user of technology. In company communications, these differences extend to logo design, color scheme, camera point of view, characters, and visual style.

A third alternative was the Dell brand, positioned as a price-driven commodity to experienced users who were confident enough to order PC's by individual specification from a catalogue (Figure 4.9).

This grid displays the various binary oppositions that characterize the Man and Machine paradigm, and breaks out the formal properties of advertising semiotics

The Man Vs. Machine Paradigm

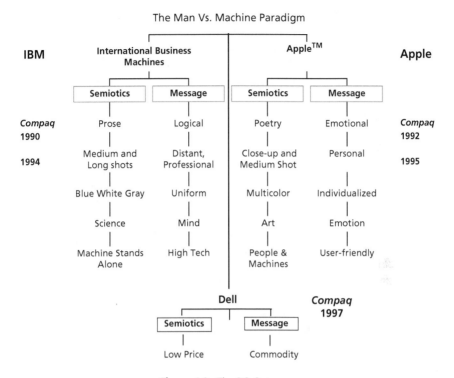

Figure 4.9. The PC Category

to the messages they communicate about the brand. The IBM logo consists of blue-and-white striped logotype of the company initials. The Apple logo is a multicolored striped apple with a bite. In advertising, IBM extends its reputation in the mainframe computer category, emphasizing the machine rather than the user. Targeted to experienced business professionals, advertising employs a minimalist style. The computer technology seems to speak for itself, displayed in medium shot against a white backdrop. The blue-and-white logo adds the only color to the austere visuals. Television advertising reiterates the minimalist style, using the limited color spectrum of blues, grays, and beige. Camera movements are also kept to a minimum, and captures business professionals in suits in objective rather than subjective angles, in medium and long shot perspectives.

Apple advertising, on the other hand, was characterized by color and detail, suggesting the more nuanced and emotional appeal of the brand to the average consumer. Advertisements feature users in relation to the machine in close-up, reiterating the more intimate and friendly relation between the user and the technology. Television advertising structures medium shot perspectives and subjective point of view camera angles in rapid montage to engage the consumer-spectator in the action and communicate the brand's intimacy with consumers.

In brief, the prose style of IBM advertising reinforces the brand associations with conformity; logic over emotion; its distant, professional relationship to consumers; and a scientific approach to personal computing. By contrast, the poetic style of Apple reinforces brand associations with innovation and creativity, with human factors over logic; its personal, accessible relationship to consumers; and a lifestyle approach to personal computing.

Positioning Compaq

To compete in this category in the 1990s, Compaq needed to identify a clear, consistent message about the relationship of computer technology to consumers. A diachronic analysis of historical advertising for the brand between 1990 and 1997 revealed that Compaq shifted constantly between the user-friendly positioning of Apple to the professional emphasis of IBM over the years. Failing to compete on brand image, Compaq ultimately identified with low price, but was edged out of that market space by Dell, the standard bearer for low-price technology.

Compaq was positioned in the 1980s as a less expensive IBM clone for business professionals. In advertising from the early 1990s, advertising emphasized the consumer benefits of the technology, featuring professionals who used Compaq technology to compete in business, with the tagline, "Compaq does it better." At the same time, advertising in the United Kingdom featured John Cleese, a creator of *Monty Python*, playing the amateur who confuses the colloquial and technological meanings of "chips" and "buses." With the launch of the Presario home computer, Compaq targeted families and students, and faced Apple head-on with a campaign featuring ways computers "Enrich our lives." This campaign emphasized the accessibility and warmth of the Compaq brand. Though all of these campaigns, taken in isolation, had appeal and entertainment value, when examined in diachronic and strategic context, they highlight the instability of brand strategy over time.

Print advertising reflected even more dramatically the shifts in Compaq brand positioning from year to year. For example, a 1995 campaign featured a gray computer against a white background, resembled IBM ads for the period; a 1997 campaign featured a metaphorical comparison between the computer and a work by Da Vinci in vivid color, resembled Apple ads for the period. Such shifts in positioning from year to year raise the question, "Would the real Compaq persona please stand up?" By the end of the 1990s, Compaq lost its competitive edge and was forced to compete on price.

The discourse analysis of brand communication illustrates how advertising, examined in the context of historical and competitive campaigns, provides a window onto the consistency and distinctiveness of brand strategy over the lifetime of the brand. Too often, management focuses on testing single campaigns with consumers when they should be asking whether the current campaign sustains a single vision and positioning over a prolonged period of time. Not only does this approach guarantee a consistent brand message but forces management to systematically monitor the brand for its internal coherence and its competitive difference.

Narrative Discourse

The previous examples illustrate the interdependency of marketing signs, brand positioning, and the culture of consumers. They also shed light on the discursive function of the brand logo, the implication of the logo in the reference and subject-address of brand discourse, and the implication of the brand in the broad cultural paradigms that structure the product category, such as the opposition of Man and Machine. In the following case study, I extend analysis to the narrative codes that structure continuity between visual elements in television advertising and engage the consumer-spectator in the brand story.

THE CASE OF KRAFT SINGLES

Over the eighteen-year period of advertising beginning in 1985, Kraft Singles advertising increasingly emphasized emotional benefits such as pleasure, humor, and fantasy, culminating in a very successful campaign called, "The Dairy Fairy". For the first time in the brand's history, the creative team not only inserted fiction and fantasy into the brand message, but deployed codes for narrative continuity and point of view to integrate product benefits into the brand fantasy featuring an animated character. The editing increased the emotional appeal of the advertising and added relevance to the brand for younger consumers. These visual strategies also engaged consumer-spectators in the illusion of a seamless narrative in which the product is the hero.

Background

Kraft Foods introduced the Kraft Singles sliced processed cheese in 1947, positioning the brand as a healthy, flavorful product for young children. At the time of this analysis, 2003, advertising for the brand had passed through several iterations and extensions of a campaign begun in the 1980s with a visual narrative showing children eating cheese sandwiches while a parental voice off-screen spoke of the health benefits of the brand, with "5 ounces of milk in every Single." The advertising evolved over a twenty-year period, and one campaign, in particular, "Dairy Fairy" (1996–8), boasted high scores in consumer response and memorability. For clients seeking to develop new advertising while retaining the essential experience of the current ad, a semiotic analysis of the codes structuring the ad is useful. To illustrate, in the following analysis, I identify the codes structuring spectator identification or engagement with the shot-by-shot organization of points of view in the ad.

A rigorous formal analysis of advertising for Kraft Singles over a twenty year period beginning in 1985[2] shows a gradual evolution in the visual style over time. These changes in style parallel changes in the culture of children as consumer. The analysis also showed how a specific configuration of codes structuring continuity and point of view in the *Dairy Fairy* campaign contributed to positive emotional associations with the brand and heightened consumer-spectator involvement in the brand world. To show how this figure evolved, I begin with a structural analysis of the story that is repeated throughout the campaign's history.

The Brand Narrative in Synchronic Perspective

Advertising originally targeted parents, but in recent years increasingly targeted children directly, reflecting the evolving importance of young consumers in the decision-making process. A consistent sequence of narrative events recurs from campaign to campaign throughout the data set, which includes twenty-nine, thirty-second spots created from 1985 to 2003. The basic sequence includes six narrative segments:

The Opening Question	A parent asks, in voice-over, some version of the question, "What makes Kraft Singles taste so good?"
Child Scene 1, lunch	On screen, a child or children eat their cheese sandwiches. A glass of milk stands next to the sandwich.
Product Benefits	A parental figure in voice-over explains that Singles taste good because, "Every three-quarter ounce Single is made with 5 ounces of milk." After 1998, the milk claim was changed to calcium benefits.
Product Demonstration	The image cuts away to milk being poured into a glass, then cuts to an "imitation" brand, "made with oil and water," and a shot of oil being poured into a glass. After 1998, this shot was replaced with a statement about calcium.
Child Scene 2, play	A shot of happy, active children are testimony to the product benefits. In the 1990s, this section included an animated fantasy scene.
End	The voice-over pronounces a tagline, such as "Experience the magic of milk" or a child spells K-R-A-F-T. The ending is accompanied by the musical jingle of five notes that correspond to the five letters of the brand name.

The Brand Narrative in Diachronic Perspective

These events recur in the historical advertising, but they do not tell the whole story, because narrative discourse is more than a summary of the action. Like any other discourse, narrative discourse consists of an interpretation of events by a narrator, traced in visual representation by means of structural elements, including rhetorical associations, camera point of view, and continuity editing. Narrative discourse also implies an addressee, the consumer-spectator, who engages with the representation by means of identification with the looks of characters in the image.

Although the basic scenario for Kraft Singles advertising did not vary much over the eighteen-year period, the tone, the visual style, and the brand message evolved in relation to changes in the target market. By the 1990s, households were becoming increasingly child-centered, and children were more involved than ever in purchase decisions. As the result, advertising targeted children themselves, not only their parents.

Whereas earlier ads were narrated by a parental voice off-screen, in the 1990s, children in the ads began speaking to the off-screen narrator about the brand, looking into the camera with confidence. The most recent campaigns engaged two children in dialogue, with very little voice-over narration. As the emotional tone of the advertising "heated up," the cold cheese sandwich was replaced by grilled cheese. Beginning in the early 1990s, an appetizing "cheese pull" shot was added to demonstrate the creamy goodness of melted American cheese. The increasingly child-centered focus of the brand is reflected in the increasing authority of children in advertising in the 1990s. Figure 4.10 maps the stages of this evolution over time from the child as icon and a character in the parents' story to the child as endorser and the empowered child.

1980s: Children as Icons

In advertisements from the early 1980s, children are the silent, passive objects of the parental voice-over narration (e.g., *Blue Eyes* 1985, *Major League* 1986). One group of ads pits children who eat Singles cheese sandwiches against children who eat "imitation" products (*Joey* 1987–8, *Mousies* 1988, *True Love* 1989). The voice-over clearly addresses other parents in the audience, not children, and appeals to the parent's need to buy the very best for their child. The children, referred to in the third person, eat cold cheese sandwiches alone or with playmates. The narrator-parent speaks in place of the child because, "He doesn't know what that big Kraft means. Glad I do" (*Major League* 1986).

The early campaigns are characterized by a static, emotionally distant editing style. Shots of kids are spliced with laboratory shots of the product, without suggesting any continuity between these contexts. Transitions are achieved by

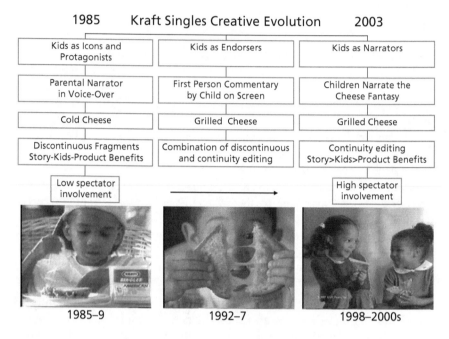

Figure 4.10. Kraft Singles Diachronic Analysis

means of fade-dissolves overlapping the previous shot with the following one. The omniscient narrative point of view engages the audience in the voice-over narrative, but keeps them outside of the story unfolding in the image.

1990s: Children as Endorsers

By the 1990s, the parental voice-over was mixed in with the voices of children speaking. Although the voice-over narrator still presents product information, such as the "5 ounces of milk in every Single," children are no longer the passive objects of a story told by an omniscient narrator; they narrate fantasies about how cheese is made and speak into the camera in the first person. They engage in dialogue with the voice-over narrator, answering questions and narrating fantasies, shown in animation shots, of the way that Kraft puts 5 oz. of milk in every Single (e.g., *Rocket* 1993, *Dr. Milk* and *Tortilla Trap* 1994, *Moonbeams* 1995). These changes imply that the target audience now includes children as well as parents.

Although the editing style is still static, the direction of looks into the camera engages the consumer-spectator directly, and the child's fantasy adds life to the traditional product display comparing the milk in Kraft to the oil in cheap imitations.

1996–2000s: Empowered Kids

With the *Dairy Fairy* campaign (1996–8), the parental voice-over narrative is reduced to a minimum because two children speaking to each other on screen take over the narration. An older child explains to a younger child how the fantasy character, the "Dairy Fairy," adds the milk to Kraft Singles cheese. The image cuts between shots of the two children talking, shots of the animated cartoon scene with the Dairy Fairy, and shots of the product demonstration.

The Cultural Subtext

The evolution of Singles advertising betrays a parallel evolution in a cultural subtext about the role of children in consumer society. In the 1980s, the off-screen voice of the omniscient narrator tells the story; on-screen children play or eat sandwiches, unaware of the camera. Over time, the growing importance of children as spokespersons and narrators in the ads reflects a kind of deconstruction of the parent–child binary not unlike the deconstruction of the masculine–feminine binary discussed early in the chapter. Children ultimately replace the parental voice off-screen and assume the voice of authority for the brand.

THE SPECTATING SUBJECT IN QUESTION

Analysis of the structure of subject-address—the formal mapping of the looks of characters on screen with the look of the spectator—structured consumer engagement in the Dairy Fairy campaign and provided a blueprint for creating a new campaign. In summary, the figure of "looking" structures continuity between narrative segments and implicates the consumer-spectator in the brand narrative. Findings illustrate how the cinematic codes structuring continuity, narrative point of view, rhetorical associations, and subject-address in visual discourse communicate the brand's accessibility, emotional benefits, and overall positioning for consumers.

Continuity Editing

The Dairy Fairy campaign received high marks in consumer testing. The effectiveness of the *Dairy Fairy* spot derives, in large part, from an apparently seamless integration of product benefits and a child's fantasy. Narrative devices such as eye-level matching and cutting on movement suture the junctures between disparate scenes of characters using a product, voice-over comments about product benefits, music, and images of the brand. At each point of contact between the brand and the child's fantasy, the advertisement builds consumer identification with the brand world.

- The spot opens with a voice-over asking a rhetorical question: "Every three-quarter ounce Kraft Single is made from 5 ounces of milk. How do they do that?

- In the next shot, Girl A answers the question, but is not responding directly to the narrator, but to a younger girl, Girl B. Girl A begins a narrative about a Fairy Queen who plays magic in the kitchen.

- The image cuts to an animated sequence with the Dairy Fairy in the kitchen.

- Next, the direction of Girl A's look traces a trajectory from left to right in shot 2, which is matched in the next shot, 4, when the Dairy Fairy flies into the kitchen from left to right. This code for structuring continuity between shots creates an illusion of continuity between the "real" conversation between the girls and the animated fantasy scene that she narrates.

- The Dairy Fairy pours milk into Singles Cheese in shot 6. Cut to the Kraft laboratory and a voice-over narrator discusses the milk that is being poured into the Kraft Single. These parallel gestures link together the Dairy Fairy fantasy and the product benefits, reinforcing the emotional benefits of the brand. Parallels between the Singles fantasy and the brand are reinforced in shot 11, when the Dairy Fairy cartoon from shot 6 is superimposed over a package of Kraft Singles in real time and space.

The Shot-Reverse-Shot

Continuity editing not only creates an illusion of a seamless flow of action in film time and space but also structures intersubjective relationships between figures in the image and between images. In moving pictures, such as film and video, relationships between characters in narrative space are organized by means of the shot-reverse-shot figure. The shot-reverse-shot rose to prominence in the classical Hollywood cinema in the 1940s and 1950s and consists of cuts between shots of two people addressing each other in the story. It consists of an establishing shot with the two characters and a series of subjective shots showing each character in separate shots, alternating between a character looking off-screen and another character being looked at from the point of view of the characters (Bordwell and Thompson, [1979] 2006).

The illusion of continuity between characters looking and the objects of their looks is reinforced by eye-line matching and the 180° rule, which stipulates that the "reverse" shot of the object of the look must be angled immediately across from the character looking (Bordwell and Thompson, [1979] 2006). In the *Dairy Fairy* sequence, the angle of vision on the "reverse"

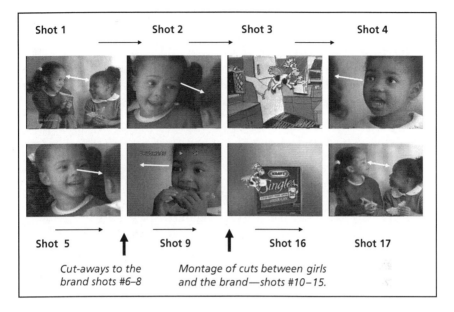

Figure 4.11. A Shot-Reverse-Shot Sequence

shots has been opened up beyond the 180° angle and addresses the consumer-spectator directly.

In the example given in Figure 4.11, I extracted the shot-reverse-shot sequence in the *Dairy Fairy* ad to illustrate the basic structure of this device. It consists of a series of alternating shots of characters looking off-screen followed by the object of their looks (see Figure 4.11).

The sequence opens with an "establishing" shot showing two girls, A on the left, B on the right, seated in a single space, talking to each other. Then the image cuts to a close-up of Girl A looking off-screen (shot 2), in the direction of Girl B. The point of view "reverses" and we then see Girl B looking back in the direction of Girl A (shot 4). The alternation of Girl A looking off-screen and the cut to Girl B looking back is repeated in shots 5 and 9, and ends with the return to the two girls talking to each other in a single space in shot 12. This technique has an advantage over a shot of two characters in the same image because it moves the camera point of view from the static, omniscient viewpoint of the impersonal camera to the dynamic, subjective viewpoints of characters in the ad.

Furthermore, the subjective viewpoints of the camera engage the spectator's identification with the story. As Metz ([1977] 1981) discovered, the spectator identifies first with the omniscient look of the camera by means of an identification of I with camera "eye" or lens. This original identification of the spectator as "I" with the camera "eye" enables them to identify secondarily with characters on screen. The Dairy Fairy ad engaged consumers in the brand narrative because the creative team inserted shots of the product and the brand fantasy into the shot-reverse-shot structure, as in the cuts between Girl A looking off-frame in shot 2 and Girl B looking back in shot 4. Inserting the cut away to the brand within a shot-reverse-shot sequence creates an illusion of seamless continuity between the brand, the story, and the consumer-spectator's imaginary.

Implications for Brand Equity

Questions of spectator identification have been carefully debated in cinema semiotics literature, particularly as they relate to the intersection of semiotics and psychoanalysis—mind and meaning—in representation (Heath, 1982; Metz, [1977] 1981; Silverman, 1983). Although space does not permit a thorough examination of these theories here, suffice it to say that by opening an imaginary space off-screen, the shots of characters looking invite the spectator to fill in the openings in the visual field, created by the looks off-screen, with their personal imaginaries. In this way, the shot-reverse-shot engages the consumer-spectator in the brand story, increasing the emotional impact and memorability of the advertisement. So, it follows that use of this editing structure in an ad campaign like *Dairy Fairy* would engage consumers more actively than through other editing styles.

A discourse analysis of the campaign showed that the figure of "looking" that I discussed earlier in the chapter played a role in the success of the *Dairy Fairy* campaign and provided management with a tool for developing successful creative strategy moving forward.

AUDIENCE RESPONSE TESTING

Although some readers may scoff at the scientific validity of psychoanalytic hypothesis, independent testing with consumers proved a strong, positive correlation between the figures for subject-address in the shot-reverse-shot sequence and consumer response to the advertisement.

Management ran an independent Link test (Milward Brown, Inc.) that supported findings from the semiotic analysis, that emotional response is strongest at the intersection of images in the shot-reverse-shot sequence, when the brand is inserted into the discourse there, where the character's look off-screen opens up an imaginary space to be filled in by the consumer-spectator (Thompson, 2003). Findings from the research highlighted those particular structural elements in the visual discourse, especially the shot-reverse-shot sequence linking characters to the brand, that could be deployed in many forms in future advertising.

Conclusion

In this chapter, I presented the basic elements of discourse and their implications for advertising and other forms of brand communication. I identified various levels of semiotic analysis from the micro-discourses that form individual texts, such as the brand logo or a single image, to the macro-discourse structuring the brand positioning and linking the brand to the broad myths and archetypes drawn from consumer culture. And I introduced the reader to the fundamentals of narrative discourse and the codes structuring narrative continuity and spectator identification in television advertising. Furthermore, the examples and cases demonstrate that semiotics provides management with actionable strategic tools for clarifying brand meanings, aligning brand meanings with the needs and wants of consumers, and engaging consumers in the brand discourse.

These findings have important implications for multicultural brand strategy and advertising research, not only to avoid cultural bias but also to extend the primary brand positioning into consumer subcultures and international markets. Without understanding the secondary codes structuring the cultural interpretation of advertising, marketers may as well be communicating with Martians. They would have limited awareness of the effectiveness of their campaign to support the brand positioning and relate to the target market. International editions of *Vogue* and *Elle*, for example, abound with unmodified fashion advertisements produced in Paris and New York, reflecting the assumption that luxury brands transcend cultural differences and appeal equally to women East and West.

Misreading the interpretive frames of consumer culture can lead to ambiguity, non-sense, and even political censorship. For example, the Chinese government banned Nike's ad showing LeBron James in a fight with Chinese martial artists because the company did not take into account the cultural subtext communicated by the ad, which seemed to denigrate Chinese traditions and boast American supremacy (Fowler, 2004).

Culture-specific codes form an interpretive frame for meaning production, particularly in the mass media. For this reason, from one consumer market to another, whether earth-bound or in Lasher's extraterrestrial world, advertising may mean different things to different consumers, thereby undermining the integrity of the overall brand message or discourse.

■ **ENDNOTES**

1. Apple management denied permission to reproduce the Apple logo.
2. Kraft Historical Advertising: 1985–2004.

ICONS AND PROTAGONISTS (6)

Kids as Icons

Blue Eyes (1985)

Major League Material (1986)

Class Picture (1986–7)

Kids as Protagonists

Joey (1987–8)

Mousies (1988)

True Love (1989)

NARRATORS AND ENDORSERS (11)

Kids as Narrators

Ta Da (1991)

Two Girls (1992)

Rocket (1993)

Dr. Milk (1994)

Big Dipper (1994)

Moonbeams (1995)

Tortilla Trap (1994)

[Cooper (1994–5)]

Tall Tale (1996–7)

Kids as Endorsers

Milk Montage (1997)

So Dee-Licious (1997)

EMPOWERED KIDS (12)

Mommy Cow (1993)

Dairy Fairy (1996–8)

Lady Bovine (2000–2)

Your Face Smiles (1997)

Calcium They Need (1998)

Lady Bovine (2000)

[Planning (2001)]

[Mooch (2002)]

[Double (2002)]

[Nails (2002)]

Lady Bovine (2002)

Construction 2% Tag (2002).

5 Mining the Multicultural Brandscape

"We all speak English, don't we?"

In consumer culture, the semiotic value of goods transcends their economic value and drives competitive advantage in the marketplace. This principle is especially salient for building brand equity, because brands consist entirely of the exchange of meaning between producer and consumer. Even customer loyalty is a function of consumers' symbolic relationships with brands. They might rely on brands to improve their self-image or to assist them in their life-stage transitions (see Aaker, 1991; Fournier, 1998; Keller, 2007). For example, an immigrant may purchase brands that remind them of home or symbolize their initiation into the new culture (Peñaloza, 1994). This symbolic appeal, which I call "brand semiotics," transcends the product benefits per se and creates value by satisfying the emotional needs of consumers. It forms an intangible asset for the company and contributes to the financial success of the company.

In previous chapters, I demonstrated the use of semiotics, the science of signs and meaning in cultural context, to grow brand equity. I showed the importance of mapping a Consumer Brandscape to guide the integration of the brand legacy (logo, icons, stories, advertising messages), the consumer target, and the cultural context in all brand-building decisions. In this chapter, I extend this principle to brand management in multicultural contexts, where consumers may speak a common language, but view the world through unique social and cultural lenses associated with their ethnic subculture. Multicultural brand strategy relies on semiotics to "translate" brand values from one cultural context to another.

I begin this chapter with an overview of the semiotic codes that structure symbolic consumption—the process of endowing goods and consumer rituals with meaning. I then show how ethnic groups rework the rituals and meanings of mass consumer culture in order to integrate them into their own culture and worldview. The dual process of projecting meanings into goods and translating mass consumer culture into local rituals and meanings has important implications for brand strategy as well. In order to target ethnic consumers, brand communication must translate the primary positioning into the signs and symbols of ethnic subcultures while retaining the essence of the brand message. In the following pages, I take the reader through the various stages of research and analysis required to build brand extensions targeted to ethnic subcultures.

Brands in Translation

Translating brands demands more than literally translating advertising from one language to another or using ethnic actors. It demands a clear understanding of a few simple concepts, including:

- How social groups rework the cultural codes structuring a product category or consumer ritual, such as preparing the holiday meal or customizing a vehicle;
- How consumers employ rhetorical operations to personalize these practices in culturally relevant discourses;
- How marketers can transfer consumer insights into brand symbolism;
- How multicultural marketers translate primary brand symbolism in advertising messages targeted to consumer subcultures.

Through research, analysis, and creative strategy, multicultural brand strategy has the potential to extend the value of the brand by making connections between the primary positioning and the culture of consumer subcultures.[1] As illustrated in the examples below, management can either follow a strict cultural segmentation strategy, and develop two separate brand positionings for each segment, or integrate the differences among consumer subcultures around single, multidimensional brand positioning. The latter extension strategy is not only more efficient but it also actually strengthens the primary brand by finding culturally relevant ways of communicating the brand across multiple segments.

A SEPARATE BUT EQUAL STRATEGY

The following example demonstrates how a "separate but equal" strategy employed by Philip Morris in the 1970s alienated the African-American market. To this day, Marlboro, the best-selling cigarette brand in the world, claims only a tiny share of market with this ethnic group.

When Leo Burnett created the Marlboro Man cowboy in the 1960s, they moved the Philip Morris brand to the top of the category. The Marlboro Man is a cool, self-sufficient, "lone ranger," who epitomizes a kind of white American hero made popular in films and on television of the period. The cowboy represents the strong, self-reliant adventurer who symbolizes

America's lost frontier legacy. Marlboro's dominance in the tobacco category and its legendary status as a cultural icon can be attributed to the brand's consistent association with this powerful image. The cowboy archetype satisfies unmet consumer needs for the freedom, adventure, and independence represented by the American West.[2]

Marlboro claims the lion's share of the mass market and dominates the category for brand awareness, loyalty, and emotional associations. However, its strength in the white mainstream is not matched in the African-American segment, where the brand claims a meager 7 percent market share (USDHHS, 2005). From the beginning, African Americans failed to identify with the cowboy character, viewing the Marlboro Man as a "loser" and loner, quite the opposite of the African-American "hero"—a family man, living in the city, and engaged in responsible roles with extended family and community (Chambers, 2008: 247–9).

To respond to this problem, Philip Morris adopted a sort of "separate but equal" brand extension strategy that targeted the African-American segment with a distinct message and brand positioning. Rather than translate the equities associated with the Marlboro Man into culturally sensitive advertising, they hired the pioneering African-American agency, Burrell, to develop a separate positioning and advertising campaign for the African-American market, focusing on everyday people and activities in the city. We see smokers at an outdoor market, driving in their cars, and talking to their friends, but no attempt at translating the powerful equities consumers associate with the primary brand into a distinctive African-American icon or story. Apart from skin color, the campaign neglected to incorporate cultural cues associated with African-American urban culture. It furthermore neglected to translate powerful brand equities, such as freedom, into culturally sensitive signs and symbols (Table 5.1).

As shown in the grid, the two campaigns present two distinct brand worlds and two unrelated consumer cultures, as represented in the lines separating the primary and secondary segments. The primary campaign targets the white

Table 5.1. The Marlboro Strategy

	A separate but equal segmentation	
Brand segment	Primary	Secondary
Ethnicity	American mainstream	African-American
Persona	The white male archetype	Other
Landscape	Rural	Urban
Personal space	Self-sufficient	Socially connected
Geography	The frontier	The community
Worldview	No boundaries	Segregated

American mainstream; the ethnic campaign targets the African-American minority segment. There is no attempt to bridge the two segments by means of shared values, beliefs, or lifestyles. The cowboy archetype has powerful nuances for the mainstream but is not replaced by an equally powerful African-American archetype in the ethnic campaign. The rural, self-sufficient, frontier mythology represented in the mainstream campaign found no counterpart in the ethnic campaign, which represents socially connected, urban consumers in routine, everyday activities.

The separate but equal approach to targeting African Americans failed in two very important ways. The ethnic campaign did not draw upon the strengths of the primary brand, which had more to do with values such as independence and freedom than cowboys per se. These intangible brand equities could have formed a line of continuity between the primary brand and the extension. The campaign also failed to exploit the rich legacy of urban African-American culture for mainstream American consumers, including musical traditions and sports icons, which could have formed another link between the two segments. The separate but equal brand strategy was a lose–lose proposition. Management's decision to develop an independent campaign for African Americans, combined with a diluted representation of a distinctive ethnic identity, alienated African Americans. To this day, the African-American target still only represents a small percentage of Marlboro's substantial market share.

A MULTICULTURAL BRAND STRATEGY

Multicultural brand strategy moderates the movement of brand meanings from the primary target to consumer subcultures by building upon, rather than departing from, the primary brand positioning.[3]

As I show in the case study featured in this chapter, a brand extension strategy built upon synergies between the white male mainstream and the African-American target would *merge*, rather than separate, the primary brand positioning and the culture of urban African Americans.

The Coca-Cola Company began a multicultural strategy many years ago and, as a consequence, continues to appeal to a broad multicultural audience successfully. In the 1970s, under the guidance of Burrell, an African-American advertising agency, Coke adopted a multicultural brand strategy, looking for ways to highlight the cultural reality of the ethnic target, while also bridging cultural differences with its primary target (Chambers, 2008: 247). In 1972, Burrell advised that the current advertising theme for the brand, "Look up, America, and see what you've got," would not resonate with black consumers, who had not yet realized the economic progress of the white middle class. He suggested a campaign that would incorporate the "real thing" tagline, "For real times, it's the real thing." The success of the campaign not only earned for Burrell the Coca-Cola account but it also demonstrated how a brand theme could be reworked to appeal to ethnic consumers. Later, Burrell developed a jingle for the African-American segment called, "Street Song," that made a hit in the black community and also became popular with the mainstream audiences as well (*Advertising Age*, 1996). The ad presents a snapshot of the urban American black experience. Some young men sit on the stoop of an urban house singing the tune in a cappella (Chambers, 2008: 247–9). The campaign won a CLIO award and was so successful that the management even incorporated the African-American jingle into ads targeted to the mainstream (see Table 5.2).

By taking a multicultural approach to ethnic marketing, the management at Coca-Cola opened channels of meaning exchange between the mainstream and subculture segments. This approach not only contributed to the success of the target extension among African Americans but also added value to the primary brand by expanding the world of meanings associated with Coke.

In the next section, I review the principles of symbolic consumption, paying close attention to the ways goods not only carry meanings for consumers but also how consumers adapt the meaning of goods and brands to their cultural agendas. And I then show how marketers can translate brand meanings from one cultural context to another.

Table 5.2. The Coca-Cola Strategy

	A multicultural segmentation	
Brand segment	Primary	Secondary
Ethnicity	Multicultural mainstream	African-American
Culture	Heterogeneous ←——→	Distinctive
Personal space	Inclusive	Integrated
Geography	One world	Community
Worldview	No boundaries	Part of the "we"
Contact point	A-A music	A-A music

Symbolic Consumption

The very notion of brands in translation is founded on the principle that the Consumer Brandscape is kind of language in which goods and rituals, rather than words, are the signifiers of meaning. In other words, in addition to the traditional economic wisdom that the marketplace is organized around supply and demand, the theory of symbolic consumption accounts for the value of the meanings associated with goods and brands in the equation (Douglas and Isherwood, [1979] 2002). In other words, if wearing a luxury watch endows the consumer with status, the symbolic or "status" value of the watch is greater than the costs associated to manufacture, market, and distribute it. The codes structuring the "language" of goods resemble a range of semiotic systems organizing social life, such as traffic signs or the Thanksgiving meal. These codes regulate transparently the behavior of consumers and structure the meaning of goods.

Symbolic consumption relies on cognitive processes that enable humans to transfer meanings from the realm of personal experience (such as memories, fantasies, or simply metaphors) to brands. As I discussed in Chapter 1, the symbolic function of goods is based on the same psychological process that enables humans to form symbols and learn language. Consumers project meanings onto goods, such as personal taste, values, and beliefs. They endow their possessions with meanings that may even exceed their material value, as with an heirloom or special object charged with memories. They also extend their own identities by internalizing the meanings of goods. The symbolic function of goods relies on psychological displacements that move meanings from the mind to external representations (see Levy, 1959; Douglas and Isherwood, 1979; McCracken, 1986; Belk, 1988; Belk et al., 1989).

Like language, symbolic consumption is also culturally codified to some extent, since the meanings consumers attach to goods and rituals derive from the collective cultural consciousness of a group. For example, the colors associated with brands may mean different things in different markets. The Chinese associate red with celebration, happiness, and good luck; so the meaning of red in logos for brands such as Coke and McDonald's fits well with this foreign market. Indians associate these meanings with the color blue; so to succeed in India, Western brands may introduce blue accents into their marketing communications.

CONSUMER CULTURES IN TRANSLATION

Symbolic consumption is a dynamic practice that not only "reflects" the meaning of a culture but also fosters cultural creativity—the process by which consumers create their personal realities by manipulating the signs of consumer culture. For this reason, the meaning of goods is not fixed in time nor shared by all members of a society. Consumers bend the meaning of goods to satisfy their own day-to-day needs from expressing solidarity with their group to participating in the mainstream culture. In this sense, symbolic consumption can be an important medium of consumer acculturation. Immigrants to the United States, for example, may use consumer goods to negotiate tensions between their dual needs to participate in mainstream society and to maintain their unique cultural identities. They may filter the new culture through the lens of the old by mixing ethnic traditions with the consumption practices of the new culture (see Peñaloza, 1994; Oswald, 1999). Consumer acculturation is an example of cultural creativity in action, where consumers "perform" the codes of culture to satisfy their own agendas, in the same way that speakers perform the codes of language in order to communicate.

Celebrating Thanksgiving in a Multicultural Context

The preparation of the Thanksgiving meal is an object lesson for the study of cultures in translation. Consumers manipulate codes such as, "Americans serve turkey at Thanksgiving" to satisfy their personal and cultural agendas. The Thanksgiving turkey is a dominant semiotic code that has come to signify a shared cultural heritage, family values, the early American legacy, and the bounty of the good life in America. Although the American household barely resembles the family perpetuated in Norman Rockwell's painting, the turkey stands for the shared meanings of Thanksgiving that transcend the diversity and fragmentation of contemporary American society (see Figure 5.1).

Figure 5.1. Rockwell (1943), Freedom from Want

Indeed, the preparation of the turkey has become a medium for consumer acculturation, an occasion to participate in mainstream culture while celebrating the family's ethnicity. In addition to the traditional oven-roasted turkey, Americans serve turkey in a variety of culturally conditioned forms, such as those listed in Table 5.3. They include African-American deep-fried turkey, Caribbean turkey casserole with rice and beans, Greek turkey *moussaka*, tofu turkey, and so on.

Such cultural performances are fundamentally semiotic activities, since, like language, they operate by means of the dialectical play between universal codes structuring meaning in a culture (such as the association of turkey with Thanksgiving) and the individual implementation of these codes in the practice of everyday life, including the contextualization of this code in the preparation of the Thanksgiving meal.

Table 5.3. Cultural Creativity at Thanksgiving

		Syntagmatic axis alignment				
	Traditional	Roasted turkey	Stuffing	Cranberries	Pumpkin pie	etc.
Paradigmatic axis substitution	Traditional African-American	Deep-fried turkey	Corn bread	Collard greens	Sweet potato pie	etc.
	Greek	Turkey Moussaka	Rice	Olives	Baklava	etc.

The Limits of Cultural Creativity

Although consumers have a fair amount of flexibility with the codes of culture, the substitution and recombination of cultural units in cultural performance are regulated by codes. In Table 5.4, each substitution on the vertical axis entails corresponding changes on the linear axis as well. For example, each term of the linear set "Charles likes pie" could be substituted by a similar term, such as "Mary likes pie" or "Charles eats cake." The flexibility of any sign system is limited, however, by cultural and semantic codes that dictate the appropriateness of such combinations. The statement "Mary eats shoes" seems false because it defies what the culture defines as edible. People do not eat shoes. Such transgressions of the code may be justified in poetic word play, but foster confusion and ambiguity in everyday cultural performance.

The same applies to other sign systems such as gastronomy. When ethnic consumers replace the traditional roasted turkey by variations, such as turkey *moussaka*, these variations entail simultaneous adjustments of the side dishes that accompany it. Changes on the vertical, paradigmatic axis must conform

Table 5.4. Linguistic Creativity

	Syntagmatic axis alignment		
	Subject	Verb	Object
	Charles	likes	pie.
Paradigmatic axis substitution	Mary	eats	pie.
	Charles	needs	shoes.
	Mary	eats	shoes.

to the cultural logic of the set of all dishes placed on the table. The traditional roast turkey is usually accompanied by some form of stuffing, cranberries, and pumpkin pie. When ethnic consumers replace the traditional roasted turkey by cultural variations, such as turkey *moussaka*, these variations entail simultaneous adjustments on the linear axis. Greek households might serve turkey *moussaka* with ethnic side dishes and desserts, such as rice, olives, and baklava. Even though such a menu digresses from the traditional Thanksgiving menu, it nonetheless constitutes a coherent gastronomic system within the ethnic Greek interpretation of Thanksgiving. However, the alignment of disparate cultural signifiers, such as Greek turkey *moussaka*, African-American collard greens, and French *crème brulé*, in a single Thanksgiving meal, threatens the semiotic coherence of the holiday meal, just as the statement "Mary eats shoes" violates the semantic categories distinguishing edible from inedible objects in the English language. These kinds of gastronomic "stews" may become the norm in the increasingly multicultural American household, but they nonetheless highlight the limits of cultural creativity, bound as it is by structural codes.

IMPLICATIONS FOR MULTICULTURAL MARKETING

The substitution and realignment of cultural units in semiotic performance is tantamount to a kind of translation. To translate the meaning of goods from one cultural system to another, consumers substitute one signifier for another on the paradigmatic axis, similar to language.

These insights have important implications for consumer behavior and brand strategy because they underscore the transparent rules often guiding the meaning of goods and the interpretation of brand meanings. They also provide a guide to creating multicultural advertising by adjusting several levels of brand communication, replacing not only the language and ethnicity of the actors but also adjusting the surrounding elements as well, including consumer rituals, symbols, and icons.

In summary, semiotic codes structure cultural rituals such as the Thanksgiving meal by means of the *alignment* of dishes served at the meal and the potential *substitution* of each dish with similar terms on the vertical axis. Roast turkey and pumpkin pie could be replaced by deep-fried turkey and sweet potato pie. In similar fashion, consumers customize products to suit their needs and interpret brands to suit their identities, by finding unique uses, wrappings, and meanings for their possessions. I develop this idea further in the case study that follows.

Brand Creativity

Selection and combination also enable consumers to adapt brands to their cultural contexts by translating the brand meaning into culturally relevant signifiers. To translate the word /car/ into French, for instance, it is necessary to find a substitute for the English term in the French lexicon that would represent the same concept, the car (see Figure 5.2).

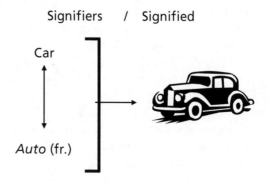

Figure 5.2. Signs in Translation

Turning a Global Brand

This same principle applies to brands in international markets. For example, to communicate the Coca-Cola brand message to Chinese consumers, management sought a local hero, Yao Ming, to represent the brand. Yao Ming was a local signifier, as it were, for the global brand.

Beginning with the essence of the brand as the "signified," marketers can develop a variety of brand representations that play within the tensions between the primary brand and the local interpretation of the brand for consumers (see Figure 5.3).

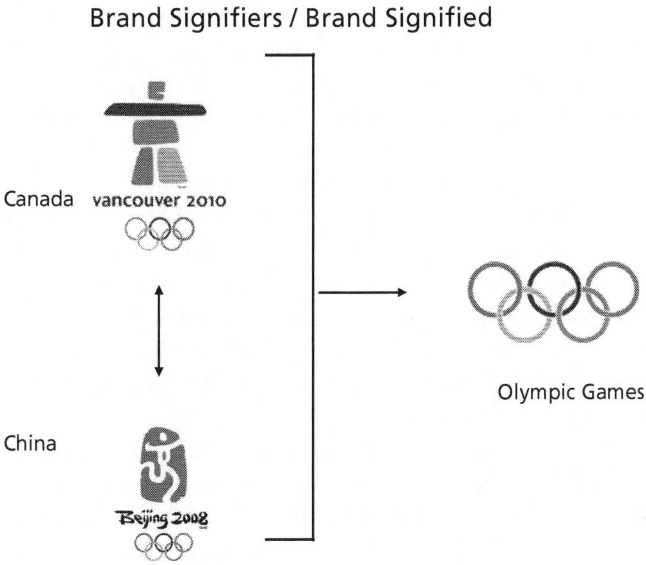

Brand Signifiers / Brand Signified

Figure 5.3. Brands in Translation

Figure 5.3 shows how different host countries "translate" the Olympic Games brand logo, consisting of five multicolored interlocking rings. When the Chinese hosted the Olympic Games (2008), they embedded the rings in imagery representing the Chinese arts, crafts, and culture. The running figure takes the form of a red seal reminiscent of those used on ancient Chinese calligraphy. The Canadians, for their part, embedded the Olympic Games logo (2010) in culturally sensitive symbols, including the Inuit symbol for peace, the Inukshuk, and also colors symbolizing that nation's natural resources, including the sun, mountains, forests, islands, and the maple leaf. These cultural symbols represent disparate worlds and values. However, each visual system translates the fundamental message of the Olympic rings, namely that the Games serve to bridge differences among people across five continents.

Brand Semiotics

BRANDS AND SYMBOLIC CONSUMPTION

Although analyzing the structure of meaning in advertising and popular culture reveals something about the cultural categories structuring brand meaning, a theory of symbol formation is needed to account for the ways consumers internalize brands and make them their own. Brand meanings derive from a dialectical exchange between the dual sign systems of advertising discourse and consumers' own personal experiences, recorded as memories in the brain. The dialectical association of externally and internally derived meanings underlies the symbolic function of goods as extensions of the emotional needs of consumers.

Brands are meaning systems that have become attached to a product or service through the repeated association of specific the signs, symbols, and icons in marketing communication. The production of brand meaning is a co-creative process involving the marketer's efforts to communicate a positioning such as Ford's "built tough," and the consumers' efforts to personalize the brand and integrate it into their own emotional needs and wants. Figure 5.4 illustrates how the mind moves meanings between these two semantic fields in an ongoing, dynamic process.

Although the movement between the internalization and personalization of brand meanings is dialectical, not hierarchical, I have outlined the various stages in the production of brand meaning from the intended meaning of marketers and creative directors to the effective meanings consumers read into brands as they use them in their daily lives.

There is a level at which the brand meaning is universal—if not, brands would never achieve strong equity across consumer segments and markets—but there is also a level at which brands become very personal. The only way to assess the unique brand perceptions produced at the level of the individual consumer or consumer subculture would be to conduct qualitative research with consumers. Figure 5.4 nonetheless illustrates the dynamic intersection of semiotics, cognitive processing, and brand strategy in the symbolic construction of brands.

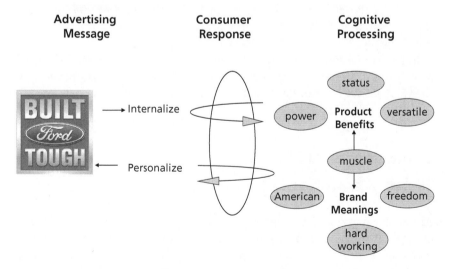

Figure 5.4. The Dialectic of Brand Meaning

The operations of similarity and contiguity make possible the unlimited creativity of sign systems such as culture, enabling consumers to rearrange, align, and expand upon the system indefinitely. As I illustrate later with a case study, they also enable consumers and marketers to translate brand meanings from one cultural system to another without losing the underlying essence of the primary brand.

IMPLICATIONS FOR ETHNIC MARKETING

This model can also be used to explain the ways that ethnic consumers rework the meaning of brands, just as they bend cultural codes to assimilate holiday rituals into their own cultural systems. They may personalize the brand by creating new product uses, replacing the packaging with their own containers, or even producing online advertising. They may translate primary brand attributes, such as "all-American," in symbols that reflect their unique cultural priorities (see Peñaloza, 1994). They may also incorporate the brand message into their own identities, the way Chinese consumers use Western brands to communicate their "modern" *savoir faire*. The brain integrates these two fields of meaning into a third, more personalized meaning, which consumers then externalize or project back onto the brand. These kinds of trade-offs account for the play of difference and assimilation in multicultural societies and contribute to the success of ethnic marketing.

Ethnic brand extensions build upon these kinds of translations and are grounded in a deep understanding of the codes structuring ethnic signifiers with brand meanings in the target culture. They also rely on advertising that builds links between the primary brand and consumers' unique memories, experiences, and cultural perspectives, while reinforcing the essence or core identity of the primary brand (Deshpande et al., 1986; Morton, 1997; Kang and Kim, 2001). In this way, ethnic brands "in translation" grow the overall value of the brand, enhancing brand awareness, loyalty, and perception of quality across multiple consumer segments.

In the next section, I present a case study that demonstrates the practical application of these concepts to multicultural advertising research. Findings include examples of:

- The Semiotics Research Process
- Building a Multicultural Brandscape
- Creating Multicultural Advertising

Case Study: From Ethnography to Creative Strategy-the Ford F-150.

The current study was prompted by Ford's need to update consumer insights in a changing automotive market that included younger drivers. To continue to lead in this segment, Ford needed to keep track of the tastes, cultural identities, and values of the F-150 buyer and potential threats from competitors. Advertising plays an important role in translating brands from one culture to another by reinforcing symbolic associations between the brand name, logo, and other brand cues to culturally relevant meanings. The Uniworld Agency were engaged to develop a new advertising campaign that would both strengthen primary brand equities such as power, masculinity, and style, and also appeal to African-American drivers. They sought a deep understanding of the values, beliefs, and lifestyles of the African-American segment, consisting mainly of middle-class, upwardly mobile male and female drivers aged 24–45. The agency created a thirty-second television spot, "Driven," based upon findings from the current study. The spot was broadcast the brand for several years. Findings from this study also contributed to long-term strategic planning for the brand.

THE FORD LEGACY AND POSITIONING

The F-150 truck has been "the best-selling vehicle in the United States for two decades" and was awarded 2004 Truck of the Year by *Motor Trend Magazine* (XmosBranding, 2004). Positioning of the primary Ford brand has focused on family, quality, upward mobility, tradition, and American patriotism since the 1940s (Lloyd, 2003). The F-150 brand positioning extends the Ford primary brand with masculine values of strength and durability. When the F-150 was launched in the 1980s with the tagline, "Built Ford Tough," it revived the Ford brand and enhanced consumer perception of vehicle performance.

At the time of this study (2003), Ford claimed 74 percent of the African-American market in the truck category, indicating strong synergies between the Ford legacy and the emotional needs and wants of this segment. Their enthusiasm for the brand was evident in the way respondents conducted themselves during the research. As compared with their counterparts in a previous, mainstream study for the J. Walter Thompson Agency (1998), African-American respondents demonstrated superior recall of F-150 advertising, brought in many more pictures to the focus groups, and could easily make metaphorical and emotional associations with Ford and competitors in projective exercises. Many remembered the anniversary tag line, "Fifty years of the F-150," from advertising several years old. They were also very familiar with the mechanical details of the truck, such as horsepower, payload, and hauling capacity.

Such dominance in the African-American segment is testimony to Ford management's consistent efforts to extend the primary brand into secondary targets rather than maintaining a "separate but equal" strategy for targeting ethnic segments. Over the years, management not only tracked cultural trends in the African-American market but also managed the meanings African Americans associate with the Ford brand.

THE SEMIOTIC RESEARCH PROCESS

The research process included three steps, including an audit of recent advertising for the F-150, in-depth research with African-American drivers in the competitive set (Ford, Dodge, GM, Chevrolet, Toyota), and a semiotic analysis that underscored connections between the primary brand and ethnic consumer culture along the lines of contrasting and consistent signs and meanings.

The Brand Audit

An audit of recent brand communication for the F-150, product benefits such as horsepower, hauling capacity, and styling are personified in scenes with strong white men in country settings. The truck is usually shown in off-road, rural landscapes, driven by white males, often viewed alone, working the land or riding bulls. Ford sponsors rodeos featuring famous cowboys, such as Kody Lostroh, and hires country music celebrity endorsers, such as Toby Keith. Ford also sponsors Nascar races and feature famous racers such as Rick Crawford in their ads. These kinds of men embody the "Ford Tough" legacy. As symbols for extreme physical endurance and mental stamina, they have aspirational value for the white mainstream target.

The "Ford Tough" persona, like the Marlboro Man, derives its strength from associations with the myth of the American frontier and the rugged free spirits who settled it. Although all trucks in the competitive set, including Chevy, Dodge, and Toyota, claim to be rugged and powerful, consumers distinguish the F-150 from the blue-collar, cowboy mythology of competitive American brands, such as Chevy, Dodge, or GMC, because of Ford's traditional positioning as an upwardly mobile, hard-working, versatile brand that is suitable for city or country, work or play. The challenge for Ford would be to translate the essence of the "Ford Tough" legacy into cultural signifiers that had power and relevance for their African-American target.

Primary Research with Consumers

To understand the culture of this consumer segment, an African-American moderator and I conducted ethnographic research that engaged with consumers at home, behind the wheel, and at social events such as family reunions and parades. A research facility recruited over twenty-four respondents in three markets. They screened respondents using narrow market criteria such as demographics, brand loyalty, and product use that had been established in advance through a large segmentation study. As a result, these findings are not generalizable to the African-American population as a whole, which is much more diverse in terms of brand choices, lifestyles, and values.

The Semiotic Analysis

While almost any qualitative research methodology can deliver a set of themes, words, and images that consumers relate to a product category and their perceptions of brands, semiotic analysis seizes upon strategic relationships between consumer culture, the brand legacy, and symbolic communication that can be leveraged to develop brand strategy. After summarizing findings from the ethnographic study, I will illustrate how a semiotic analysis contributed to a multicultural creative strategy for the F-150 truck.

AFRICAN AMERICANS AND THE F-150

Just as ethnic consumers rework the traditional Thanksgiving menu to participate in American culture, African-American consumers "translate" the meaning of the Ford brand in culture-specific ways. They employ an African-American vernacular to describe the truck, they redesign the truck using aftermarket accessories, they use the truck as a prop in social rituals, and they rely on the truck to realize the American Dream of financial independence.

Language

African Americans in this study replace standard automotive terms with slang, metaphors, and symbolic language. In this way they customize the brand in the same way they customize their vehicles. For example, they filtered the tagline, "Ford Tough," through their own cultural lens. In addition to "hard-working," "powerful," and "resilient," respondents associate "Ford tough" with integrity and ambition. Respondents used slang, word play, and rhetorical figures to personalize their vehicles and weave their personal stories into the semiotic landscape of the brand. They associate "Ford Tough" with an urban "thug," an inner city hero made popular in rap music, who succeeds in life by overcoming difficult conditions through hard work and determination.

"I want to look like a regular common guy even though I have a Master's Degree. A Denzel-type. Tough . . . thuggish." (M.D.)

"(The Ford driver ...) She's a thug woman. Looks cute but straight from the street; like ghetto fabulous. Truck is souped up like the boys." (T.A.)

Respondents condensed the multisensory dimensions of brand perceptions in rhetorical language, merging sight, sound, touch, and even taste in words like "smooth." The F-150 is "smooth like jazz," "smooth as the taste of an expensive cognac," smooth to the touch, and "smooth looking, like Denzel [Washington]." Women used metaphors to express their passion for their trucks, the embodiment of the tough male. "The truck is my husband," said one woman. Another said that in her truck she was "the Woman." Yet another respondent said the Ford has "the pick-up of an Energizer Bunny." Respondents also use African-American slang to describe the design and use of the truck.

Truck Design

Most respondents in the study personalized their trucks with after-market accessories from sound systems to external trim. However, younger drivers personalize their trucks with enhancements to the body itself, including a chrome grill or exhaust pipes, 20–26 inch rims. They rev up the engine by adding a new computer chip. They also use African-American slang to describe these activities. They "slam" the truck down by lowering the suspension close to the ground. They "trick out" the truck to describe this behavior, while older, more conservative drivers used expressions such as "dressed out," "bowed out," or just "customized."

Social Life

Respondents also used the F-150 as a prop to facilitate social events such as parties, parades, family reunions, and family fun. For example, at an African-American tailgating event near the Atlanta Falcon's stadium, consumers towed a long steel drum, used as a barbecue pit, to the parking lot, where they spent the afternoon grilling barbecue. Truck beds were the site of buffet tables, card games, and the DJ stand for the music. There was ample room for the 4-foot speakers, the sound system, and other accessories necessary for providing an essential component of the party—the music.

Younger drivers in the inner city participated in "flossing" parades to show off their tricked out trucks. Researchers accompanied a respondent to the inner city in south Dallas, Texas, to observe this ritual. On Sunday afternoons during the summer months, drivers go to the car wash, then spend the afternoon flossing up and down the main road, "lookin' good, rollin' down the road." This display gives rise to socializing with passersby in the parking lot and picking up women. "Guys really customize trucks to get the attention of women. That's the sole purpose.... And for other guys to say, 'Whoa, look at that. Who's that in that Big Body? That's $100,000 worth of car.'"

The American Dream

Participants belonged to an emerging African-American middle class that did not take money, success, or a comfortable lifestyle for granted. For them, brand attributes such as power, versatility, convenience, and styling transcended their mechanical functions and became means of surmounting class barriers and achieving economic independence. African Americans working their way up into the middle class traditionally develop side jobs to carry them through in difficult times (LaGuerre, 1994). Respondents in this study were no exception. They relied on the truck to work at informal side jobs delivering goods and helping people move. Some respondents were developing informal work into businesses in beauty care, manufacturing, and delivery services. For these drivers, the F-150 symbolized access to the American Dream of self-determination and freedom.

"It's an African American male thing. A man has to take care of his family. Will he survive?" A.S.

"You can make lots of money with the truck," "It opens the door to the entrepreneurial spirit." M.D.

BUILDING A MULTICULTURAL BRANDSCAPE

Brand Culture Creativity

Brands, like the holiday meal, are cultural systems structured by codes. Just as ethnic consumers rework the Thanksgiving menu by substituting traditional American dishes with ethnic foods, consumers too customize brands by interpreting the brand essence through the lens of their culture. In order to adapt the primary brand to ethnic markets, management can substitute primary brand signifiers, such as the color red, with ethnic signifiers, such as the color blue, as I mentioned with regard to Indian marketing. In this way, a multicultural brand strategy keeps the primary brand intact while extending it to new markets. In Table 5.5, I demonstrate how the consumers in the African-American segment adapted the Ford F-150 brand equities to their cultural perspective.

From left to right, the brand elements include the target segment, the brand metaphor, the culture, music, brand personality, and the personal signs consumers use to personalize their trucks. The F-150 primary brand is targeted to the white mainstream. It is positioned as a workhorse, which

Table 5.5. Brand Culture Creativity

The F-150 in the African American Market

Syntagmatic Axis
Alignment

	Target	Culture	Metaphor	Music	Personality	Personal signs
White mainstream	White mainstream	Cowboys Rodeo NASCAR	Work Horse	Country Toby Keith	"Tough"	Decals Bug shield Interior details
African American	African American	"Thugs" Music Festivals Reunions Self-employment	Cowboy Cadillac	R&B Bo Diddley	"Smooth"	"Bling" Chrome trim and wheels, etc. Low ride.

(PARADIGMATIC AXIS / SUBSTITUTION on left margin)

reflects the rural context in which the brand tends to be embedded in advertising and sponsored events. In this world, the F-150 is associated with cowboys, rodeos, NASCAR racing, country music, featuring Toby Keith and a "tough" personality. African Americans interpreted these categories differently. They associate a strong personality with an urban "thug," a term derived from gang culture but generally meaning strong and independent. They associate trucks with tailgate parties, family reunions, and self-employment. Their musical preferences leaned to jazz and rhythm and blues. The personality of the brand is "smooth," rather than "tough." African Americans even differ from the mainstream in their style of after-market decorations. White drivers apply decals to the windows, install chrome bug shields on the front fender, and decorate the interior. African Americans generally shun decals, favoring ostentatious chrome trim and wide chrome wheels. They may also add a plate that states the size of the engine.

Consumer Metaphors

Furthermore, consumer metaphors linked these ethnic preferences to the core equities of the primary brand, including the brand legacy, the product benefits, and consumer experiences. Figure 5.5 illustrates the complexity of the meta-phorical system. Here the displacement of focus from one realm of experience, such as the senses—"Smooth"—to another, such as product benefits—drive, steering, image—motivates strong, polyvalent brand symbolism.

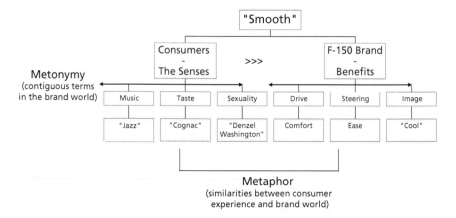

Figure 5.5. The Logic of Consumer Metaphors

Consumers in the study blended a range of sense experiences in a kind of poetic synesthesia along a common element, "smooth." The word "smooth" was also the vehicle for linking consumers' sense experiences to the brand benefits. The F-150 reminded them of listening to smooth jazz, tasting smooth cognac, touching smooth skin, because the drive was "smooth," the leather felt "smooth," the steering was "smooth," and the driver looked cool and "smooth" behind the wheel.

Advertising

The Uniworld Agency employed similar figures to condense primary brand signifiers and ethnic symbolism into a thirty-second TV spot titled "Driven." The ad narrative ties brand benefits such as power, hauling capacity, and styling to African-American cultural signifiers such as R&B music, an urban backdrop, and showing off in the truck.

THE ADVERTISING NARRATIVE

The narrative structuring "Driven" condenses research findings into a thirty-second montage of images, movements, narrative commentary, and music. The soundtrack alternates between the lyrics of a blues song, "I'm a Man," sung by Bo Diddley, and a voice-over narration. The scenario can be summarized as follows.

Soundtrack	Visuals
Music: "I'm a Man..." *Narration: What is it about a man in his truck?*	The ad opens on a good-looking black male driving around in his black F-150 at night in the city. The camera moves with the truck for the entire ad, sometimes showing the driver's face, sometimes the scene outside the truck. Red shadows and streetlights cast a glamorous glow onto the urban scene. An African-American couple walks along the sidewalk.
Music: "I'm a full grown man..."	The couple on the sidewalk looks at the driver going by; close-up on the woman as she smiles toward the driver.
Narration: Does a steel frame that's stronger than ever before remind you of his strength?	Cut back to the driver, smiling; cut to a Hispanic man working in a manhole on the sidewalk, wearing a welding mask. The worker raises his mask and gazes toward the truck going by.
Music continues in background. *Narration: Does the quietest cab in class and a distinctive new design make you see him any differently?*	Cut to a close-up of white leather seats.
Stronger, sleeker, "badder" than ever before.	The truck passes by a skyscraper, a fountain in front. A red F-150 drives by the black one, suggesting the life-style range of the brand from formal to informal lifestyle.
The only truck that's earned the right to be *Motor Trend*'s truck of the year: the next F-150	The truck moves out of the city into the suburbs and pulls up to an up-scale white house, a fountain in front.
If you haven't seen a ford lately—hand stamp of the Ford Tough Logo—look again.	A hand with a branding iron stamps the "Ford Tough" logo onto a surface.

Visual Rhetoric

The ad draws upon the consumer metaphors described earlier linking brand benefits, consumer culture, and personal identity along a trajectory formed by the term "smooth." The smooth montage style creates seamless transitions between visual elements and between sound and image, cutting on movement and creating an illusion of continuity from one shot to the next, one semantic category to the next. The editing style parallels the smooth handling and feel of the vehicle as the driver navigates the road. The smooth music resembles the smooth ("cool") driver, who is admired by people on the street. The editing condenses a long drive from city to suburb into thirty seconds, emphasizing the easy versatility of the truck.

The truck adapts smoothly from city to country scenes, passing by an apartment building, a concert hall, an underpass, and a skyscraper with a fountain in front. The drive ends up at an upscale white house with a fountain in front. The fountain in front of the skyscraper and the house anchor the association of town and country along the lines of a common element. The water shooting straight up from these two fountains suggest an erotic under-tone to the scene, reflecting the passion to drive that consumers associate with the F-150.

Consumer Culture

The blues music on the soundtrack complements the rhythmic pace of the visual track, while referencing the driver's musical heritage. The action itself resembles a kind of flossing parade, referencing the culture-specific behavior of drivers in the study. Unlike mainstream ads, which show characters moving heavy loads and navigating rough terrain, this ad shows an African-American driver enjoying the sheer pleasure of driving an F-150 and drawing the attention of passers by, including a man in a construction helmet and a woman who turns away from her boyfriend to look up at the driver in the F-150. Cross-cuts between the driver looking out and people looking back establish a circle of consumer desire linking the styling, the status, and the performance of the brand to the driver's identity, culture, and emotional needs.

THE VALUE ADDED

The campaign has important implications for multicultural branding, since it represents a creative strategy targeted to the ethnic segment that extends, rather than reinvents, the primary brand positioning. The ad translates the "Ford Tough" message by focusing on an urban interpretation of "tough" as cool, urban, and "smooth," and uses editing to merge these attributes with product benefits (such as handling and performance). The TV spot emphasizes culture-specific details drawn from consumer insights, such as the need for self-presentation, upward mobility, sex appeal, and "smooth" music. However, the ad suggests a blending of mainstream and ethnic cultures. The

Bo Diddley song, "I'm a Man," is an example of the blues tradition that has widespread appeal in the American mainstream, as illustrated by the success of films such as *The Blues Brothers*. And the movement from the dark city street to the white house in the suburb suggests a play between black and white that is cooperative rather than mutually exclusive.

As consumer markets become more fragmented, and media more narrowly focused, targeting smaller consumer subcultures has become standard industry practice. To succeed in the multicultural, global marketplace, marketers can no longer rely on cultural stereotypes, nor can they simply recycle a standard advertising campaign using ethnic actors in place of Caucasians. They must take into account how cultural codes structure the interpretation of goods and brands in the target market and incorporate these codes in brand communication.

This study highlights the value of ethnographic research and semiotic analysis for achieving this goal by identifying new sources of meaning and value in the target market and extending the primary brand into ethnic markets. The ethnography uncovered ways ethnic consumers rework the primary brand to suit their personal and cultural agendas.

Furthermore, the semiotic analysis of research data provided means of developing consumer insights into positioning and creative strategy for the brand. First of all, the semiotic analysis extended the primary brand meaning from basic product benefits such as power, performance, and torque, to the intangible, emotional associations consumers make with these benefits, including self-expression, sex appeal, musical enjoyment, and socializing. Analysis tracked semantic trajectories linking product benefits to the culture of consumers, including the icons, rhetorical devices, and music they associate with the truck category. The semiotic analysis provided a blueprint for condensing these meanings into advertising that targeted African Americans while appealing to a broad audience. This inclusive approach to brand strategy and creativity adds value to the brand by broadening the reach and cultural richness of the primary brand, while also growing loyalty in the African-American segment.

ENDNOTES

1. For more on consumer subcultures, see Deshpande et al. (1986), Deshpande and Stayman (1994), Schouten and McAlexander (1995), Morton (1997), Aaker et al. (2000), Dimofte et al. (2003), and Torres and Gelb (2003).

2. For an image of the Marlboro Man icon, see <www.google.images.marlboro man.com>.

3. For further reading on brand extensions, see Keller (2007).

6 The Semiotics of Consumer Space

"Spaces speak."

Semiotics is a social science discipline devoted to the study of sign systems in cultural perspective. The word "semiotics" also refers generally to the sign system itself, as in "brand semiotics," or "the semiotics of a retail setting." In this second sense, the word "semiotics" refers to the visual or verbal cues structuring a text or environment that communicate something to consumers. However, the semiotic analysis, as defined in this book, goes beyond interpreting individual texts or describing sign systems, and examines the complex process of *semiosis*, a form of meaning production that engages material signs, consumer response, and cultural codes in a dialectical process.

Charles Sanders Peirce (1955), a nineteenth century philologist, introduced the Greek term *semiosis* into modern usage to describe specifically the triadic model of meaning production, which he conceptualized as the interaction between three types of signs: the icon, the index, and the symbol. In the present discussion, we open up the term "semiosis" to include meaning production in general and also introduce the question of the subject or consciousness of the speaker and receiver of a message.

Semiosis, in the broad sense used here, is a dialectical process that engages the consumer in the symbolic structure of texts as various as traffic signs, advertising, and retail design. Consumers participate in semiosis as reader, spectator, or shopper. In consumer culture, the process of semiosis transforms consumer goods, activities, and messages into symbolic experiences that transcend their practical functions and satisfy the emotional needs of consumers. Consumers engage in semiosis every time they personalize a holiday meal, interpret advertising, internalize brands, and translate brand meanings into ethnic contexts. Semiosis is a multidimensional process that operates at the levels of the material, the conventional, the contextual, and the performative dimensions of sign systems.

- *The Material.* To analyze a sign system at all, it must be intelligible to perception, though the material itself may consist of sounds, words, images, gestures, or other media.

- *The Conventional.* Next, sign systems are structured into discourses by codes or conventions specific to the system: linguistic codes structure language, visual codes structure paintings, cinematic codes structure cinema, architectural codes structure buildings, and so on.

- *The Contextual.* Next, the meaning of the system is subject to influence from the context of the communication event. An apple, for example, takes on a whole new meaning in the context of the Apple brand logo.

- *The Performative.* Finally, and most importantly, semiosis relies on human subjects—in the form of speakers, viewers, consumers, and so on—to interpret, relay, translate, and participate in the production of meaning in relation to other subjects. Although subjectivity is a psychological concept, it has a semiotic dimension. Subjectivity can be traced in discourse by means of indexes, such as the personal pronouns in narrative, the looks of characters in film, the frames articulating consumer participation in architectural space, and the codes linking one site to another in cyberspace.

In the present chapter, I look at the ways consumers "read" and experience dwellings and branded retail sites. The spaces of consumption transcend the blueprint or design of the physical environment because they are multidimensional sites of meaning production. These dimensions, from floor plan and décor to furnishings, form a kind of *Signscape*—a semiotic system that structures consumer space as a form of discourse created by someone for a consumer. I distinguish the term *Signscape* from Sherry's notion of the Servicescape (1998) in order to create a rubric for embracing a range of consumer spaces, including homes, entertainment venues, and organizations, as well as stores.

For example, a home is structured by the floor plan, the room dimensions, the traffic pattern linking one area or room to another in that plan, and the disposition of furnishings, both movable and immovable, within each area. In addition to furniture, there are personal objects, decorations, electronics, flooring, acoustics, and lighting. A store is structured by architectural design and merchandising elements that function to move traffic through the store and communicate the brand experience. Branded retail sites, including theme parks and restaurants, stage the movement of consumers through the brand experience as if they were participants and spectators in a spectacle or a film (see Kozinets et al., 2002). Floor plan, traffic flow, signage, and product display can all potentially be used to control consumers' brand perceptions and behaviors in the store (see Sherry, 1998). However, as Kozinets et al. (2002, 2004) point out, retail design does not rigidly structure consumers' behavior in a retail environment such as ESPN, but organizes a dialectical process of engaging consumer agency—consumers' choices about their moment-to-moment actions in the store—around a series of design guideposts.

In discussions that follow, I explore the basic principles of spatial semiotics, articulate a research methodology for decoding the spaces of consumption, and present examples and case studies where the application of semiotics to consumer settings contributed to brand value.

Problem 1
A North American health organization wanted to develop an advertising message targeted to chronic pain sufferers who abused over-the-counter (OTC) medications instead of seeking professional help. In order to promote alternative treatments for pain, the organization first needed to understand how patients experienced and defined pain, and how pain created specific unmet consumer needs that the new treatments could satisfy. The challenge for researchers was to identify a vocabulary to discuss pain symptoms, since the experience of pain is very subjective and abstract. Semiotics research uncovered a consistent, unexpected consumer narrative that could be leveraged in public health advertising for this segment.

Problem 2
In 2002, a fast-food chain developed a range of new sandwich items to provide variety and excitement to their menu. They developed appealing advertising and even displayed large pictures of the new meals outside restaurants. However, by the time consumers got to the cashier, they ordered the usual burger and fries. Semiotics research identified barriers to new product trial at the point of purchase and recommended solutions.

A Semiology of Space

In the first instance, consumers relate to their physical environments along the lines of a *phenomenology* of space structuring the ontological essence of "being in the world" (Merleau-Ponty, [1945] 2002). Sense perception is the means by which human subjects take in the world, relate it to their own experiences, and construct a sense of reality.

Gaston Bachelard ([1958] 1994) extends phenomenology to the interpretive agency that enables humans to project their subjective states onto an environment, therefore constructing meaning along the lines of a "poetics of space" that conforms to the individual's memories, previous experiences, and free associations. Bachelard claims, for instance, that our experiences of domestic space are shaped by our memory of the home we were born in. Whether a new space triggers feelings of security or anxiety, the meaning of this space for the individual is to some extent driven by their subjective experiences. Consumer memory plays an important role in the value they attach to places. Realtors report that buyers often make purchase decisions based on something in a new house that triggers memories of their childhood home.

The phenomenology of space forms a philosophical framework for conceptualizing how consumers internalize their surroundings. However, phenomenology does not account for the way spaces "speak" to consumers through the media of architecture, design, and other codes in an environment. It is, rather, a *semiology* of space—a symbolic process—which engages consumers in a discourse structured by cultural codes. Whether the codes derive from the disciplines of architecture, merchandising, design, or the psychology of proxemics, they are ultimately cultural in nature, inasmuch as they regulate collective consumer behavior.

The relationship between the structure of space and consumers' subjective states has been theorized in the context of "experience retailing."[1] I propose a general semiology of space that moves beyond phenomenology inasmuch as it accounts for the role of culture in the construction of reality. It entails a dialectical play between cultural codes structuring consumer environments and consumers' manipulation of those codes to suit their personal needs (see Figure 6.1).

THE SPACE AND PLACE OF CONSUMPTION

The Signscape is first of all a text, a system of signs that has definite limits. The semiotician could define the text as a home, a single room, a shop, or a smaller area within these spaces. As a text, the Signscape is also a form of discourse that engages consumers in the formal system structuring a site. As a discourse, the Signscape is more than a set of design elements—it is a medium of communication structured by codes. It is also a surface on which consumers

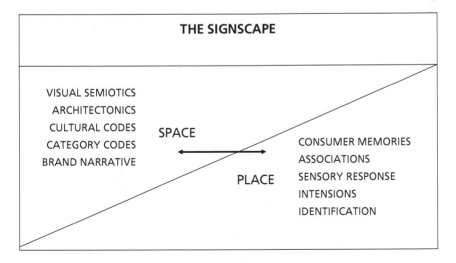

Figure 6.1. The Semiology of Space

project their own meanings. In this sense, the consumer environment is both a space and a personal place. The line joining/separating the space and place of consumption parallels the material "énonciation" or statement, in discourse, inasmuch as it represents the material surface where the codes structuring the physical environment meet the interpretive actions of consumers. The implication of spatial codes in the consumer's subjective processes accounts for the ways consumers transform the space of consumption into a personal space (see Oswald 1996).

Since the physical environment does not "speak" in the manner of linguistics, does not unfold in the manner of cinema, the imprint of "voice" or subjectivity in space is not as immediately clear as the pronoun "I" or the narrative point of view of the camera. However, there are other ways of tracing voice in nonverbal semiotic systems. Benveniste (1971) expanded the linguistic notion of voice from the pronouns per se to any markers for the subject's personal manipulations of the code—the literal meaning—in various ways. For example, metaphors and other rhetorical figures, adjectives, adverbs, or irony reflect the speaker's subjective states and therefore trace the instance of "voice" in verbal or visual discourse. Similar markings trace the instance of "voice" in spatial semiotics.

The traces for voice in spatial discourses are more subtle but nonetheless evident by highlighting the codes structuring a specific environment, such as the blueprint, the disposition of furnishings, the private and public areas, and the staging of visual perspective in branded retail sites. The personal stamp of the consumer or the marketer on these spaces can be traced in the various manipulations of these codes, as evidenced in the unique arrangement of furniture or the open or closed movement of traffic between rooms in a dwelling. In a branded retail setting, branding cues may be evident in the design of the counter, the merchandising, and the disposition of products on the shelves. Spaces "speak" by means of the structure, design, and experience of consumer space as a kind of narrative space.

THE SPACE OF CONSUMPTION

Although professionals such as architects, designers, or marketers command to some extent the consumer's experience of an environment, their designs and ideas are steeped in the conventions structuring private and commercial spaces in a culture. They are subject to structural, cultural, and social codes.

Cultural Codes

Cultural codes reflect the traditions or routines associated with the arrangement of spaces in a certain culture, such as the location of the cash register in a supermarket. As cultures evolve, the use of space evolves also. For instance, at some point at the end of the 1980s, the dining room in American homes became practically obsolete, and the kitchen opened up into a large family room. This change represented the increasing informality of American family life and the breakdown of rigid barriers between cultural categories such as cooking and dining that characterized the Victorian home.

Social Codes

Social codes regulate the movement of consumers through public space. For example, the decision to drive on the right or left side of the road is not a personal choice but is dictated by the rules of the road governing social behavior in a given society. Children in primary school may be taught to walk to one side or the other of a corridor to facilitate traffic flow. These social norms contribute to the nonverbal, "silent language" identified by Edward T. Hall (1973) in his study of the spatial effects of human interactions. This kind of silent language eventually influences the way consumers are guided through retail sites such as supermarkets and theme parks, where signage and walkways move consumers through commercial space by building upon these deeply engrained patterns of social behavior.

I will discuss the semiotics of space in more detail as I present the case studies. Suffice it to say here that the spaces of consumption are structured environments that conform to the cultural priorities of social groups. Whether it concerns the structure of the home or the retail site, semiotic codes perpetuate the normative dimensions of consumer space and moderate consumer expectations and behaviors associated with spaces of consumption. They also invite consumers to make choices and explore consumption spaces on their own (see Kozinets et al., 2004).

THE PLACE OF CONSUMPTION

The codes structuring the space of dwellings, commercial sites, and even the Internet are responsible for articulating a consumption space from the surrounding environment, organizing the disposition of consumers and objects within that space, and staging consumer experiences according to social norms. However, spatial codes form only part of the story, since consumers construct meanings from the environment by transforming *space* into an individualized *place* of consumption. The "place" of consumption is formed by an act of interpretation, which molds the normative codes structuring a site, such as the blueprint of a home, store signage, traffic flow, and the location of the cashier—to the personal expectations, intentions, and memories of the consumer. For example, since the layout of stores within a category is dictated more or less by convention, consumers may move through the supermarket automatically, paying only limited attention to signs and directions. The spatial conventions structuring supermarkets speak for themselves.

In Chapter 1, I discussed how goods take on a symbolic function by means of the meanings consumers project into them. Just as projection and introjection structure the symbolic dimension of goods, they also structure the transformation of consumption sites into personal places of consumption for consumers.

Projection

Consumers may have limited ability to modify the fixed structure of a consumption site, such as a home or store, but they respond to these spaces in personal ways. They project personal memories, sensory reactions, intensions, and other meanings into spaces of consumption. Consumers may express the chaos of their inner lives by hoarding goods and garbage throughout their home. They may visit a monument because it reminds them of family holidays. Travelers experience vacation spots through the lens of the travel brochures and hype they consumed in advance (Borgerson and Schroeder, 2003). They may be gratified to experience first hand the fantasy they dreamed of or may be disappointed because the reality of the place did not match their expectations.

Introjection

Consumers also internalize the meanings communicated by retail spaces. The design of a retail space may influence their perceptions of a brand and their shopping experiences. For example, if shoppers associate the health food category with small, specialty shops, they may turn away from Whole Foods' new hypermarkets because they remind them of WalMart stores. Furthermore, traffic flow and proxemics—the structure of personal distances from others and objects—also communicate meanings such as clear or cluttered, distant or intimate. These meanings then guide consumers' experience of commercial sites, their interpretation of the company or brand, and even their ultimate product choice.

Case Studies

By reading consumer environments as texts that reflect needs and wants of consumers, semiotic analysis can identify the visual triggers that prompt consumers to react in specific ways to their environments. As the following case studies illustrate, this type of research has valuable applications for consumer research. The first study leads to a new brand positioning by drawing inferences between the subjective states of pain sufferers and the structure of their home environments. The second study leads to changes in retail design by uncovering contrasts between consumers' expectations of a fast-food brand, as communicated in advertising, and the structure of the restaurant.

Case I: The Meaning of Chronic Pain

In the following case study, I developed a methodology for identifying the subjective states of consumers suffering from chronic pain, then drew parallels between consumers' subjective states and the semiotics of their lived environments. In the process, I discovered unmet needs of consumers that could be leveraged in public service advertising targeted to chronic pain sufferers.

RESEARCH DESIGN

In 2002, a public health organization in North America asked me to investigate the meaning of pain and pain relief among patients who suffer from chronic pain. The purpose of the research was to develop a campaign that would deter patients from abusing OTC medications such as ibuprofen and offer them alternative, nonchemical treatments. Findings were used to position and develop communication strategies for the new treatments.

Data Set

Accompanied by a videographer, I interviewed twenty-four consumers at home in three North American markets. They included men and women, ranging in age from 35 to 65. They had been suffering from chronic pain for durations ranging from one year to ten years or more. All respondents had reported using OTC products in addition to pharmaceuticals to treat their pain. All respondents reported looking for alternative ways of managing pain.

Methods

Pain is an abstract, very subjective experience. As a result, consumers have difficulty expressing pain in so many words or finding values for measuring the effects of pain treatments. The challenge for researchers was to discover a methodology for identifying concrete expressions of respondents' experiences of pain and pain relief without relying on first hand, literal statements. As the result of this approach, we discovered the essence of pain and pain relief for these consumers and also identified a system of signs for eventually communicating the benefits of the new pain relief program in advertising and packaging.

Ethnographic Design

The symptoms of chronic pain leave traces on the individual's external environment, in their personal grooming, their lifestyle choices, and social relationships. For example, if an individual cannot raise their arms comfortably, this limitation will be expressed in their grooming and housekeeping. I therefore designed an ethnographic research protocol for interviewing respondents at home. The home is a rich semiotic field for investigating consumers' values, mental states, and social lives. It is a space that has been transformed by consumer actions into a "place" imbued with their inner thoughts and experiences. Furthermore, talking to consumers at home enables researchers to balance respondent statements against the meanings communicated in their décor, housekeeping, and the disposition of products in the home. It enabled researchers to observe how pain had left its mark on their physical and social milieus, and how they disposed of treatment products and regimen within the home.

Projective Tasks

A key component of the methodology consisted of projective exercises designed to elicit indirectly the subjective thoughts and feelings consumers associate with pain that they could not express directly. The task I will discuss here involves a picture sort technique used to stimulate associations between pictures and the topic under study.

So as to avoid respondent identification with characters or specific scenes, I chose a set of abstract paintings as stimuli. Respondents were exposed to two dozen pictures by abstract modern artists such as Appel, O'Keefe, Picasso, Mondrian, Kandinsky, Pollack, and Delaney. They were asked to choose five images that most reminded them of their pain. They were then asked to pick five images that reminded them of pain relief. This approach enabled respondents to identify their subjective experiences with the forms and colors in the images. Respondents also ranked their picture choices from one to five, enabling researchers to identify the most commonly chosen images and look for consensus across the respondent group.

In the course of this elicitation task, respondents developed terminology for discussing pain based on symbolic associations between forms in the pictures and various experiences of pain and pain relief. This approach guided researchers and respondents through the difficult discussion about pain and enabled respondents to objectify their experience as a sign system. It also led to development of a visual "lexicon" of signifiers for pain that rang true across all interviews. All respondents chose similar abstract symbols, such as colors and shapes, to describe their experiences. In fact, out of a random sampling of twenty-four respondents, recruited not from a database but from the phone book, a majority of respondents even chose the same few pictures to symbolize pain and pain relief. For example, the color blue symbolized the self, jagged lines symbolized the disorder that pain created in their lives, red symbolized the heat of the pain, and so on. In the course of twenty-four interviews, there was universal agreement among respondents about the correlations between visual signifiers (such as colors) and the meaning of pain for respondents. These findings enabled us to generalize the pain lexicon into a visual esthetic and message for use in advertising.

A SEMIOTICS OF PAIN

Results from the picture sort exercise suggest that the existential effects of pain far outweigh its physical effects. Respondents most frequently selected the top image in Figure 6.2 to symbolize pain. The work titled *Angry Landscape* (1967) is by the Dutch artist Karen Appel. Red, yellow, and black splashes of color moving haphazardly over the canvas express emotions out of control. The jagged lines, the eerie faces, and the splashes of red, yellow, and orange

The sharp, stabbing effects of pain are expressed in stark, primary colors, jagged forms, and chaos.

Figure 6.2. Signs of Pain—A

against the black background communicate the sharp emotional intensity of the figures and the dark mood of the painting. A bright streak of yellow traverses the canvas on a diagonal from top to bottom of the frame, adding intensity and heat to the color scheme. A patch of blue cools down the palette at the lower-right corner of the canvas, but does not mitigate the overall expression of violence and lack of control communicated by the work.

Respondents focused on the disorderly, jagged forms in the image, stating that pain, like the image, is chaotic, unpredictable, moving, and capricious. They never knew when it would come or go. Only secondarily did they speak of the heat communicated by the color red and sharp, jabbing experience of pain on the body, as represented by the color yellow and the jagged lines. Respondents compared the black in the background to the effects of pain on the mind as deadening, depressing, and dark.

Respondents also identified the menacing, face-like forms top left and right of the image with inner demons that hound them day and night. Black outlines set the faces apart from the surrounding swirl of colors and outline eyes and teeth that threaten the viewer. Respondents identified the color blue with the self, which is being reduced and pushed aside by the other colors/ experiences. As one respondent put it, "Blue is me being blocked by pain."

Respondents also chose most frequently the image in *Untitled* (1954) (Figure 6.3) by the American artist Beaufort Delaney. Though splashes of red, yellow, and green are toned down by touches of blue and the white background, the painting is characterized by the chaotic, swirling movement of brush strokes on the canvas. In reaction to this picture, respondents again

Pain is capricious, chaotic, twisted, disordered, and out of control.

Figure 6.3. Signs of Pain—B

emphasized the effects of pain on the self rather than the body. Pain causes mental confusion, loss of control, and disorder. It covers up the "blue," that is, the self, as the lines in this picture cover up the blue color, rendering it a shadow of its former life. From one interview to the next, respondents consistently associated the same symbols with their various sensory and emotional experiences of pain. By keeping track of the consistent use of these symbols over time, researchers identified a lexicon of terms that referenced the various emotional and sensory experiences of pain (see Table 6.1).

Table 6.1. A Visual Lexicon for Pain

Symbol	Experience
Red	The intensity of the pain
Yellow	Heat
Black	(a) The numbing of the brain from pain; (b) the dark mood associated with pain
Blue	The self
Jagged lines	(a) Chaos; (b) jabbing sensations
Wiggly lines	Chaos, disorder, and lack of control

By the end of each interview, researchers found that respondents stopped using words like "pain" or "heat" and used symbols from the pain lexicon instead.

As we moved through the exercise, respondents were asked how pain relief felt. They would respond with statements such as "The blue gets bigger," "The red softens to pink," "The black goes away," and "The lines smooth out." Respondents most often selected images for pain relief that softens the colors into pinks, blues, and other pastels swimming in a sea of blue. Black [mind numbing] and yellow [heat] are either absent or under control (see Figure 6.4).

Respondents most frequently chose O'Keefe's painting, *Music Pink and Blue, II* (1918), to represent pain relief (Figure 6.4). They identified relief with soft, flowing streams of color, including red and pink. In these kinds of images, the blue, representing the self, mitigates the violence of the hotter colors of the palette, but does not eliminate them entirely. Respondents said repeatedly, "The medication doesn't remove the pain, it reduces its control." Blue cools down the impact of reds and yellows. Relief brings order to jagged lines. The black is omitted altogether.

Respondents chose the Rothko painting, *White Center (Yellow, Pink and Lavender on Rose)* (1950), seen in Figure 6.5, to represent pain relief. The pastels soften the force of the yellows and reds that respondents associated with pain. In addition, there is symmetry between the top and bottom of the canvas, articulated by the black-and-white lines separating the two halves of the composition. The overall composition communicates the sense of order,

Soft lines, pastels, smooth forms express pain relief.

Figure 6.4. Signs of Pain Relief—A

Order, geometrical lines, clarity express order and personal control over the chaos of pain.

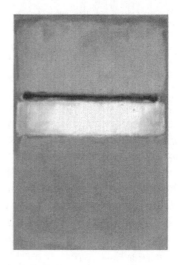

Figure 6.5. Signs of Pain Relief—B

control, and clarity respondents associate with pain relief. They said this image represented the cooling down of the heat, enhanced personal control, and an expansion and unfolding of the possibilities of life when pain remedies enable the individual to organize their lives and keep chaos at bay. The black line dividing the canvas across the middle reminded respondents that pain was ever present even though medication may provide relief.

THE DYSFUNCTIONAL SIGNSCAPE

The picture sort exercise gave form to a shared consumer discourse about the subjective states respondents associated with pain. They insisted that chronic pain is more than a physical symptom; it diminishes the individual's social life, lifestyle, and aspirations. In the picture association exercise, respondents discussed the effects of pain on their subjective states, lifestyles, and life projects. In order to create a positioning and brand communication for the new pain relief treatment, however, the research team sought to clarify a specific message for the brand that would communicate the lifestyle benefits of the new brand, not just the vague promise that the brand "relieved pain." The solution emerged as we moved analysis from the picture sorts to the lived environments of consumers.

Respondents reported difficulty completing the simplest daily tasks, from making the bed to doing laundry, because pain not only made movements difficult but also increased their fatigue. Chronic pain often led to depressive states where respondents just gave up on these basic tasks. The challenges of homemaking, cleaning, and completing small projects in the home and yard seemed to increase with the duration and intensity of chronic pain. As a result, the effects of chronic pain became visible in the organization of respondents' homes and yards, which became increasingly messy, unorganized, and chaotic, the longer they lived with chronic pain.

A dwelling space is a kind of text, codified by formal codes and cultural conventions. The disposition of rooms in the average home is usually beyond the control of consumers. The placement of spaces within the home follows a predictable logic, designed to provide convenience, safety, and comfort. The home is also a cultural space inasmuch as the meanings associated with cooking, dining, socializing, and bathing dictate how entire social groups arrange rooms, activities, and possessions within the home.

The home is also a personal place that takes on the personality and lifestyle preferences of consumers. For chronic pain sufferers, the disposition of goods in the home mirrored the chaotic states of mind they described in the picture sort exercise. As the fieldwork progressed, we noticed that the longer the respondent had lived with chronic pain, the more likely were they to lose the ability to manage and maintain order in their homes. The normative order of goods in the home was gradually overcome by a dysfunctional order of goods. Domestic space had become a surface on which consumers inscribed their inner turmoil.

The Normative Order of Goods

Social norms influence the way consumers manage their homes and possessions, as reflected in popular proverbs such as "cleanliness is next to godliness." Storage areas, such as cabinets, closets, and shelves, regulate the disposition of goods within the home. Closets and drawers serve to organize goods by category, that is, clothing, shoes, boxes, foods. Consumers set aside special spaces for storing off-season clothing and outerwear. Shelves and file cabinets keep books, papers, and toys at arms reach while clearing spaces for human activity.

Moreover, the function of each storage area is codified by function and cultural norm. Consumers relegate goods that they want to save but rarely use to the attic, out of reach and out of sight. They store tools, automotive accessories, and yard equipment in the garage, a transition space between the home and the outdoors. Sacred and profane realms of consumption also influence storage decisions. Pharmaceuticals belong in the designated "medicine cabinet" in the bathroom, for example, while candy may be on display in the living room. Although individual consumers may reinterpret these spaces based on convenience or lifestyle preferences, they nonetheless conform to a storage system in order to keep goods "in their place" and in the service of the consumer.

The Dysfunctional Order of Goods

In the homes of chronic pain sufferers, sacred and profane areas of the home become blurred, because abandoned goods eventually take over all areas of the home. Findings suggest that the disorder of goods in chronic pain sufferers' home' evolves in pace with the advance and duration of the pain. As shown in Figure 6.6, in the early stages of chronic pain, the respondent's home seems very orderly. At this stage, consumers stored pain medication in the medicine cabinet or a special closet, out of view. By hiding the visible signs of dysfunction behind doors, consumers at this stage of illness could remain in denial about the effects of pain on their personal lives. Upon closer look, the respondent would dump unwanted goods in a closet and shut the door.

Order   Chaos

Early Stage Patient   Advanced Stage Patient

Figure 6.6. Spaces Speak

This closet was then designated as off-limits for normal use, out of sight and out of mind.

Hoarding and Dumping

Respondents in the advanced stages of pain suffering could no longer hide their mess behind doors, since hoarded goods encroached on every available space in the home. As time goes on, the mess spreads to a spare room, then to several rooms, which were then closed off from the rest of the house. Old clothing fills up hallways and bedrooms; discarded boxes and newspapers crowd the living room; old appliances, utensils, and dishes overwhelm kitchen cabinets and furniture. In one case, the researchers were asked to enter by the back door of the home because the respondent had blocked the front door and hallway with discarded newspapers, Christmas ornaments, and boxes. The stove, sink, and table in the kitchen were likewise piled high with dirty dishes, pans, and refuse. In these kinds of households, researchers had to remove junk from chairs and sofas in order to find space to sit down for the interview. Even respondents' beds were piled high with clothing and papers, leaving only a small space for the individual to sleep.

These behaviors reflect a breakdown of cultural paradigms such as sacred and profane, public and private, conventional space and personal place in the household. Hoarding differs from storing, since it is a means of holding onto things which are no longer of use, such as old newspapers and clothing. Hoarding also demands little planning in the order and placement of goods. Hoarders abandon the conventions that send waste to the garbage, Christmas ornaments to the attic, and clothing to the closet. Ultimately, the possessions of these consumers take over their domestic space, leaving little room for moving about, sitting down, eating a meal, or even going to bed. The goods in these homes seemed to possess the individual, rather than the other way around.

The placement and storage of their medications also reflected a gradual decline in the sacred and profane realms of goods, such as the distinction between everyday products and medical treatments. Consumers in the advanced stages of chronic pain stopped storing their prescription medications in special cupboards or cabinets, leaving them in public spaces such as coffee tables, kitchen counters, and bookcases in the public spaces of the home. Pain treatment consumed their daily lives, leading some of them to addictive behaviors, such as taking double and triple the recommended dose of OTC medications such as ibuprofen. They purchased generic ibuprofen in large bottles at WalMart and treated the drug as if it were candy. During our trips to local WalMart stores, we discovered that consumers' association of ibuprofen with candy was aided and abetted by the organization of products on the shelf. WalMart managers displayed the large packages of ibuprofen alongside rows of candy, disposable cameras, and other "fun" products. They also placed them near the check-out lines alongside the magazines and confectioneries offered as impulse purchases. Thus the organization of products in retail space forms a kind of discourse, as truly as the verbal association of ibuprofen and candy in the structure of metaphor.

Dissociation

In summary, the experience of pain permeates every area of consumers' lives and transforms conventional spaces of consumption into places of dysfunction. Interestingly, as the chaos in the home increases, consumers' tendency to dissociate themselves from their surroundings increases. They seem frozen in a state of mental denial about their dysfunctional homes. For example, I was interviewing a junior high school teacher surrounded by heaps of old junk in the family room, when her teenage son returned home from school. He walked through the mess and clutter up to the equally messy upstairs area, apparently screening out the disaster of his home life. In other words, the effects of chronic pain not only disrupted the orderly disposition of goods in the home but also disturbed the consumers' experience of identification with their domestic places of consumption. This kind of dissociation is symptomatic of the individual's self-alienation and psychological disintegration over time.

Theory and Evidence

To "read" an environment as a text demands acceptance of the underlying theory of projective identification derived from the Freudian tradition in psychoanalysis. The semiotic analysis supports theory with analysis of the codes structuring meaning in the data. It begins with tracing recurring patterns of meaning in the data, such as the association of pain with clutter and confusion, and the reiteration of these patterns in multiple registers of consumer discourse. In the case of the chronic pain sufferers in this case study, these registers include emic and etic accounts of the consumer environment. The emic account includes the respondents' own words as they describe the effects of pain on their thinking and their lives. It includes consumer analogies between abstract paintings and the experiences of pain. The etic account includes the researchers' observations of consumer's homes, analysis of consumer statements about pain, and in the meanings constructed by the placement of pain medications in the WalMart stores where respondents shopped.

The semiotic analysis emphasizes the complex dynamic structure of meanings in a category, a research site, and/or a consumer segment. Rather than simply describe the paradigmatic structure of findings, it exposes tensions within the category that shape consumer needs. For example, a cursory analysis of advertising for the pain relief category as a whole, including OTC and pharmaceutical treatments, reveals a general emphasis on the effects of medication on the body, including vague promises about freedom from pain and increased physical movement. Not only do these claims ring false, since patients realize they will never be "pain free," but they limit the potential benefits of medication to physical symptoms.

Since culture is structured like a language, any single cultural category, such as the body, entails consideration of its binary opposite, such as the soul or spirit. Respondents distrusted commercial messages that emphasized the effects of medication on the body, because they promised unrealistic results, including "pain free" experiences and full mobility. They were also suspicious of messages that represent escape rather than engagement with the real world. On this, the "spirit" side of the equation, we plotted consumers' own fears that pain relief treatments take them out of life, make them feel drugged and "zoned out" (Figure 6.7).

However, deconstructing the body/spirit dialectic on the semiotic square exposed a new cultural space—consumer well-being, that plays within the tensions between the mind and body. Consumer well-being does not depend upon a complete absence of pain, which respondents realized they would never achieve, but on the ability to manage pain so as to live a productive and orderly life. Furthermore, the new treatment produced by our client is not a drug, so they did not want to associate the brand with zoning out or emotional escape. By locating the new brand on the well-being quadrant of

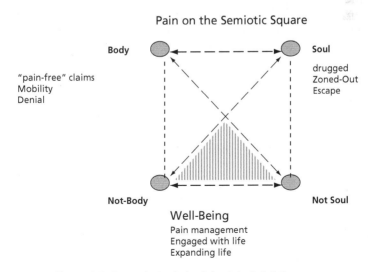

Figure 6.7. Strategic Analysis of the Pain Relief Category

the semiotic square, we identified a unique brand positioning for our client that emphasized the lifestyle and emotional benefits of the new pain treatment, not the body. This led to development of a unique message for the brand that centered on resolving the chaos in consumers' lives, enabling them to complete projects, realize plans, and live expansive, fulfilling lives.

Implications

By conducting a two-pronged investigation of both consumers' subjective states and the semiotics of their home environments, semiotics research identified the essence of pain for chronic pain sufferers. In all phases of research, including the in-depth interview, the picture sort, and the observations, findings revealed that the residual effects of pain on consumers' personal integrity and domestic space outweighed their physical symptoms. By tracking the effects of pain over time, the analysis also provided means of segmenting consumers by degree of dysfunction. Findings led to the development of a positioning for the new pain treatments in terms of unmet consumer needs for personal control, integrity, and order. Furthermore, findings from the picture sort exercise provided the basis for developing creative strategy based on the symbolic cues that consumers associated with pain and pain relief in the picture sort exercise.

Navigating The Branded Signscape

The branded retail setting adds another dimension to the semiology of space: the brand discourse. The brand "speaks" to consumers through the medium of the merchandising elements of the store. As shown in Figure 6.8, the dialectical structure of the branded shopping experience engages consumers

Figure 6.8. Semiosis in the Branded Signscape

in the brand discourse by means of the codes structuring sign systems such as architecture, design, and merchandising.

Successful retail design does not stop at decorating the environment; it integrates all merchandising elements from the floor plan and lighting to the ambient sounds and packaging around a single value proposition. This approach explains the success of Target's retailing strategy, for instance. The Target Company changed consumer perceptions of the brand and the discount category by imitating the branding strategies of high-end department stores. While consumers associate discount shopping with drab, generic stores, Target invested in brand development, creating the red Target logo and creative, attention-grabbing advertising. They also integrated the Target value proposition—discount shopping with style—into the smallest details of the merchandising repertoire from the décor and floor plan to the shopping carts and decorated shopping bags.

As illustrated in Figure 6.8, the retail design itself only accounts for part of the semiology of the retail setting. The other part consists of the expectations consumers bring to the store. They "read" the retail setting through the lens of their brand perceptions, their memories of other stores, and their expectations of the retail category itself. They also respond to sensory cues such as colors, icons, and sounds. For example, the color red may remind them of the holidays. In this way, they make the retail space into their own personal "place."

THE SEMIOTICS OF SPACE

Retail design, like language, is a communication system. Just as linguistic codes ensure the shared, social function of speech, cultural codes and category conventions ensure the shared, social function of branded retail sites. Secondary codes rework the standard conventions to form a unique brand discourse and engage consumers in the brand experience. In Victoria's Secret, for example, the décor, placement of mirrors, and product displays engage shoppers in the brand promise of hedonistic indulgence. The visit is staged from the entrance to the back rooms in order to move shoppers through a series of sensory experiences from looking to trying that culminate in the purchase. Shopping and browsing become a kind of performance in which consumers and marketers "co-create" meanings across the symbolic and material structures forming the retail site (Sherry, 1998).

In summary, three kinds of codes structure the communication function of branded retail space:

- Merchandising codes or conventions associated with retailing in general and specific retail categories in particular, such as the placement of the cashier;

- Cultural codes associated with the meaning of shopping in consumer culture; and
- Branding codes related to the unique positioning and identity of the brand.

Merchandising Codes

In the same way that social codes structure the normative meaning of words or traffic signs, retailing conventions structure the meaning of retail space and provide consistent experiences from one store to the next. These conventions form the "deep structure" of the retail experience—a system of codes that can be modified and reworked but that nonetheless transcend the structure of any individual store. Codes structure the organization of retail operations in a store, including management, product displays, customer service, checkout, and stocking areas. They also guide consumers from one area of the store to another along a kind of logic derived from the product categories themselves. This flow is supported by signage, lighting, and even sounds. Shelves, cases, bins, and doorways organize products into intelligible categories.

Cultural Codes

The "deep structure" of retail space is not only a formal grid; it is a cultural blueprint regulating the social experience called shopping. A structural analysis of retail design across categories revealed several dominant cultural codes that regulate the disposition of retail functions, spaces, and shoppers in a setting. They include the bifurcation of retail space into sacred and profane areas of retailing, and the organization of the visual field along perspective lines leading from consumer vantage points to key vanishing points on the horizon.

Sacred and Profane Dimensions of Retailing

In superstores, department stores, groceries, boutiques, malls, and theme parks, the primary function of spatial semiotics is to perpetuate the cultural divide between sacred, consumer-centered spaces of consumption and profane, commercial-centered spaces of consumption. Design strategies conceal the profane, pecuniary functions of retailing behind the counter, behind the service window, and behind closed doors. These codes are so embedded in consumer culture that consumers automatically avoid the spaces designated for customer service, stocking, and cash registers.

Design strategies not only conceal the commercial objectives of retailing from the consumer; they distract consumers from the transactional objectives of their visit by embellishing the consumer-centered spaces with entertainment value. Although the "retail-tainment" phenomenon motivates the design of all kinds of retail outlets, it has particular relevance for boutiques, entertainment venues, and specialty stores, where the consumer's in-store experience adds substantial value to the brand.

The hedonistic value of shopping contributes increasingly to the bottom line of branded retail chains such as boutiques, flagship stores, and fast-food restaurants (Pine and Gilmore, 1999). Management coordinates all design functions from the floor plan, lighting, and color scheme to the music, product displays, and merchandising cues. In this, the experience-centered retail environment, money does not seem to matter. The commercial realities of production, profit, and credit card debt are moved off-stage and out of sight to leave way for what Rob Shields (1992: 7) calls a "spectacle" of consumption.

THE RETAIL SPECTACLE

The organization of the retail spectacle draws upon the conventions that structure the illusion of perspective and depth in the visual arts. The principles of visual perspective were developed from the science of optics by the Quattrocento school of art in the fifteenth century. Quattrocento artists such

The diminishing scale of elements along perspective lines create the illusion of depth in narrative space.

Vantage point meets vanishing point on the horizon, organizing the visual field into a narrative discourse.

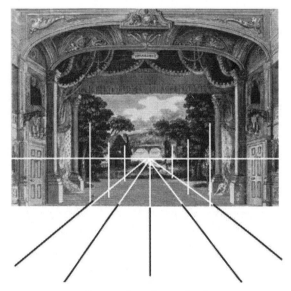

Proscenium Stage Design

Figure 6.9. The Perspective Structure of Spectacle

as Leonardo Da Vinci used mathematical formulas to organize the visual field in line with human vision. Besides adding depth and realism to art, theatrical design, and architecture, perspective re-created the depth of field seen through the human eye (see Figure 6.9).

Perspective principles have been used for centuries to create an illusion of depth on a flat or shallow surface and engage spectators in visual discourse. Perspective lines on either side of the frame regulate the illusion of depth and focus vision toward a vanishing point at the center of the horizon. The gradual centering of vision from the surface to depth toward the horizon, as well as the diminishing scale of the walls along these lines from front to back, creates an illusion of great depth and distance on a simple stage and also inscribes dramatic point of view and spectator-address in the space of spectacle. In line with this tradition, a proscenium arch frames the stage. The proscenium has two functions. It marks the divide between the space of spectacle and the space of the spectator; and it engages the spectator's gaze on the scene unfolding on stage.

Perspective and Retail Design

Although one usually associates the principles of perspective with the representation of space in the fine arts, these codes are deeply embedded in the visual culture of the West. They orient the consumer experience of public space in cinema, architecture, and retailing around deliberate points in the visual field. They guide the consumer through a course—real or imaginary—drawn by the director, builder, or retailer. Perspective techniques also engage consumers in the pleasure of shopping. Perspective lines organize visual perception in relation to window displays and service counters that re-create the disposition of the voyeur at the window. Perspective thus transforms retail space into narrative space and displaces consumer desire from goods themselves to the pleasurable experience of looking and possessing with the eyes (Oswald, 1996, 2009).

Narrative Space

Although branded retail sites resemble spectacles (Kozinets et al., 2002), "engaging the consumer's senses in the spectacular display of goods and commodities" (Shields, 1992: 7), they also function as discourses delivering the brand message from the retailer to the consumer. The traffic flow, product placement and décor, the scents and music not only enhance retail atmospherics (Pine and Gilmore, 1999; Oswald, 1987; Underhill, 2001; Ailawadi and Keller, 2004) but also organize the disposition of goods, consumers, and store dimensions into a kind of brand story narrated by a virtual designer-narrator. Design elements in this way trace the visible effects of the retailing "discourse" organizing the consumer's experience, brand relationship, and brand perceptions in line with the brand positioning and story.

Example: Disneyland

The theme park represents the ultimate use of perspective to engage consumers in a retail spectacle. At Disneyland, designers employ theatrical techniques to engage consumers in a seamless fantasy of American life, untroubled by conflict, cultural difference, and the other tensions associated with real life. From the moment the visitors enter the park, they are guided by Disney characters, signs, attention-grabbing foods and rides, and optical illusions through a seamless fantasy experience with nothing left to chance (Oswald 1989).

At Disneyland, the designers used the principles of perspective to move visitors through the park as if they were in a Disney movie. Even the scenery is scaled to give visitors the impression that they are actors in the Disney story, rather than observers. Klingmann (2007: 71) reports that Disney architects employed a series of forced perspectives to create the illusion that objects are closer or further away. The architects reduced down the buildings along Main Street to increasingly smaller scales from the ground floor, at nine-tenths of a standard size, to the top floor, at five-eighths the standard size. Even the trees on Magic Mountain are scaled down smaller and smaller, moving from bottom to top of the structure.

These kinds of optical illusions match the visitor's line of vision, their "eye," with the narrative positioning of the brand, the "I" of the Disney brand discourse. Although visitors choose among a variety of options as they walk through the park, the physical design orients the visitor's experience around the brand experience, symbolized in the Magic Kingdom towering above the park. From any given vantage point in the park, the castle appears centered on the horizon, anchoring the visitor's experience in line with the brand positioning.

The theme park is unusual inasmuch as it has the capacity to hold consumers hostage in the brand world. However, the same principles of consumer engagement apply to store design.

- Every detail in the store must reflect the brand message and personality from the décor to the product displays and shopping bags.
- Design elements from the architecture to the signage must be deliberately organized in order to stage the shopper's experience in line with the brand story. Store design can communicate intimacy or distance, formality or casualness, freedom or control.
- Retail design should keep up with emerging trends in the retail category in general.

Case Study II: The Branded Restaurant Space

This case study focuses on the impact of the environment on consumer choice at a fast-food chain in the United Kingdom, which I will call Best Burger. Periodically the company develops new sandwiches and meals to satisfy consumer needs for variety and to increase dining occasions at their restaurants. To promote these innovations, the company spends millions on advertising and special promotions because increasing the product line has the potential to grow traffic to the store and grow brand value. The current study draws attention to the impact of the retailing experience on consumer acceptance of new products in the fast-food venue.

BACKGROUND

The case in point concerns the launch of new sandwiches and meals in 2002. Although the new products won kudos in consumer testing and new product messaging came through loud and clear in advertising, these efforts did not succeed in selling the new products at point of purchase.

Obviously, retailing strategies alone cannot account for consumer decisions and choices. If the core target at Best Burger prefers burgers and fries to salads and wraps, marketing alone will not change their behaviors. If the target is motivated primarily by low price and promotions, retailing activities alone will probably not persuade them to try something new. However, in the branded retail business, pricing strategy, consumer habits, and store design work together, not separately, to influence retail brand loyalty, perception of quality, and product choice (Ailawadi and Keller, 2004). In the following discussion of retailing semiotics, I discuss how the semiotic structure of a retail environment can influence brand perception, consumer choices, and ultimately brand value. The Best Burger case illustrates how design and merchandising tactics in a fast-food restaurant can create barriers to brand acceptance and threaten the success of new product launches.

Semiotics research and participant observation at a dozen Best Burger restaurants in several markets revealed that in spite of consumers' willingness to try new products upon entering the store, they changed their minds by the time they reached the service counter. Consumers may have been thinking about the new sandwiches at Best Burger when they entered the restaurant, but ultimately resorted to the "burgers and fries" default decision when they made their orders.

A cursory analysis of the spatial semiotics of a dozen Best Burger restaurants suggested that design factors may have contributed to this behavior. Findings from the research confirmed that the spatial semiotics of the restaurants undermined management's new product strategy and also limited consumer perceptions of the restaurant's range of offerings. Semiotic analysis uncovered simple measures for correcting the problem.

Research Design

The branded retail experience gains meaning according to a "semiology of space" that implicates consumers' subjective states in the formal structure of a retail venue. For example, consumers enter the fast-food venue with memories of the stores they have just shopped, other fast-food restaurants they have patronized, and other kinds of restaurants in their dining repertoire. They also bring expectations of the brand formed by advertising and other brand experiences. Even the perception of price is affected by consumers' expectations and previous experiences of stores and restaurants. Therefore, to understand how consumers interpret the Best Burger retail experience, it does not suffice to understand the design experience of Best Burger, or even all fast-food restaurants, but to look at a broad range of retail experiences that form consumer expectations of a store.

Data Set and Methods

For the present study, researchers examined the spatial semiotics of several kinds of stores, including (*a*) competitive fast-food stores, (*b*) "convenience food" restaurants serving cold prepackaged meals, (*c*) boutiques, (*d*) department stores, and (*e*) street kiosks. Findings led to the identification of a set of codes structuring emerging trends in retailing in general and fast-food restaurants in particular. I used this information to highlight potential conflicts, at the level of retail design, between consumer expectations and their actual experiences at Best Burger restaurants.

THE FAST-FOOD VENUE

Researchers visited a dozen Best Burger stores in several markets in the United States and the United Kingdom, in addition to another dozen visits to a range of other branded fast-food restaurants, including Burger King, Wendy's, Subway, Sonic, and other local brands. Armed with a grid that outlined the standard semiotic dimensions of fast-food restaurants, such as the layout and décor, researchers kept track of the details of each store. At the analysis stage, researchers compared and contrasted restaurants, identifying underlying codes that were common to all, as well as unique features that distinguished one brand from another. Researchers also spoke with adult consumers before and after they purchased meals to assess how their store experience influenced their purchase decisions.

The Code

The design of fast-food restaurants has been codified over time by conventions that balance consumer needs for quick service with the need for a clean, pleasurable, and trustworthy brand experience. Marketers manipulate these codes in order to inscribe a specific brand discourse in the spatial structure of the restaurant.

Branded fast-food restaurants share a basic blueprint. A large service counter usually divides the restaurant into the spaces of production in the depth of the store—the kitchen, the cash register, the management—and the spaces of food consumption out front. A menu board above the counter includes photographs of the food items with prices and serving sizes. Between the counter and the seating area, there are usually self-service kiosks for napkins, condiments, and sometimes beverages are served. The seating areas are normally up front near windows and doors and may include booths as well as tables and chairs (see Figure 6.10).

Figure 6.10. The Fast-Food Venue

Staging the Fast-Food Experience

As shown in Figure 6.10, the fast-food layout is divided into service, dining, and staging areas for the meal service. The service counter distinguishes fast-food venues from traditional restaurants because it exposes the management and food preparation areas behind the counter, though keeping them strictly off-limits to consumers. Like the proscenium arch framing a theatrical stage, the service counter is the gateway between the spaces of food consumption and production. It is the site of transactions and a showcase for the menu, service, and brand message. As such, the service counter forms the focal point of the site, the spot on the horizon toward which all of the design elements ought to converge.

Returning again to Figure 6.10, the fast-food restaurant orients all design elements toward the proscenium opening at the service counter, turning the physical space of the site into a branded narrative space for consumers. The disposition of pathways, furnishings, and decorative elements center the gaze, the movements, and the intentions of customers on a trajectory leading toward a visual horizon behind the service counter. The space in front of the service counter forms a staging area for the serving and dining functions. Kiosks, garbage bins, and dividers should be strategically placed to support the flow of movement from front to depth of the store. Accents such as lighting, color scheme, signage, and even the pattern of tiles on the floor should reinforce the branded design strategy of the store.

The Brand Discourse

Spaces "speak" inasmuch as they trace the intervening hand of the designer/marketer in the construction of the retail experience. The spatial discourse consists of primary and secondary codes structuring the meaning of space for consumers. First, retailing conventions dictate to a large degree the physical layout and the optical organization of the fast-food restaurant. Second, the brand positioning, identity, and relationship to consumers ideally structure the unique interpretation of the conventions by specific companies.

Analysis of the layout of a dozen fast-food restaurants revealed that even slight manipulations of the structural elements could create very distinct restaurant experiences and communicate distinct meanings about the brand. The dimensions of the service counter, the disposition of the kitchen, and the direction of the traffic flow, for example, communicate emotional dimensions of the brand, such as the personality, the relationship to consumers, and trustworthiness.

In the best cases, the visual orientation of the restaurant moves customers toward the service counter quickly while creating a mood, atmosphere, and visual discourse that supports the brand message. Even the floor tiles reinforce the traffic pattern by marking pathways to the service counter. In the worst cases, confusing traffic flow or structural barriers between restaurant functions—ordering, servicing, dining—limits consumer freedom and creativity, and influences their choice of new products.

Although the color scheme, logo, décor, and signage are the most obvious media for branding the store, modifications of the service counter and traffic flow can have dramatic impact on the store experience. For example, the service counter is both a barrier and an opening between consumers and the brand. From one restaurant brand to the next, the design of the service area communicates either intimacy and transparency or distance and opacity. At one extreme are local fast-food venues that use the counter as an eating area and cook the sandwiches right before the eyes of diners. The Billy Goat's Restaurant in Chicago is a good example of this. The exposed kitchen and management areas of the restaurant communicate a personal relationship between the brand and the diner, as if the diner was in the manager's kitchen. Furthermore, the close physical proximity between diners and service staff emphasize the intimacy and casual personality of the brand.

At the other extreme are the large global brands such as Best Burger, Burger King, and McDonald's, where the counter serves to manage transactions and to market new menu items. Within this category, subtle differences in the structure and use of the service counter vary from one brand to another. At Burger King restaurants in London, for instance, the countertop was waist-high and uncluttered. Cashiers took orders on laptop computers rather than behind heavy cash registers. The physical structure of the service counter provided a direct, open line of vision between consumers and service staff and communicated an accessible, transparent brand relationship. Furthermore, the wall behind the counter was open, exposing the kitchen and the meal production process. In this sense, the service counter at Burger King resembled the service spaces at smaller fast-food chains, where the personal and casual tone of the restaurant is reinforced by the open, intimate space separating the kitchen from the diner. By contrast, as I discuss in detail further on in the chapter, at Best Burger the space between the consumption and production of the food formed a barrier to access and communicated a guarded, untrustworthy brand.

RETAILING TRENDS

In order to identify any emerging trends in the structure of retail space, I extended the fieldwork to other types of stores beyond the fast-food category per se. Researchers observed convenience food restaurants, boutiques, and department stores and discovered that in general stores were offering more flow and freedom in consumer's movements and more independence in their selection and scrutiny of product choices. These trends form a context for

Figure 6.11. The Convenience Food Service Space

consumers to compare and contrast their experiences in fast-food restaurants with the many retail sites they visit throughout the day.

Convenience Food Restaurants

Researchers observed the growing popularity of the "quick" food service category, a kind of "convenience food service restaurant" that served pre-packaged sandwiches and fresh coffee. This category includes gourmet coffee chains and cold sandwich stores such as Costa Coffee or Prêt à Manger, a British company. Unlike traditional fast-food outlets, which have to serve food fresh from the griddle behind the counter, the "convenience food restaurant" serves cold, prepackaged sandwiches, wraps, sushi, side dishes, and beverages displayed in cases facing out toward the consumer. Only the coffeemakers remain behind the counter (see Figure 6.11).

Next, the design strategy of fast-food restaurants is focused on speedy service, while convenience food stores, invite more casual shopping, strolling, and looking at goods. In malls and other concourse sites such as airports and train stations, convenience food restaurants are often structured as open, free-standing kiosks. This layout breaks down the rigid bifurcation of the restaurant into the production and consumption areas, and invites consumers to browse the display and even pick up and examine products before they make a choice. Traffic flow is dictated more by consumers' passion to see and touch products than by the purchase function alone (see Figure 6.12).

Figure 6.12. The Food Service Kiosk

Figure 6.13. The Fast-Food Concourse Window

In the same concourse areas, fast-food venues are typically recessed into walls, communicating with consumers through a service window, forming a barrier to consumer choice, freedom, and sensory contact with the brand in the selection process (see Figure 6.13).

Figure 6.14. Niketown Self-Service Kiosks, London

Peripheral Retail Categories

The emphasis on consumer choice and flow in retailing was also evident in other retail categories. In boutiques, branded flagship stores, and department stores, design elements such as windows, racks, display cases, and mirrors reached out toward consumers as if to break down the barrier between front- and back-space functions of the store.

At Bath and Body Works, signs invite consumers "Try me," next to cosmetic displays. At Niketown, shoes are displayed behind self-service windows that encourage shoppers to open the door, look inside, and examine first-hand the latest innovations in shoe wear (see Figure 6.14).

Even at the stuffy department stores on London's Bond Street—where the cosmetic counter is traditionally the sacred realm of expert sales staff—the cosmetics display has been reconfigured to encourage shoppers to touch, try, and play with products (see Figure 6.15).

The previous discussion of branded retail strategies focused attention on several design principles that contribute to a successful fast-food experience. They include:

- Aligning the structural and merchandising elements of the store along perspective lines leading from all consumer vantage points toward a vanishing point on the horizon beyond the service counter.

- Designing the disposition of furnishings, signage, décor, and lighting to stage a consumer experience that conforms to the brand personality, that is, friendly or distant, formal or casual.

- Responding to the effects external retailing trends have on consumer expectations of the restaurant.

Try me!

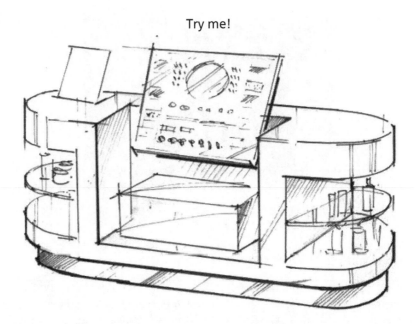

Figure 6.15. Department Store Cosmetic Bar

IMPLICATIONS FOR BEST BURGER

In the course of visits to twelve Best Burger restaurants at multiple locations in London, researchers interviewed a random selection of diners before and after their purchases to take stock of their perceptions of the store. Many consumers remarked that when they entered the restaurant they were considering purchasing the new menu items advertised outside, but by the time they reached the service counter, they ordered their usual fare, burgers and fries. Although they did not always reference specific factors that influenced their purchase decisions, most diners said they were in a hurry and it was easier to order their usual choices than to try something new. A structural analysis of the restaurants revealed that design elements communicated confusion, lack of trust, and ambiguity, which may have contributed to consumers' experience that they just "didn't have time" to try the new products. Semiotic analysis identified a lack of focus and flow in the visual layout, traffic flow, and the disposition of furnishings and signs, which may have slowed down and muddled the decision-making process, creating barriers to the trial of new menu offerings.

Layout and Traffic Flow

Since fast food is in large part evaluated on the speed of service, a clear and uncluttered line of traffic toward the service counter takes priority over shopping or loitering. By contrast, the retail design at Best Burger caused confusion rather than clarity, slowed down traffic flow rather than speeding it up. Furthermore, it interfered with the branding process rather than creating a branded narrative space for staging the consumer experience. They interfere with the projective lines that usually focus consumer perceptions and experiences toward the proscenium of the service counter. Designers seemed to have overlooked the experiential and strategic functions of traffic flow and focused more on fitting as many seats and promotional signs as possible in the restaurant.

In the apparent absence of a clear and focused physical layout, kiosks and other immovable furnishings interrupted the direct line joining the serving and dining areas. The floor tiles were organized randomly rather than supporting the organization of the visual field along perspective lines leading to the service counter.

Promotional Signs

Next, an abundance of promotional signs competed for consumers' attention. Signs advertising new products, specials, and other messages hung from the ceiling, decorated the walls, and stood atop the kiosks, scattering consumer attention in many directions. Rather than guide the diner to a desired destination or product choice, the signage interferes with the optical clarity and direction of retail space and creates confusion. Ultimately, the excessive signage at these restaurants detracts from the nonverbal, emotional dimensions of the restaurant experience. By treating retail space merely as a surface for selling, management misses an opportunity to leverage the experiential value of the store that distinguishes the brand from competitors and builds trust, loyalty, and emotional attachment with consumers.

The Service Counter

The transactional focus of the restaurants was most evident in the design and function of the service counter. Rather than a proscenium opening for inviting consumers into the brand world, the service counter at Best Burger formed a physical and psychological barrier between consumers and the service staff, and ultimately the brand. The counter was raised six inches higher than those at other fast-food outlets by a ledge. On top of the ledge, a variety of paper signs promoting desserts, discounts, and other offerings competed for space and attention. In addition to the high, cluttered service counter, stainless steel cabinets and walls blocked consumers' view of the kitchen, as if management had something to hide. These kinds of barriers communicated a lack of transparency and trust, and inevitably contributed to consumers' reluctance to try new products.

Retail Trends

Fast-food brands generally suffer from a lack of transparency, flow, and spontaneity. The tables and chairs are anchored to the floor, the food is hidden behind counters and walls, and the service staff controls product delivery. These shortcomings not only interfere with consumer pleasure at restaurants such as Best Burger; they also contrast sharply with emerging trends in retail design that encourage customer experimentation, creativity, and play. Emerging trends inevitably shape consumer expectations of stores generally, which may contribute to their dissatisfaction with the Best Burger restaurant experience.

Strategic Implications

Besides creating barriers to new product trial, design factors at Best Burger undermined, rather than communicated, the brand legacy and promise. In advertising, public relations, sponsored programs, and social networking sites, Best Burger communicates a brand positioning associated with intimacy, civic responsibility, transparency, trust, and innovation. However, the retail design communicated distance, commercialism, opacity, distrust, and stagnation.

THE SEMIOTIC SOLUTION

Best Burger management responded to the findings of this research by lowering the counter, exposing the kitchen, and managing the signage. It is impossible to measure the direct effects of these changes on consumer choices or even restaurant traffic. Nor is it possible to measure the exact effects of any given advertising campaign, marketing strategy, or design tactic for that matter on consumer behavior. However, research has shown that retailing factors such as layout, availability of service staff, and product variety influence consumer perceptions of the brand value, product quality, and even pricing strategy of retail brands (Ailawadi and Keller, 2004). Studies have also shown that consumers also delay making shopping decisions because, among other reasons, they do not have enough time, they need more information about the product, or they find the shopping experience unpleasant (Greenleaf and Lehmann, 1995). By clearing up the clutter at Best Burger, management restored clarity and transparency to the retail experience and facilitated a smoother, more thoughtful decision-making process.

Theoretically, these changes would account for the increase in traffic and new product trial at Best Burger in subsequent months.

I would add that the perceived value of the retail atmosphere has less to do with any single design element, no matter how attractive, and more to do with the orchestrated effects of all design elements on a coherent brand experience or narrative. Retail branding, like product branding, creates value by forming a consistent, unified message across all media that differentiates the brand from competitors and engages the target market in a relevant brand world. Ultimately, it is consumer trust in the brand that encourages new product trial and repeat business.

Since low prices and value meals drive profits at fast-food companies such as Best Burger, management may underestimate the role of retail semiotics for increasing customer loyalty and new product trial. They may even neglect the importance of brand strength altogether for increasing traffic to the store. However, research suggests that consumers develop perceptions of value from multiple factors, only one of which is the price itself (Alba et al., 1994). Consumers at branded retail sites evaluate the quality of their purchases by balancing the benefits of low price with the perceptions of quality associated with a strong brand, a comfortable store experience, and the expectations they bring to the category.

In this chapter, I studied consumption environments from the point of view of the dynamic of semiosis that implicates the consuming subject in the "semiotics" of consumer environments. The semiotics of space provides a complex, dialectical account of consumer experiences of their environments and takes account of the intersection of the structural codes regulating the normative dimensions of social spaces and the individual manipulations of those codes by marketers and consumers. In this sense, the semiotics of space defines an epistemological order, an understanding of the world as essentially a world of meanings, defined by codes derived from culture, not nature.

Structural codes organize the cultural world into binary categories, such as private and public, background and foreground, consumer space and commercial space. They account for the ability of whole societies to navigate social spaces with common expectations. On the other hand, the performative or interpretive dimensions of spatial semiotics account for the ways individuals personalize environments, either by reworking the actual structures or by projecting their personal expectations, mood states, and thoughts into them.

Semiotics defines both an epistemological understanding of the world and also a method of analysis. The semiotician approaches the consumer environment as a textual system in which multiple codes work together to produce a statement or discourse. By articulating the code from the personal interpretation of the code, the semiotics of space highlights parallels between the structure of consumer environments and language, whose communication function is regulated by socially shared conventions and rules. Spaces "speak" to consumers by means of the complex, dialectical movement between the code structuring spatial meanings or discourse, and consumers' active participation in meaning production.

Semiotics research embeds the structural analysis of social spaces in the broader culture of consumers. For example, the meaning of space is essentially regulated by cultural codes and conventions, such as the laws of perspective, which transcend any given environment or text. These codes standardize the way consumers interpret and participate in social spaces and structure the environment as a form of discourse. Since these codes are culture-specific, they may give rise to different interpretations, experiences, and expectations based on the consumer segment, culture, or national identity.

The semiotics of space has important applications for retailing and consumer research. First, by analyzing consumer environments such as dwellings and retail sites in terms of codes, semiotics can tease out the controllable dimensions of the retailing mix (such as a store layout) from uncontrollable dimensions of the retail experience (such as the subjective states and memories that consumers bring to the store). Furthermore, the theory of codes enables researchers to infer cause–effect relationships between specific physical structures such as the disposition of the service counter and consumer experiences. Even in the absence of direct, primary research with consumers, semiotics draws upon the conventions structuring the retail environment to anticipate the effects of retailing tactics on consumers and to plan retailing strategy and design accordingly.

■ ENDNOTES

1. Thompson and Haytko (1997) propose a dialogic relation between the marketer's manipulation the staged retail experience (sign domination) and consumers' creative "sign experimentation" (sign manipulation). Kozinets et al. (2002) propose a "co-creative" dialectic between consumer play and marketing spectacles in branded flagship stores. Diamond et al. (2009) explain it in terms of consumers' identification with the "retail brand ideology" represented consistently throughout the themed "brandstore."

7 New Directions in Marketing Semiotics

"Expanding markets, unlimited semiosis."

Semiotics embraces a broad range of social science disciplines, theoretical constructs, and methods, and has broad applications to the fields of advertising, brand management, and consumer research. In this short book, I have presented only a few of them. In concluding, I will suggest directions for future research in two emerging areas: Internet marketing and global brand strategy.

Surfing the Virtual Brandscape

Computer experts have been writing about the implications of semiotics for computer information for decades, but there is still a limited body of research on the applications of semiotics to marketing, public policy, and consumer behavior on the Internet. Mihai Nadin (2001) calls the computer a "semiotic machine." He states that, "Computation is about meaning, not electrons. [...] Whether electron, light, quantum, or DNA-based, the computer is a medium for sign processes! Numbers turned into images, simulations, database operations, etc. are examples of how the signs of the object of our practical interest are processed according to our goals."[1]

Peter Bøgh Andersen ([1990] 1997) emphasizes parallels between the interdisciplinary nature of semiotics and structure of information on the Internet. Semiotics can be used to bridge computer technology, the social sciences, and the arts. He states, "This is useful in designing computer interfaces, since computers are inherently multimedia where codes from these diverse fields meet and amalgamate in practice" (ibid.: 15). The basic principle is that the Internet is a medium of communication, and is therefore susceptible to the same conditions of analysis as language, advertising, and consumer space. However, few writers have teased out the distinctions between these more traditional forms of communication and computer communication in particular.

Neumüller (2001) emphasizes that the web site is a kind of hypertext unfolding through time and virtual space in several dimensions and media simultaneously. The nature of the web site as a hypertext has several implications for the semiotics of Internet marketing. It places in question the phenomenology of consumer response and the nature of meaning, and pose a potential threat to brand integrity that these suggest.

First of all, the hypertext is a multimedia, multidimensional system of meaning. A user can be watching a video ad from one source while scrolling a menu for more options in another window, and communicating with another user on yet another page. Furthermore, on the Internet, consumers can simultaneously participate in range of interpersonal relationships, social roles, and personal identities with ease. Thus, consumer identity and self-hood are transitory and polyvalent, not easily targeted by traditional segmentation methods.

Next, in order to engage with information on the Internet, consumers "interface" with the hypertext rather than simply read it. Even as they are guided periodically by signposts such as hyperlinks that direct them to new contents and resources in cyberspace, consumers make decisions about which links to follow from one content node to another. Consumers thus navigate a web site as creators, not passive receivers of a message. They construct meaning by building sequences of information that may or may not constitute coherent discourses. They nonetheless form inferences and analogies among units of content by means of the point-to-point navigation of search options on the Web. Thus the nature of the hypertext demands a rethinking of the ways persuasion operates on the Internet, how consumers respond to advertising, and how marketers can test the effectiveness of a marketing program online.

Most of the computer semiotics research draws upon semiotic theory to understand how meaning is organized on the Internet as a medium of communication. They apply Peirce's typology (1988/1955) of sign forms to the analysis of hyperlinks, to account for the nature of the signs signaling the transitions consumers make as they navigate the Web. Some authors emphasize the role of icons and metaphors in marketing links between nodes or information containers. These sign types highlight a relationship of similarity between the source and target page (Sherson, 1999). Other computer semioticians emphasize the inherently indexical nature of these links and their role in integrating multiple pages and media in a multidimensional search (Codognet, 2002). Indexical transitions create contiguity between multiple sites in the virtual space of the Web and have the potential to draw inferences and implications between multiple, even disparate, information.

Moritz Neumüller (2003, 2001) points out that the scope of computer semiotics and its applications to the commercial uses of the Internet have yet to be defined. He underscores the importance for marketers and web designers to account for the consumer's unique interface with the semiotic structure of the hypertext as a nonlinear, multimedia, performative medium when designing web sites and planning strategy. Neumüller does not give specific examples of how semiotics could be applied to marketing and advertising in the computer hypertext or its implications for consumer behavior, social network marketing, or online retailing.

The current application of semiotics to marketing online falls short of accounting for the distinct hypertextual structure of advertising on the Web and its implications for advertising response research, online marketing, and consumer behavior. For example, Tsotra et al. (2004) exposed consumers to advertisements posted on the web sites for Ericsson and Nokia phones in order to gauge the importance of culture on their responses to the ads. They discovered a positive correlation between the cultural identity of respondents and their opinions of the ads.

Unfortunately, the authors of that study did not add to our knowledge of computer semiotics, because they analyzed self-contained advertising images on these web sites as if they were print ads. As a result, they overlooked the very important difference between advertising response—a one-way interpretive process characteristic of linear media—and the complex, two-way dynamic constructing consumer interface with the hypertext. The limitations of this approach reinforce the need for future research into hypertext semiotics as it relates to Internet advertising, consumer interface with computers, and marketing online.

In the following section, I summarize a business case that shows, in a very rudimentary fashion, how computer semiotics can be used to strategic advantage. Internet marketing has obviously evolved since the time of this event, but it nonetheless serves to illustrate the potential applications of semiotics to Internet marketing, public policy, and consumer behavior.

In this case, I applied semiotics to a trademark dispute over the meaning and reference of language on the Internet.[2] As an expert witness in a trademark litigation case for Playboy Enterprises (PEI) in 1999, I proved that the search engines, Excite and Netscape, committed trademark violation when they keyed the search terms "playboy" and "playmate" to unsponsored adult entertainment sites, in order to divert Web traffic from Playboy Enterprises content to those sites. The Appellate Court of the Ninth Circuit overturned a ruling of the Circuit Court of Southern California and ruled in favor of PEI. The court ruled that Excite and Netscape violated PEI's trademarks by confusing consumers, blurring Playboy brand distinctions, diluting Playboy brand equity, and tarnishing the Playboy brand.

CASE: IS IT "PLAYBOY" OR PLAYBOY?

Trademark ownership contributes to brand equity because it protects companies' most valuable assets—the meanings and brand legacy consumers associate with the logo and brand name. Semiotic theory can be used to justify the trademark claims of companies whose brand names might be misconstrued and exploited as common names by competitors, particularly on the Internet. The Playboy (PEI) litigation focused on the practice of "keying" or linking the search terms consumers type into the search box to advertising on a webpage. The problem is particularly acute when common words that can be found in the dictionary acquire trademark meanings in the course of branding activities by companies.

The International Trademark Association defines the problem of fair use on the Internet in the following statement:[3]

The proper trademark analysis in a 'keyword' case, just as in any infringement case, should begin with an examination of whether the defendant's use is a use of the plaintiff's mark in its secondary or trademark sense. If not, then the word is being used in its dictionary sense and is a descriptive fair use.... If, however, the word is used in its secondary, trademark sense, then the inquiry turns to: (1) whether the direct or indirect use is likely to cause confusion, and (2) where appropriate, defenses such as nominative fair use or nonconfusing comparative advertising.

Advertisers can purchase the right to appear on the results page above or below the search term. There is trademark infringement if search engines deliberately key ("link") search terms for brand names to competing web sites. For example, if consumer types the word, "Harvard MBA" in the search box, a competing university may legitimately purchase advertising space on the results page to attract users to their sites. However, if advertisers deliberately confuse consumers by keying branded search terms, such as "Harvard," to a less renowned brand, such as a school in Harvard, Texas, they could be accused of pilfering Harvard University's brand equity and even diluting the Harvard brand by association with a less prestigious school.

Playboy charged Excite and Netscape of trademark violation for selling banner advertisements for unsponsored adult content web sites that were keyed to the terms "playboy" and "playmate" in the search box. They claimed that Excite *confused* consumers, *blurred* distinctions between the PEI brand and the other adult entertainment sites, *diluted* the Playboy brand name, and even *tarnished* Playboy's brand by association it with x-rated sites. Playboy also claimed that Netscape violated its marks by displaying the same ads in partnership with Excite. The judge summarizes the complaint in the following way.

The plaintiff has a trademark on "Playboy®" and "Playmate®." The plaintiff contends that defendants are infringing and diluting its trademarks (*a*) by marketing and selling the group of over 450 words, including "playboy" and "playmate," to advertisers; (*b*) by programming the banner ads to run in response to the search terms "playboy" and "playmate" (i.e., "keying"); and (*c*) by actually displaying the banner ad on the search results page. As a result, the plaintiff contends that Internet users are diverted from the plaintiff's official web site and web sites sponsored or approved by the plaintiff, which generally will be listed as search results, to other adult entertainment web sites. The plaintiff further argues that defendants intend to divert the users to the non-PEI sites.[4]

Findings and Arguments

The sexual connotations the words PLAYBOY and PLAYMATE were the direct result of PEI marketing actions, including Playboy Magazine and other PEI activities beginning in the mid-1960s.

Playboy and other PEI activities produced an adult lifestyle and culture for which Playboy and Playmate became legitimate and tacit trademarks in the minds of consumers.

The meaning of search words on the Internet cannot be defined in isolation from the context. The organization of the web page forms the context for defining the precise meaning of words in the key word search box. Excite and Netscape make implicit references to the Playboy trademark by means of the juxtaposition and analogies between the brand and unsponsored adult sites on their search page. Excite and Netscape were therefore responsible for confusing consumers, blurring and depleting the Playboy trademark, and tarnishing the brand in consumers' minds.

Confusion

The basis for confusion rests with the double meaning of common nouns such as playboy and playmate—the generic term found in the dictionary, and the secondary trademark meaning created by a company. Lawyers for the defense claimed that Playboy Enterprises did not own the terms "playboy" and "playmate" on the Internet because they could be found in the dictionary. They argued that these terms have always been associated with sexual meanings.

However, a historical review of words "playboy" and "playmate" in literature and dictionaries, beginning in the seventeenth century, disproved this claim, since these terms had never been associated with sexual meanings until the creation of *Playboy Magazine* in 1954.[5] The generic meanings of playboy and playmate are defined in the sources we studied in the following terms:

Companion in play. Good time girl.	Playboys are moved by some impractical notion or other.	Gay, hilarious, rowdy, outspoken.
Funny gentleman.	A Playboy couldn't do a man's job.	Lives a life devoted chiefly to the pursuit of pleasure.
Blatantly silly.	Player, reveler.	

Through *Playboy Magazine* and other company activities, PEI created a culture of adult entertainment symbolized in the flashy lifestyle of Hugh Hefner. *Playboy Magazine* created the sexual connotations of Playboy and Playmate and popularized them in the popular imagination, where they became the trademarks for this lifestyle. To further support this claim, I list below the meanings "playboy" and "playmate" had acquired in the popular culture after 1960, when Playboy had achieved worldwide recognition.[6] They include:

Erotic	Concubine, playmate	Pin-up, centerfold girl, bunny
Voyeuristic	Free, openness	Upscale, glamorous
Recreational sex	Casanova	Sophisticated
Pleasure	Nudity	Mainstream press
Doll, sex kitten		

Blurring

Meaning production on the Internet is entirely contextual and results from a network of intersecting references and associations in the search process. A structural analysis of the Excite web page showed that Excite and Netscape reinforced the branded meaning of "playboy" and "playmate" by associating these key words with the Playboy trademark in juxtapositions and analogies. In this way, defendants blurred Playboy's hard-fought distinctiveness in the competitive environment and sent consumers to sites that had not developed a brand identity.

Figure 7.1 is an outline of a typical Search Results page generated by the words PLAYBOY and PLAYMATE on the Excite search engine in 1999. (For

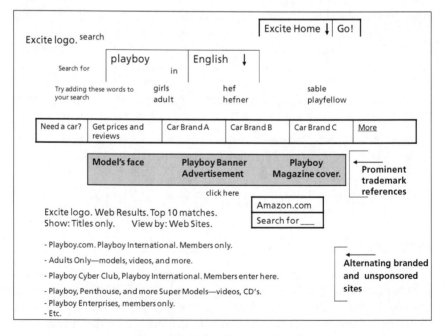

Figure 7.1. Excite Web Page Analysis

proprietary purposes I did not reproduce logos or advertiser's brand identities). On the original site, the organization of the various elements of the page takes on a rhetorical dimension. Though these findings are only summarized here, throughout the original web page, the juxtaposition of the keyword "playboy," or "playmate," with references to Playboy International in the "Try These First" lists, site Directories, and Web results, point to the secondary, trademark use of the words PLAYBOY and PLAYMATE.

If the keyword PLAYBOY is juxtaposed with a list of the Related Search words that are associated with Playboy Enterprises, such as Hefner and Playboy Magazine, this association creates a first identification between the word PLAYBOY and the secondary meaning or trademark for Playboy Enterprises. When this list is then juxtaposed with an unsponsored banner ad for adult entertainment, the consumer will infer a connection between the Playboy trademark and unsponsored adult entertainment on the web. This analogy is further reinforced when the banner ad is juxtaposed with a "Top 10" list on which Playboy Enterprises is prominently featured.

Next, on the list of Web results itself, the alternating juxtaposition [A/B/A/B] of the sites for PEI [A] with the unsponsored adult sites [B] implicates Playboy Enterprises in an undifferentiated list of sites for unsponsored adult entertainment. This rhetorical device effectively blurs distinctions in consumers' minds between the Playboy trademark and the unsponsored sites.

Dilution

Brand meaning and keying activities create the Internet Brandscape. This movement, rather than any given key word taken in isolation, constantly refines the meaning of words, links them to specific semantic categories, and integrates them into a coherent brandscape. When a competitor reroutes these links to content unintended by the trademark owner, they disrupt this coherence and threaten the integrity of the trademark owner's brand. By referencing the Playboy brand, then associating the brand trademarks with unsponsored adult entertainment sites, Excite and Netscape not only stole traffic from the Playboy company but also diluted the Playboy trademark by linking it to generic sites.

Tarnishment

Playboy Enterprises prides itself on being at the high end of the adult entertainment industry, having avoided association with "hard core" adult entertainment such as *Hustler* and *Penthouse*. In their corporate report, management claims that the Playboy trademark references a world of ideas, culture, and politics, not only the magazine centerfold. On page 4 of the 10-K form is a list of American Presidents, prominent writers, artists, and celebrities interviewed in the Magazine, as well as special features on cultural trends, politics, and art. Moreover, Playboy Enterprises is associated with a mainstream, upscale market, as proven by the choice of advertisers in *Playboy Magazine.*

Lawyers for PEI claimed that Excite and Netscape degraded its equity by linking the keyword "playboy" to an array of hard-core web sites other than Playboy Enterprises. That is, when a user typed the word "playboy" into the search box, the Excite search engine produced a list of links to unsponsored pornographic sites. Netscape also tarnished the Playboy brand by positioning Playboy banner ads next to links keyed to unsponsored pornographic sites. Not only did Excite commit trademark violation by drawing business away from Playboy to these other sites; they also *tarnished* the Playboy brand by associating it with unsponsored pornographic content on the Internet.

The Circuit Court of Southern California ruled against Playboy, but they won on appeal. The judgment from the 9th Circuit Court of Appeals in California agreed with our argument that Playboy Enterprises (PEI) had created a new, proprietary meaning for the noun "playboy," by means of advertising and marketing activities over a long period of time. They agreed that by creating Internet links and rhetorical associations between Playboy trademarks for "playboy" and "playmate" and X-Rated sites, Excite and Netscape *confused* consumers, *blurred* hard-fought distinctions between Playboy trademarks and unsponsored adult entertainment, diluted the Playboy brand equity, and tarnished the Playboy brand name.[7]

In the brief summary of this business case, I have suggested some of the implications of semiotics for Internet marketing as they relate to marketing, public policy, and intellectual property on the Internet, and the important distinctions between common words and their secondary, trademark meanings. However, I have only scratched the surface of the potential applications of semiotics to marketing on the Internet. For example, the current research on consumer engagement in visual discourse does not address the unique interface of consumers with the computer hypertext, which is dynamic, multimedia, and performative.

Furthermore, there is a need to understand how consumers create symbolic environments in cyberspace—not just the fictional identities that they can create on sites such as Second Life[8] but also the virtual environments they create on retail sites, from the single-brand boutique to the broad context of an Amazon.com. And there is an urgent need to understand how consumers interface with meaning in the social network. Social networking produces a unique form of discourse in which the consumer interfaces with multiple sites, cyber-mates, and sponsored messages in the virtual community of online communication.

Global Brand Strategy

In the flat, multicultural, and polyglot world of global marketing, semiotics is indispensable for calibrating global brands to the local culture of consumers, particularly in developing markets. As I show below, to market global brands it is not enough to translate the words used in advertising from one language to another. It is a matter of understanding how consumers in these markets construct the meaning of goods in the first place. Do they view the world in terms of similarities or differences, for example.

In the section below, I map the structural dimensions of brand meaning in Western culture and show the limitations of this structure for consumers in China, based on a study of the luxury sector in Shanghai.

THE STRUCTURAL DIMENSIONS OF BRAND MEANING

In the West, consumers construct brand meanings along two dimensions—the grouping of brands into product categories, and the differentiation of brands into unique personalities.

In Figure 7.2, I have mapped these dimensions along two axes of meaning formation. They include the paradigmatic association of all brands in a category on the vertical axis and the syntagmatic association of individual brand meanings on the horizontal axis.

Syntagmatic Axis—Set of unique brand attributes   Contiguity

	AWARENESS	QUALITY	SOCIAL STATUS	PERSONALITY	RELATIONSHIP
Dior	Expensive	Rare	Celebrity	Sexy, young	Erotic
RL	Expensive	Rare	Old wealth	Conservative mature	Envy
Gucci	Expensive	Rare	Nobility	Refined, sporty	Admiration
LV etc.	Expensive	Rare	Achievers glamour	Mythical Iconic	Emulation

Similarity

Paradigmatic Axis—
Set of all luxury brands.

Figure 7.2. The Structural Dimensions of Brand Meaning

The Paradigmatic Axis

Consumers in the West group brands together into a category, such as luxury, on the basis of the more general and functional brand benefits they share. The category forms the "paradigmatic" or vertical axis of this grid. For the luxury category, these include high price, high perception of quality, and social status, though the symbols for social status may change from one brand the next, as from "celebrities" to "nobility."

The Syntagmatic Axis

Marketers expect consumers to relate to brands with increasing degrees of intensity, from awareness to a personal relationship, as shown in Figure 7.2. At the same time, they expect to create increasing differentiation among brands on the basis of more emotional attributes, such as desire. These attributes are linked to each other on a continuum that forms the brand world. For the luxury category, these include the more nuanced and emotional brand benefits consumers associate with particular interpretations of luxury, such as the association of Dior with sexy, young, and erotic.

The brand continuum forms the *syntagmatic* or horizontal axis of this grid. As consumers' brand perceptions move from left to right on this axis, they may even report that the brand contributes to their self-esteem, prestige, or happiness. These unique associations form the cornerstone of brand equity because they differentiate brands from each other and clarify the brand positioning. These are tried and true assumptions of marketing professionals in the West.

The Role of Culture

To participate in brand culture, consumers learn to navigate the paradigmatic and syntagmatic axes of meaning production, alternatively grouping together brands that share the same product category and differentiating brands that stand for different meanings. This is a complex and fairly sophisticated process. Marketers may err in assuming that consumers in developing markets, such as the People's Republic of China, move through the brand relationship cycle "just like us." Consumers in China may belong to the first or second generation of their families to purchase brands rather than trading vouchers for commodities, as was common during the Cultural Revolution. Consequently, they may not be accustomed to the conventions structuring symbolic consumption at all. On the other hand, their responses to brands may be due to the fact that they structure meaning differently from consumers in the West, just as their language structures meaning differently from Indo-European languages.

A CONSUMER ETHNOGRAPHY IN CHINA

Findings from an ethnographic study I conducted with affluent consumers in Shanghai (2007–9) suggest that consumers in developing markets do not move through these stages of brand relationship naturally or in the same order as consumers in the West. Many consumers failed to grasp the more nuanced meanings symbolized by brands, and were far from using brands to enhance their identities (Aaker, 1997) or fulfill their life projects (Fournier, 1998), concepts that marketers in the West take for granted. As the result of their low engagement with brand meanings, respondents did not draw clear qualitative distinctions among luxury brands.

Between 2007 and 2008, working with Chinese researchers,[9] I conducted sixteen ethnographic interviews with affluent consumers in Shanghai to assess their interpretations of luxury, the kinds of products they usually purchased, and their perceptions of European luxury brands, as communicated in advertising, retailing, and packaging.[10] We limited research to product categories such as fashion, leather goods, clothing, watches, and perfumes. In this brief review, I will limit analysis to one section of the interview protocol devoted to a brand audit exercise. We exposed consumers to a limited set of advertisements for Western luxury brands taken from Chinese magazines. We assessed consumers' perceptions of global brands such as Louis Vuitton, Dior, Patek Philippe, and Ralph Lauren in order to understand the intensity of their response to these brands and their ability to distinguish one brand from another on the basis of emotional and esthetic attributes. To create a base line from which to gauge consumer responses to the brands, I also conducted similar interviews with affluent consumers in Paris, France.

Findings Summary

Most respondents in Shanghai purchased luxury goods such as watches, bags, and cosmetics, without engaging with the emotional attributes and fantasies that create value for European luxury brands. They claimed that luxury purchases did not express their own personalities, and that luxury advertising fell short of helping them personalize their brands. Most respondents did not relate to brands on emotional and personal levels, and failed to make qualitative distinctions between brands on the basis of brand culture, personality, and esthetics. As a result, consumer responses to European luxury focused on the most general meanings of luxury, such as price. In linguistic terms, their responses betrayed tensions between the meaning and reference of brand symbolism: the CG logo signifies "expensive," LV must be successful because they are so well known—but these brands do not conjure up any emotional experience, fantasy, or image that the consumer can relate to.

Furthermore, consumers in Shanghai struggled to find a luxury brand that expressed their personal values, lifestyles, and fantasies. Some reported losing interest in their LV bags once they got them home, leaving them in the closet with indifference. As the goods piled up in their closets, these same consumers expressed strong interest in finding a "match" with a brand that satisfied their need for self-expression and met their expectations, fueled by advertising, that luxury consumption would enrich their self-image and help them express their deeply felt values and beliefs (Belk, 1988).

By contrast, their counterparts in Paris readily identified brand distinctions. Affluent consumers in Paris could describe the emotional and esthetic factors that led them to prefer one brand to another. They formed emotional relationships with their brands, and used brands to express their personal and social identities. The marketing challenge is to understand these different responses to brand meanings, and to identify marketing actions that could mitigate these differences.

The Marketing Semiotic Perspective

As I have reiterated throughout this book, the marketing semiotic perspective looks at the cultural factors that lead consumers to read the world of brands in one way or another. By bringing semiotics to bear on this business problem, I discovered that the response of Chinese consumers to luxury brand symbolism is not simply the result of their recent entry into the culture of consumption. Chinese consumers enter global consumer culture from a dramatically different culture and ideology of origin than consumers in the West. Their interpretations of brands naturally stem from their unique worldview. Returning to Figure 7.2, most Chinese respondents focused on the paradigmatic axis, the axis of similarity, rather than the syntagmatic axis, the axis of contiguity. They identified the attributes brands in a category had in common rather than the unique attributes that differentiated brands from each other.

Several factors influence the way consumers perceive brands. They include the cultural factors associated with the history, language, and worldview of consumers. And they include marketing factors associated with strategic planning and communication tactics. I will begin with a discussion of cultural factors.

CULTURAL FACTORS

History and Ideology

History, ideology, and culture affect Chinese consumers' ability to make qualitative distinctions between brands and to use luxury brands to express their identities. One hundred and fifty years of wars, colonization, and communism have disrupted the Chinese history of luxury. The widespread Confucian ideal of frugality may also explain why Chinese consumers have trouble relating to the luxury category. The signs and symbols of luxury represented in European ads fail to reference a tradition of luxury in consumers' personal lives or cultural background. This may be responsible for the somewhat superficial responses of consumers to luxury brands from Europe.

The Philosophy of Language

Language difference may be a significant cause for the different brand perceptions of affluent consumers in China and the West, because language shapes consumers' interpretation of the world of phenomena. Proponents of the sociolinguistic tradition of linguist Benjamin Lee Whorf (1956) argue that language structures thought; therefore, the formal and semantic structures of languages influence the way social groups in different parts of the world interpret and structure reality. These insights have important implications for the current study, because they suggest that structural differences between Chinese ideograms and Indo-European languages such as French or English also structure radically different cultural constructions of the world. Consumer researchers find that these linguistic differences influence, in turn, consumer responses to advertising and brand meaning.[11]

Consumers in the West read the world of phenomena in terms of binary oppositions, because binarism is the underlying formal relationship structuring Indo-European languages. By extension, Western consumers also make sense of the marketplace by classifying the world of meanings, culture, and brand identity into distinct binary categories. This explains why even college students in the West could easily classify luxury perfumes into discrete paradigms of meaning.

A Binary Analysis of Luxury Perfume Brands

For example, in Chapter 2, I discussed the binary oppositions structuring the luxury perfume category into two styles and two interpretations of the feminine, French and American, at the end of the 1990s. In Figure 7.3, I take the analysis further and identify lateral distinctions within each set of brands. Given all French luxury perfumes, there are distinctions between the positioning of Guerlain, Paloma Picasso, and Dior based on binary contrasts and comparisons within the set. The same is true for the American brands, Estee Lauder, Calvin Klein, and Ralph Lauren.

Two sets of binary patterns structure the distinctiveness of these brands in the luxury perfume category. On the one hand, as discussed in Chapter 2, one set of advertisements characterizes the French interpretation of Woman as a

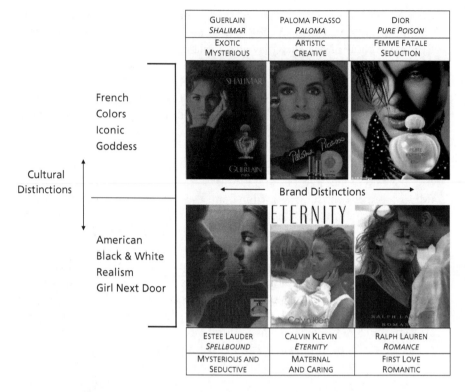

Figure 7.3. A Binary Analysis of the Luxury Perfume Category

Goddess shown in rich colors, removed from the world. The other set characterizes the American interpretation of everyday women in realistic black-and-white photography, as the Girl Next Door.

The second set of binaries structures contrasts and distinctions among brands themselves, within the French and American groups of ads. A cursory description of these brand positionings highlights the qualitative differences between these brands as communicated in the choice of model, color scheme, and "story," in each advertisement. When I expose American college students to these ads, they readily make these kinds of distinctions.

By contrast, based on findings from research in Shanghai, very few of the young affluent consumers we interviewed in China would identify these distinctions. The research on Chinese language and philosophy provides an answer to this riddle. Unlike consumers in the West, who intuitively structure the world in terms of dialectical pairs and contrasts, Chinese consumers interpret the world in terms of flow and complementarity, of "yin" and "yang."

François Julien ([1995] 1999) describes Chinese thought in terms of the flow of meaning through things, rather than the logic of meaning imposed by the mind. He speaks of the alternation of poles within this flow, as opposed to their opposition. This may explain why consumers in Shanghai, despite their education, *savoir faire*, and income, did not readily make distinctions among brands in the luxury category. They were perhaps predisposed to finding similarities among brands, therefore leaning toward the paradigmatic associations on the left of Figure 7.2, rather than seeking distinctions aligned on the syntagmatic axis.

MARKETING FACTORS

Some consumers in China had actually mastered the rules of brand communication and were able to differentiate luxury brands and engage with brand meanings. Their brand perceptions seemed to be influenced by their experiences living abroad or their professional role in marketing organizations in China. This finding suggests that marketers may be able to mitigate cultural differences by means of a consumer acculturation process that would move them toward greater identification with brand symbolism.

Consumer Segmentation

During the fieldwork, I identified three consumer segments based on the intensity of their involvement with luxury brands as mapped in Figure 7.2. These segments include the New Rich, Passionate Trend Setters, and the Mature New Rich, and correspond to the stages consumers had reached in the brand acculturation process.

The New Rich. Consumers in the New Rich segment may be the first generation in their family to advance economically and enjoy luxury goods. Luxury brands are a "badge" of success, not a passion. This segment is characterized by low identification with the luxury category as a whole due to their more practical lifestyles and values. They express very low brand differentiation. In other words, they place high value on the luxury category, but lower value on any given brand.

The brand perceptions of the New Rich stop at the levels of brand Awareness and the Perception of Quality. They read the literal meaning of the logo or brand name rather than its poetic meaning, that is, "Louis Vuitton is a famous luxury brand from France." Their perception of quality is to some extent driven by the high price, for example, "Louis Vuitton is expensive and well made."

Passionate Trend Setters. Passionate Trend Setters enjoy luxury as a reward for their hard work. Their lifestyles, as well as their length of time in the affluent segment of the economy, influence their luxury brand perceptions.

This segment is characterized by high involvement in the luxury category as lifestyle choice. They may choose large-scale "masstige" brands like LV and Armani for their high recognition factor and because they do not appreciate the finer distinctions of more discrete brands such as Dior or Hermes. Focus on perception of quality, status, and *savoir faire*. They do not engage with brands on a visceral, personal level. Frustrated because they seek a "match" or relationship with brands that express their personal myth or identity. Consumer behavior is characterized by frequent purchases and low brand identification.

The brand perceptions of the Passionate Trend Setters stop at the level of social status. They share a high degree of brand familiarity and perception of quality with the New Rich segment, and also appreciate the value of the brand as measured by others, for example, "Wearing Louis Vuitton communicates that I am successful and possess savoir faire."

The Mature New Rich.   Consumers in the Mature New Rich segment may be second or third generation luxury consumers. They no longer seek luxury brands as badges for their social success. They recognize the qualitative differences among brands, and choose brands that communicate something about their personal style and culture. They represent a small portion of the respondent sample, and their brand behavior has been influenced by travel abroad, a commitment to learning about brands, or work in a marketing field.

The brand perceptions of the Mature New Rich segment resemble Western consumers' brand perceptions. They personify brands and use them to express or extend their own identities. They can also distinguish the more popular "masstige" brands such as Louis Vuitton from more subtle brands such as Dior or Hermes. Masstige brands such as LV are mass marketed and therefore not rare or special. They might give their secretary a gift from Louis Vuitton, knowing that he/she will recognize the value of the brand. However, they would give their close friends more discrete brands that have a personal connection to the person.

The Marketing Challenge

The marketing challenge consists of moving Passionate Trend Setters into the Mature New Rich segment by adopting measures that both promote the brand and initiate consumers in brand culture. Research has shown that to succeed in developing markets, marketers must engage in a two-way process of understanding and appreciating the complex cultural systems of the brand culture on the one hand, and the local consumer culture on the other, for successful brand adoption (Burke, 1996; Calya and Eckardt, 2008). Findings from our research in China suggest that marketers need to change their approach in order to acculturate Chinese consumers into luxury culture and branding. Recommendations are listed as follows.

- Rely less on the single-image magazine ad so characteristic of luxury advertising. The single-image approach isolates the brand from the lived context and experience of consumers and privileges visual culture over other forms of communication. Research has shown that a full spectrum of marketing events, including special events and even personal selling, may be required to initiate consumers into the culture of brands (Burke, 1996).

- Chinese consumers do not currently anchor their perceptions of Western luxury in a collective culture of luxury because recent political events have damaged the cultural legacy of luxury. Marketers need to contextualize luxury brands in a broader, more detailed experience of the brand world and the culture of luxury.

- Account for deep, philosophical differences between consumers in the East and West in order to appreciate the distinct worldviews of these two markets, and communicate these differences in all marketing activities.

Implications for Brand Equity

Luxury consumption in China continues to grow at an annual rate of 17 percent. At this rate the Chinese market will soon account for 29 percent of global luxury consumption, even though the Chinese have participated in branded global consumer culture for a relatively short time. Luxury consumption in developing countries as a whole has been driving double-digit growth in the European luxury sector for the past fifteen years. Without a clear understanding of the consumer culture factors underlying growth in emerging markets, some researchers warn that the luxury industry may lose touch with consumers and lose their hard-won success in these markets (Allérès, 2005; Sicard, 2006).

Furthermore, since brand image drives profitability in the luxury sector, consumers' low identification with brand meanings in China has important implications for the overall growth of this market. Luxury brands enjoy margins of up to 80 percent because of they are valued precisely because of the emotional, social, and esthetic attributes they communicate to consumers through marketing. Since Chinese consumers do not, for the most part, relate to the deep emotional dimensions of luxury brands, manufacturers face the risk of losing market share over time, as New Rich consumers of luxury evolve into mature consumers and demand more from their brands than flashy signs of success. Furthermore, there are indications that local businesses are developing a Chinese national culture of luxury that may draw market share away from Western brands. Consumers may also seek more relevant signs of their success and *savoir faire* than fashion brands, investing their disposable income in real estate, automobiles, and private jets.

As I demonstrated in this brief summary of an ethnography of affluent consumers in Shanghai, semiotics research can help marketers face these challenges by guiding them through a strategic planning and communications process that takes into account the distinct ways consumers in developing markets construct meanings and relate to brand culture.

As these examples illustrate, the marketing semiotics approach provides a conceptual framework and mode of analysis appropriate to the complexity of meaning production and consumption in the marketplace, including virtual markets on the Internet and global markets in the developing world. Semiotics can be applied to a range of business problems to create value for consumers and the firm, by clarifying the symbolic dimension of brands and aligning brand meanings to the culture of consumers. Though some readers may be put off by the technical terminology and theoretical constructs that seem to go hand in hand with the academic discourse, I have sought throughout this book to clarify these challenges in order to make semiotics accessible, relevant, and practical for students, scholars, and marketing professionals.

ENDNOTES

1. Neumüller (2001: 178), quotes Nadin, "Semiotics for the HCI Community," 2001, <http://www.code.uni-wuppertal.de/uk/hci/>.
2. U.S. District Court Case No. CV 90-320 AHS EE. Related case: Sa CV 99-321 ahs (eex).
3. Statement from a Brief of Amicus Curiae submitted by the International Trademark Association (INTA) in support of Playboy's appeal to the 9th Circuit Court, No. 9-56239 and No. 99-56231.
4. Ibid., Case CV 90-320 and 321.
5. Sources are attached to the original pleading filed in Case CV 90-320 and 321.
6. Sources are attached to the original pleading filed in Case CV 90-320 and 321.
7. United States Court of Appeals for the Ninth Circuit; No. 9-56239 and No. 99-56231; DC# CV 99-321.
8. The Linden Lab company developed Second Life, a virtual world that users can access via the Internet by downloading a program called the Viewer. Users can interact with other users via avatar identities, create virtual environments, and travel anywhere in the Second Life Universe.
9. In 2007, I employed Lingli Wang at BBR Consulting, Shanghai, to recruit thirteen respondents in Shanghai and conduct simultaneous translations during the interviews. In 2009, Professor Jeff Wang recruited eight more respondents in Shanghai. Professors Wang and Xin Zhao conducted simultaneous translations of the interviews.
10. For a more detailed account of this study, see Oswald (2010*b*).
11. See Schmitt et al. (1994), Pan and Schmitt (1996), and Schmitt and Zhang (1998).

■ REFERENCES

Aaker, David A. (1991). *Managing Brand Equity*. New York: Free Press.

—— (1995). *Building Strong Brands* (8th edn). New York: Free Press.

—— (1996). *Building Strong Brands*. New York: Free Press.

—— (2007). *Strategic Market Management*. New York: Wiley.

Aaker, Jennifer L. (1997). "Dimensions of Brand Personality," *Journal of Marketing Research*, 34/3 (August): 347–57.

—— Brumbaugh, Anne M., and Grier, Sonya A. (2000). "Non-Target Markets and Viewer Distinctiveness: The Impact of Target Marketing on Advertising Attitudes," *Journal of Consumer Psychology*, 9/3: 127–40.

—— Benet-Martinez, V., and Berrocal, J.G. (2001). "Consumption Symbols as Carriers of Culture: A Study of Japanese and Spanish Brand personality Constructs," *Journal of Personality Psychology*, 81/3: 492–508.

—— Fournier, Susan, and Brasel, S. Adam (2004). "When Good Brands Do Bad," *Journal of Consumer Research*, 31 (June): 1–16.

Advertising Age (1996). June 3, C1–C15.

Ailawadi, Kusum L., and Keller, Kevin Lane (2004). "Understanding Retail Branding: Conceptual Insights and Research Priorities," *Journal of Retailing*, 80: 331–42.

Alba, Josepth W., Broniarczyk, Susan M., Shimp, Terence A., and Urbany, Joel E. (1994). "The Influence of Prior Beliefs, Frequency Cues, and Magnitude Cues on Consumers' Perceptions of Comparative Price Data," *Journal of Consumer Research*, 22/2 (September): 219–35.

Allérès, Danielle (2005). *Le Luxe . . . Strategies de Marketing*. Paris: Economica.

Andersen, Peter Bøgh ([1990] 1997). *A Theory of Computer Semiotics: Cambridge Series on Human-Computer Interaction*. Cambridge, UK: Cambridge University Press.

Apple Computer Corp. (2009). "The Apple Logo," <http://www.theapplemuseum.com>, accessed January 14, 2010.

Aristotle (1984 edition). *The Rhetoric and Poetics of Aristotle*, trans. W. Rhys Roberts and Ingram Bywater. New York: Random House.

Arnould, Erik J., and Wallendorf, Melanie (1994). "Market-Oriented Ethnography: Interpretation Building and Marketing Strategy Formulation," *Journal of Marketing Research*, 31/4 (November): 484–504.

Austin, John ([1962] 2005). *How to Do Things with Words* (2nd edn). Cambridge, MA: Harvard University Press.

Bachelard, Gaston ([1958] 1994). *The Poetics of Space*, trans. Maria Jolas. Boston: Beacon Press.

Baker, Julie, Parsuraman, A., Grewal, Dhruv, and Voss, Glee (2002). "The Influence of Multiple Store Environment Cues on Perceived Merchandise Value and Patronage Intentions," *Journal of Marketing*, 22 (April): 120–41.

Barthes, Roland ([1964] 2000). *Elements of Semiology*, trans. Annette Lavers and Colin Smith. New York: Hill and Wang.

Barthes, Roland ([1967] 1983). *The Fashion System*, trans. Matthew Ward and Richard Howard. New York: Hill and Wang.

—— (1972). *Mythologies*, trans. Annette Lavers. New York: Hill and Wang.

—— (1977a). "Rhetoric of the Image," in Roland Barthes (ed.), *Image, Music, Text*, trans. Stephen Heath. New York: Hill and Wang, 32–51.

—— (1977b). "The Third Meaning," in Roland Barthes (ed.), *Image, Music, Text*, trans. Stephen Heath. New York: Hill and Wang, 52–68.

Batra, Rajeev, and Homer, Pamela M. (2004). "The Situational Impact of Brand Image Beliefs," *Journal of Consumer Psychology*, 14/3: 318–30.

Beasley, Ron, and Danesi, Marcel (2002). *Persuasive Signs: The Semiotics of Advertising*. The Hague: Mouton de Gruyter.

Belk, Russell W. (1987). "Identity and the Relevance of Market, Personal, and Community Objects, in Jean Umiker-Sebeok (ed.), *Marketing and Semiotics*. The Hague: Mouton de Gruyter, 151–64.

—— (1988). "Possessions and the Extended Self," *Journal of Consumer Research*, 15/2: 139–68.

—— Pollay, R.W. (1985a). "Images of Ourselves: The Good Life in Twentieth Century Advertising," *Journal of Consumer Research*, 11 (March): 887–97.

—— —— (1985b). "Materialism and Status Appeals in Japanese and U.S. Print Advertising: A Historical and Cross-Cultural Content Analysis," *International Marketing Review*, 2/12: 38–47.

—— Sherry, John, and Wallendorf, Melanie (1989). "The Sacred and the Profane in Consumer Behavior: Theodicy on the Odyssey," *Journal of Consumer Research*, 16 (June): 1–39.

Belk, R. W. (2006). *Handbook for Qualitative Research Methods in Marketing*. Cheltenham: Edward Elgar Publishing.

Benveniste, Émile ([1966] 1971). "Man and Language," in Émile Benveniste (ed.), *Problems in General Linguistics*, trans. Mary Elizabeth Meek. Coral Gables, FL: Miami University Press, 195–248.

Biel, Alexander (1993). "Converting Image into Equity," in David A. Aaker and Alexander L. Biel (eds.), *Brand Equity and Advertising: Advertising's Role in Building Strong Brands*. Hillsdale, NJ: Lawrence Erlbaum Associations, 67–82.

—— Danesi, Marcel (2002). *Persuasive Signs: the Semiotics of Advertising*. The Hague: Mouton de Gruyter.

Bordwell, David, and Thompson, Kristin ([1979] 2006). *Film Art: An Introduction*. New York: McGraw-Hill.

Borgerson, Janet, and Schroeder, Jonathon (2003). "The Lure of Paradise: Marketing the Retro-Escape of Hawaii," in Stephen Brown and John F. Sherry, Jr. (eds.), *Time, Space, and the Market: Retroscapes Rising*. London: M. E. Sharpe Publishers, 219–37.

Borghini, Stefania, Diamond, Nina, Kozinets, Robert V., McGrath, Mary Ann, Muniz, Jr., Albert M., and Sherry, Jr., John F. (2009). "Why Are Themed Brandstores so Powerful? Retail Brand Ideology at American Girl Place," *Journal of Retailing*, 85/3: 363–75.

Bourdieu, Pierre de ([1979] 1984). *Distinction: A Social Critique of the Judgement of Taste*, trans. Richard Nice. Cambridge, MA: Harvard University Press.

Burke, Timothy (1996). *Lifebuoy Men, Lux Women: Commodification, Consumption and Cleanliness in Modern Zimbabwe*. Durham and London: Duke University Press.

Chambers, Jason (2008). *Madison Avenue and the Color Line*. Philadelphia: University of Pennsylvania Press.

Chandler, Daniel (2002). *Semiotics Basics*. New York: Routledge.

Codognet, Philippe (2002). "Ancient Images and New Technologies: The Semiotics of the Web," *Leonardo*, 35/1. MIT Press.

Collins, Sara, Davis, Karen, Schoen, Cathy, Doty, Michelle M., and Kriss, Jennifer L. (2006). "Health Coverage for Aging Baby Boomers: Findings from the Commonwealth Fund Survey of Older Adults," *Wall Street Journal*, January 20, A7.

DeBerry-Spence, Benét, and Izberk, Elif (2005). "Consumer Comforting: How African Americans Create Comfort in African Clothing," *Advances in Consumer Research*, 105–18.

Deeley, John (1990). *The Basics of Semiotics*. Bloomington: Indiana University Press.

Deshpande, Rohit, and Stayman, Douglas M. (1994). "A Tale of Two Cities: Distinctiveness Theory and Advertising Effectiveness," *Journal of Marketing Research*, 31 (February): 57–64.

—— Hoyer, Wayne D., Donthu, Naveen (1986). "The Intensity of Ethnic Affiliation: A Study of the Sociology of Hispanic Consumption," *Journal of Consumer Research*, 13 (September): 214–20.

Diamond, Nina, Sherry, Jr., John F., Muñiz, Jr., Albert M., McGrath, Mary Ann, Kozinets, Robert V., and Borghini, Stefania (2009). "American Girl and the Brand Gestalt: Closing the Loop on Sociocultural Branding Research," *Journal of Marketing*, 73/3: 118–34.

Dimofte, Claudia V., Forehand, Mark R., and Deshpande, Rohit (2003). "Ad Schema Incongruity as Elicitor of Ethnic Self-Awareness and Differential Advertising Response," *Journal of Advertising*, 32/4: 7–17.

Douglas, Mary, and Isherwood, Baron ([1979] 2002). *The World of Goods: Toward an Anthropology of Consumption*. New York: Routledge Press.

Dyer, Linda M., and Ross, Christopher A. (2000). "Ethnic Enterprises and their Clientele," *Journal of Small Business Management*, 38/2: 48–62.

Eco, Umberto (1976). *A Theory of Semiotics*. Bloomington: Indiana University Press.

—— (1979). *The Theory of Signs*. Bloomington: Indiana University Press.

Editors (2004). "Motor Trend 2004 Truck of the Year Winner: Ford F-150," *Motor Trend*, February. <http://www.motortrend.com>, accessed November 21, 2009.

ElBoghdady, Dina (2002). "At McDonald's, Supersize Problems: With Sales Flat, Chain Revises Menu, Marketing," *Washington Post*, September 18, E01.

Floch, Jean-Marie ([1990] 2001). *Semiotics, Marketing and Communication: Beneath the Signs, the Strategies*, trans. Robin Orr Bodkin, with foreword by John F. Sherry. New York: Palgrave.

Fournier, Susan (1998). "Consumers and their Brands: Developing Relationship Theory in Consumer Research," *Journal of Consumer Research*, 24 (March): 343–73.

Fowler, Geoffrey A. (2004). "Nike's Kung Fu Ad Trips up in China," *Wall Street Journal*, December 7, B14.

Freud, Sigmund ([1898] 1955). *The Interpretation of Dreams*, vol. v of *The Standard Edition of the Complete Works of Sigmund Freud*, trans. and ed. James Strachey. London: Hogarth Press.

—— ([1898] 2010). *The Interpretation of Dreams*, trans. from German and ed. James Strachey. New York: Basic Books.

—— ([1909] 1955). "Analysis of a Case of Phobia in a Little Boy" (Little Hans), *The Standard Edition*, x. 5–149.

—— ([1920] 1955). "Beyond the Pleasure Principle," *The Standard Edition*, xviii: 14–15.

—— (1976). *The Interpretation of Dreams*, vol. iv of the Penguin Freud Library, trans. James Strachey. Middlesex: Penguin Books.

Gaffey, Sheila (2004). *Signifying Place: The Semiotic Realization of Place in Irish Product Marketing*. Hants: Ashgate Publishing.

Genelius, Susan (2009). "Interbrand Group Announces 100 Best Global Brands," <http://www.corporate-eye.com/blog/2009/09/interbrand-announces-100-best-global-brands-2009>.

Genette, Gerard ([1972] 1982). "Métonymie chez Proust," in *Figures III*. Paris: Le Seuil, 41–66.

Goldman, Robert, and Papson, Stephen (1996). *Sign Wars: The Cluttered Landscape of Advertising*. New York: the Guildford Press.

Grayson, Kent, and Shulman, David (2000). "Indexicality and the Verification Function of Irreplaceable Possessions: A Semiotic Analysis," *Journal of Consumer Research*, 27 (June): xx.

Greenleaf, Eric A., and Lehmann, Donald R. (1995). "Reasons for Substantial Delay in Consumer Decision Making," *Journal of Consumer Research*, 22/2 (September): 186–99.

Greimas, Algirdas ([1966] 1984). *Structural Semantics: An Attempt at a Method*, trans. Daniele McDowell, Ronald Schleifer, and Alan Velie. Omaha: University of Nebraska Press.

Hall, Edward T. (1973). *The Silent Language*. Garden City, NY: Anchor-Doubleday.

Harvey, Michael, and Evans, Malcolm (2001). "Decoding Competitive Propositions: A Semiotic Alternative to Traditional Advertising Research," *Journal of International Market Research*, 23/2: 171–87.

Have, Paul ten (2004). *Understanding Qualitative Research and Ethnomethodology*. Thousand Oaks, CA: Sage Publishers.

Heath, Stephen (1982). *Questions of Cinema*. Bloomington: Indiana University Press.

Hegel, G.W.F. ([1807] 1979). *The Phenomenology of Spirit*, trans. A.V. Miller, with forward by J.N. Findlay. New York: Oxford University Press.

Hirschman, Elizabeth C., and Holbrook, Morris B. (1992). *Postmodern Consumer Research: The Study of Consumption as Text*. Newbury Park, CA: Sage Publications.

—— Scott, Linda M., and Wells, William D. (1998). "A Model of Product Discourse: Linking Consumer Practice to Cultural Texts," *Journal of Advertising*, 27 (Spring): 33–50.

Hoeffler, S.K., and Lane Keller, Kevin (2003). "The Marketing Advantages of Strong Brands," *Journal of Brand Management*, 10/6: 421–45.

Holbrook, Morris B., and Hirschman, Elizabeth C. (1993). *The Semiotics of Consumption: Interpreting Symbolic Consumer Behavior in Popular Culture and Works of Art*. The Hague: Mouton de Gruyter.

Holland, Jonna, and Gentry, James W. (1999). "Ethnic Consumer Reaction to Targeted Marketing: A Theory of Intercultural Accommodation," *Journal of Advertising*, 28/1: 65–80.

Holt, Douglas (2003). "What Becomes an Icon Most?" *Harvard Business Review*, March1.

—— (2004). *How Brands Become Icons: The Principles of Cultural Branding*. Boston: Harvard Business School Press.

Hoshino, Katsumi (1987). "Semiotic Marketing and Product Conceptualization," in Jean Umiker-Sebeok (ed.), *Marketing and Semiotics: New Directions in the Study of Signs for Sale*. The Hague: Mouton de Gruyter, 41–57.

Humphreys, Ashlee (2010). "Semiotic Structure and the Legitimation of Consumption Practices: The Case of Casino Gambling," *Journal of Consumer Research*, 37 (October).

Interbrand Group (2007). "All Brands Are Not Created Equal: Best Brands of 2007," *Business Week*, July 10, <http://www.interbrand.com/best_brands_2007.asp>, accessed May 7, 2008.

Jakobson, Roman ([1956] 1990). "Two Aspects of Language and Two Types of Aphasic Disturbances," in Linda Waugh and Monique Monville-Burston (eds.), *On Language: Roman Jakobson*. Cambridge, MA: Harvard University Press, 115–33.

—— (1960). "Closing Statement: Linguistics and Poetics," in Thomas Sebeok (ed.), *Style in Language*. New York: Wiley Press, 350–77.

—— Fant, C. Gunnar, and Halle, Morris ([1956] 1990). "The Concept of Distinctive Feature," in Linda Waugh and Monique Monville-Burston (eds.), *On Language: Roman Jakobson*. Cambridge, MA: Harvard University Press, 242–58.

Johar, Gita Venkataramini, Holbrook, Morris B., and Stern, Barbara B. (2001). "The Role of Myth in Creative Advertising Design: Theory, Process, and Outcome," *Journal of Advertising*, 30 (Summer): 1–26.

John, Deborah Roedder, Loken, Barbara, Kim, Kyeongheui, and Basu Monga, Alokparna (2006). "Brand Concept Maps; A Methodology for Identifying Brand Association Networks," *Journal of Marketing Research*, 43 (November): 549–63.

Julien, François ([1995]1999). *The Propensity of Things*, trans. Janet Lloyd. New York: Zone Books.

Jung, C. (1969). "The Structure and Dynamic of the Psyche," in Sir Herbert Read (ed.), *Collected Works of C. G. Jung*, Vol. 8. Princeton: Princeton University Press.

Kang, Jikyeong, and Kim, Youn-Kyung (2001). "The Effects of Ethnicity and Product on Purchase Decision Making," *Journal of Advertising Research*, 41/2: 39–48.

Kapferer, Jean-Noel (2003). *Strategic Brand Management: Creating and Sustaining Brand Equity Long Term* (2nd edn). London: Kogan Page.

Kassarjian, Harold H. (1977). "Content Analysis in Consumer Research," *Journal of Consumer Research*, 4 (June): 8–18.

Kehret-Ward, Trudy (1987). "How Syntax of Product Use Affects Marketing Decisions," in Jean Umiker-Sebeok (ed.), *Marketing and Semiotics: New Directions in the Study of Signs for Sale*. The Hague: Mouton de Gruyter, 219–38.

Keller, Kevin Lane (2007). *Strategic Brand Management*. New York: Prentice-Hall Publishers.

——(1993). "Conceptualizing, Measuring, and managing consumer-based brand equity," Journal of Marketing, Vol. 57 (Jan), 1–22.

——Lehmann, Donald R. (2006). "Brands and Branding: Research Findings and Future Priorities," *Marketing Science*, 25/6 (November–December): 740–59.

Klein, Melanie (1975). "Envy and Gratitude (1946–1963)," in *The Collected Writings of Melanie Klein*, Vol. iii. London: Hogarth Press.

Klingman, Anna (2007). *Brandscapes: Architecture in the Experience Economy*. Cambridge, MA: MIT Press.

Kozinets, R.V., Sherry, J.F., DeBerry-Spence, B., Duhachek, A., Nuttavuthisit, K., and Storm, D. (2002). "Themed Flagship Brand Stores in the New Millennium: Theory, Practice, Prospects," *Journal of Retailing*, 78: 17–29.

Kozinets, Robert V., Sherry, Jr., John F., Storm, Diana, Duhachek, Adam, Nuttavuthisit, Krittinee, and DeBerry-Spence, Benet (2004). "Ludic Agency and Retail Spectacle," *Journal of Consumer Research*, 31 (December): 658–72.

Lacan, Jacques ([1953] 2002). "The Function and Field of Speech and Language in Psychoanalysis," in *Écrits: A Selection*, trans. Bruce Fink. New York: W. W. Norton, 197–268.

Laguerre, Michel S. (1994). *The Informal City*. New York: St. Martin's Press.

Lentini, Nina M. (2008). "Kodak CMO Makes Hay While 'Celebrity Appearance' Shines," March 31, <http://www.mediapost.com>, accessed November 21, 2009.

Lévi-Strauss, Claude ([1958] 1963). *Structural Anthropology,* trans. Claire Jacobson and Brooke Grundfest Schoepf. New York: Basic Books.

—— (1962). *Tristes Tropiques.* Paris: Union Générale d'Éditions.

—— ([1964] 1969). *The Raw and the Cooked.* New York: Harper Torch Books.

Levitt, Theodore ([1960] 2004). "Marketing Myopia," Reprint from *The Harvard Business Review,* Cambridge, MA.

Levy, Sidney J. (1959). "Symbols for Sale," *Harvard Business Review,* 37 (July–August): 117–24.

—— (1981). "Interpreting Consumer Mythology: A Structural Approach to Consumer Behavior," *Journal of Marketing,* 45/3 (Summer): 49–61.

—— (1987). "Semiotician *Ordinaire,*" in Jean Umiker-Sebeok (ed.), *Marketing and Semiotics: New Directions in the Study of Signs for Sale.* The Hague, Netherlands: Mouton de Gruyter, 13–20.

—— ([1974] 1999). "Myth and Meaning in Marketing," in *Brands Consumers Symbols, and Research: Sydney J. Levy on Marketing.* Thousand Oaks, CA: Sage, 241–46.

Lloyd, Shawn (2003). "Ford Tough?" <http://www.writing.fsu.edu/cwc/sp02/jszcz1/shawn.htm>, accessed March 10, 2006.

Lohr, Steve (2004). "Is Kaiser the Future of American Health Care?" *New York Times,* October 31.

Lotman, Yuri (2000). "Semiotic Space," *Universe of the Mind: A Semiotic Theory of Culture.* Bloomington: Indiana University Press, 123–50.

Lunt, Penny (2005). "How to Tap into the African American Market," *ABA Banking Journal,* 87/1: 45–9.

Martin, Andrew (2009). "At McDonald's, the Happiest Meal Is Hot Profits," *New York Times,* January 11.

Maslow, Abraham H. (1943). "A Theory of Human Motivation," *Psychological Review,* 50: 370–96.

McCracken, Grant (1986). "Culture and Consumption: A Theoretical Account of the Structure and Movement of the Cultural Meaning of Consumer Goods," *Journal of Consumer Research,* 13 (June): 71–84.

—— (1991). *Culture and Consumption: New Approaches to the Symbolic Character of Consumer Goods and Activities.* Bloomington: Indiana University Press.

—— (1993). "The Value of the Brand: An Anthropological Perspective," in David A. Aaker and Alexander L. Biel (eds.), *Brand Equity and Advertising.* Hillsdale, NJ: Lawrence Erlbaum Publishers, 125–42.

McLuhan, Marshall (1951). *The Mechanical Bride: Folklore of Industrial Man* (1st edn). The Vanguard Press, NY; reissued by Gingko Press, 2002.

McQuarrie, Edward, and Mick, David Glen (1992). "On Resonance: A Critical Pluralistic Inquiry into Advertising Rhetoric," *Journal of Consumer Research,* 19 (September): 180–97.

—— —— (1996). "Figures of Rhetoric in Advertising," *Journal of Consumer Research,* 22 (March): 424–38.

Mendes, George (2005). "What Went Wrong at Eastman Kodak?" The Strategy Tank, at <http://www.thestrategytank.org>, searched on April 4, 2010.

Merleau-Ponty, Maurice ([1945] 2002). *The Phenomenology of Perception,* trans. Colin Smith. New York: Routledge.

Messaris, Paul (1997). *Visual Persuasion.* Thousand Oaks, CA: Sage Publications.

Metz, Christian ([1971]1991). *Film Language*, trans. Michael Taylor. Chicago: University of Chicago Press.

—— ([1977] 1981). *The Imaginary Signifier: Psychoanalysis and the Cinema*, trans. Celia Britton, Annwyl Williams, Ben Brewster, and Alfred Guzetti. Bloomington, IN: Indiana University Press.

Mick, David Glen (1986). "Consumer Research and Semiotics: Exploring the Morphology of Signs Symbols, and Significance," *Journal of Consumer Research*, 18 (September): 196–13.

—— Buhl, Claus (1992). "A Meaning Based Model of Advertising Experiences," *Journal of Consumer Research*, 19 (December): 317–38.

—— Oswald, Laura (2007). "The Semiotic Paradigm on Meaning in the Marketplace," in Russell Belk (ed.), *The Handbook of Qualitative Research Methods in Marketing*. Cheltenham: Edward Elgar, 31–45.

—— Burroughs, James E., Hetzel, Patrick, and Brannen, Mary Yoko (2004). "Pursuing the Meaning of Meaning in the Commercial World: An International Review of Marketing and Consumer Research Founded on Semiotics," *Semiotica*, 152/1–4: 1–74.

Moon, Youngme, Herman, Kerry, Kussmann, Erika, Penick, Emma, and Wojewoda, Susan (2003). *Burberry Case*. Cambridge, MA: Harvard Business School Press, October 1.

Moos, Bob (2008). "Baby Boomers may Find Bridge to Health Insurance," *Dallas Morning News*, 12 February.

Morton, Linda (1997). "Targeting Minority Publics," *Public Relations Quarterly*, 42/2: 23–30.

Mulvey, Laura (1975). "Visual Pleasure and Narrative Cinema," *Screen*, 16/3 (Autumn): 6–18.

Muniz, Albert M., Jr., and O'Guinn, Thomas C. (2001). "Brand Community," *Journal of Consumer Research*, 27 (December): 412–32.

NASA (2007) NASA website, 2007 http://www.nasa.gov/centers/ames/missions/archive/pioneer.html, March 26.

Neumüller, Moritz (2003). Hypertext Cemiotics in the Commercialized Internet, Hamburg, Diplomica GmbH.

—— (2001). *Hypertext Semiotics in the Commercialized Internet*. Dissertation submitted to the University of Vienna, Vienna, Austria (October).

Nunberg, Geoffrey (1995). "Transfers of Meaning," *Journal of Semantics*, 12/2: 109–32.

Oswald, Laura (1984). "The Subject in Question: New Directions in Semiotics and Cinema," *Semiotica*, 48/3–4: 293–317.

—— (1987). "Toward a Semiotics of Performance: Staging the Double in Jean Genet," Poetics Today, Vol. 8, No. 2 pp. 261–283.

—— (1989). "New Directions: The Semiotics of Spectacle," *Semiotica*, 75/3–4: 327–34.

—— (1996). "The Space and Place of Consumption in a Material World," *Design Issues*, 12/1: 48–62.

—— (1999). "Culture Swapping: Consumption and the Ethnogenesis of Middle Class Haitian Immigrants," *Journal of Consumer Research*, 25/4: 303–18.

—— (2010). "Developing Brand Literacy among Affluent Chinese Consumers: A Semiotic Perspective," in Margaret C. Campbell and Jeff Inman and Rik Pieters (eds.), *Advances in Consumer Research*, Vol. 37. Duluth, MN: Association for Consumer Research, Pages: NA.

—— (2010a). "Marketing Hedonics: Toward a Psychoanalysis of Advertising Response," "Marketing Hedonics," *Journal of Marketing Communication*, 16/3: pp. 107–31.

Oswald, Laura, and Mick, David (2008). "The Semiotic Paradigm in Consumer Research," in Russell Belk (ed.), *The Handbook of Qualitative Research Methods in Marketing*. London: Edward Elgar Publishing Ltd, 31–45.

Otnes, Cele, and Scott, Linda (1996). "Something Old, Something New: Exploring the Interaction between Ritual and Advertising," *Journal of Advertising*, 25/1 (Spring): 33–50.

Packard, Vance ([1956] 1984). *The Hidden Persuaders*. New York: Pocket Editions.

Pan, Yigang, and Schmitt, Bernd (1996). "Language and Brand Attitudes: The Impact of Script and Sound Matching in Chinese and English," *Journal of Consumer Psychology*, 5: 263–77.

Peirce, Charles Sanders ([1955] 1988). "Logic as Semiotic," in Justus Buchler (ed.), *The Philosophical Writings of Charles Sanders Peirce*. New York: Dover Press, 98–119.

Peñaloza, Lisa (1994). "Atravesando: Border Crossings. A Critical Ethnographic Exploration of the Consumer Acculturation of Mexican Consumers," *Journal of Consumer Research*, 21/1 (June): 32–54.

Pine, Joseph B., and Gilmore, James H. (1999). *The Experience Economy: Work Is Theater and Every Business a Stage*. Cambridge, MA: Harvard Business School Press.

Ricoeur, Paul (1976). *Interpretation Theory: Discourse and the Surplus of Meaning*. Fort Worth: Texas Christian University Press.

Ries, Al, and Trout, Jack ([1981] 2000). *Positioning: The Battle for Your Mind: How to Be Seen and Heard in an Overcrowded Marketplace*. New York: McGraw-Hill.

Saussure, Ferdinand de ([1916] 1983). *The Course in General Linguistics (Cours de linguistique générale)*, Paris: Payot, trans. Roy Harris. London: G. Duckworth publishers.

——([1916] 1967). Cours de linguistique générale. Paris: Payoy.

Schouten, John W., and McAlexander, James H. (1995). "Subcultures of Consumption: An Ethnography of the New Bikers," *Journal of Consumer Research*, 22/1: 43–61.

Schultz, Ellen E. (2004). "More Retirees May See Health Cuts: Provision in New Tax Bill Allows Employers to Alter How Benefits are Trimmed," *Wall Street Journal*, October 14, A5.

Schmitt, Bernt H. (1999). *Experiential Marketing: How to Get Customers to Sense, Feel, Think, Act and Relate to your Company and Brand*. New York: Free Press.

—— Pan, Yigang, and Tavossoli, Nader T. (1994). "Language and Consumer Memory: The Impact of Linguistic Differences between Chinese and English," *Journal of Consumer Research*, 21/12: 419–31.

Scott, Linda M. (1990). "Understanding Jingles and Needledrop: A Rhetorical Approach to Music in Advertising," *Journal of Consumer Research*, 17 (September): 223–36.

—— (1994a). "The Bridge from Text to Mind: Adapting Reader-Response Theory to Consumer Research," *Journal of Consumer Research*, 21/4 (December): 461–80.

—— (1994b). "Images in Advertising: The Need for a Theory of Visual Rhetoric," *Journal of Consumer Research*, 21/2: 252–73.

—— Batra, Rajeev, eds. (2003). *Persuasive Imagery: A Consumer Response Perspective*. New York, NY: Routledge Press.

—— Vargas, Patrick (2007). "Writing with Pictures: Toward a Unifying Theory of Consumer Response to Images," *Journal of Consumer Research*, 34 (October): 341–56.

Sebeok, Thomas A. (1972). *Perspectives in Zoosemiotics*. The Hague: Mouton.

Setha, M. Low (2009). "Towards an Anthropological Theory of Space and Place," *Semiotica*, 175 (June): 21–37.

Sherry, John F., Jr. (1987). "Advertising as a Cultural System," in Jean Umiker-Sebeok (ed.), *Marketing and Semiotics: New Directions in the Study of Signs for Sale.* New York: Mouton de Gruyter Press, 441–61.

—— (1990). "A Socio-Cultural Analysis of a Midwestern American Flea Market," *Journal of Consumer Research*, 17 (June): 13–30.

—— (1998). "The Soul of the Company Store: Niketown Chicago and the Emplaced Brands-cape," in John F. Sherry, Jr. (ed.), *Servicescapes: The Concept of Place in Contemporary Markets.* Chicago: NTC Business Books, 112–33.

—— (1998). "The Soul of the Company Store," in John F. Sherry, Jr. (ed.), *Servicescapes: The Concept of Place in Contemporary Markets.* Lincolnwood, IL: NTC Business Books, 109–38.

—— Camargo, Eduardo G. (1987). "'May Your Life Be Marvelous': English Language Labelling and the Semiotics of Japanese Promotion," *Journal of Consumer Research*, 14/3 (September): 174–88.

—— Eileen Fischer (eds.) (2009). *Explorations in Consumer Culture Theory.* New York, NY: Routledge Press.

Shields, Robb (ed.) (1992). *Lifestyle Shopping: The Subject of Consumption.* London: Routledge.

Silber, Kenneth (1999). *Pioneer 10's Remarkable Afterlife*, Staff Writer, posted: 02:23 pm ET, August 5, 1999. <http://www.space.com/news/pioneer_update.html>, accessed September 17, 2007.

Silverman, Kaja (1983). *The Subject of Semiotics.* New York: Oxford University Press.

Schmitt, Bernd, and Zhang, Shi (1998). "Language Structure and Categorization: A Study of Classifiers in Consumer Cognition, Judgement and Choice," *Journal of Consumer Research*, 25: 108–22.

—— Pan, Yigang, and Tavassoli, Nader T. (1994). "Language and Consumer Memory: The Impact of Linguistic Differences between Chinese and English," *Journal of Consumer Research*, 21: 419–31.

Sherson, Grant Warren (1999). "The Relevance of Semiotics to the Internet: How Web Designers use Metaphors in Web Development," Master's Thesis, Department of Communications, Victoria University of Wellington (May).

Smith, D.C. and Park, C.W. (1992). "The Effects of Brand Extensions on Market Share and Advertising Efficiency," *Journal of Marketing Research*, 29 (August): 296–313.

Stam, Robert, Burgoyne, Robert, and Flitterman-Lewis, Sandy (1992). *New Vocabularies in Film Semiotics: Structuralism, Post-Structuralism, and Beyond.* New York: Routledge.

Stern, Barbara B. (1989). "Literary Criticism and Consumer Research: Overview and Illustrative Analysis," *Journal of Consumer Research*, 16 (December): 322–34.

—— (1991). "Who Talks Advertising? Literary Theory and Narrative Point of View," *Journal of Advertising*, 20 (September): 9–22.

—— (1993a). "A Revised Communication Model for Advertising: Multiple Dimensions of the Source, the Message, and the Recipient," *Journal of Advertising*, 23: 25–36.

—— (1993b). "Feminist Literary Criticism and the Deconstruction of Advertisements: A Postmodern view of Advertising and Consumer Responses," *Journal of Consumer Research*, 19 (March): 556–66.

Stern, Barbara B. (1995). "Consumer Myths: Frye's Taxonomy and the Structural Analysis of Consumption Text," *Journal of Consumer Research*, 22 (September): 165–85.

Stern, Barbara B. (1996a). "Deconstructive Strategy and Consumer Research: Concepts and Illustrative Exemplar," *Journal of Consumer Research*, 23 (September): 136–47.

—— (1996b). "Textual Analysis in Advertising Research: Construction and Deconstruction of Meanings," *Journal of Advertising*, 25/3 (Fall): 61–73.

—— (1999). "Gender and Multicultural Issues in Advertising: Stages on the Research Highway," *Journal of Advertising*, 28 (Spring): 1–9.

Thompson, J.W. (1998) (Ch. 5)—Internal documents of the J. Walter Thompson Company.

Thompson, J.W. (2003) (Ch. 4)—Internal documents of the J. Walter Thompson Company.

Thompson, Craig J. and Zeynep Arsel (1994). "The Starbucks Brandscape and Consumers' (Anticorporate) Experiences of Glocalization," The, *Journal of Consumer Research*, 31 (December), 631–642.

—— and Haytko, Diana L. (1997). "Speaking of Fashion: Consumers' Uses of Fashion Discourses and the Appropriation of Countervailing Cultural Meanings," *Journal of Consumer Research*, 24/4 (June): 15–42.

Torres, Ivonne M., and Briggs, Elten (2007). "Identification Effects on Advertising Response," *Journal of Advertising*, 36/3: 97–108.

—— Gelb, Betsy D. (2003). "Hispanic-Targeted Advertising: More Sales?" *Journal of Advertising Research*, 42/6: 69–75.

Tse, David K., Belk, Russell W. and Zhou, Nan (1989). "Becoming a Consumer Society: A Longitudinal and Cross-Cultural Content Analysis of Print Ads from Hong Kong, the People's Republic of China, and Taiwan," *Journal of Consumer Research*, xx: 457–72.

Tsotra, Danai, Janson, Marius, and Cecez-Kecmanovic, Dubravka (2004). "Marketing on the Internet: A Semiotic Analysis," *Proceedings of the Tenth Americas Conference on Information Systems*. New York, NY, 4210–20.

Umiker-Sebeok, Jean, ed. (1987). *Marketing and Semiotics: New Directions in the Study of Signs for Sale*. The Hague: Mouton de Gruyter.

Underhill, Paco (2001). *Why We Buy: The Science of Shopping*. New York City: Texere Press.

United States Court of Appeals for the Ninth Circuit (2004); No. 9-56239 AHS; DC #CV99-320, *the Case of Playboy Enterprises, inc. versus Netscape Communications, Corporation*; and No. 99-56231; DC# CV99-321 AHS, *the case of Playboy Enterprises, inc. versus Excite, Inc.*

United States District Court, Central District of California, Southern Division (2000). *Playboy Enterprises, Inc., Plaintiff, V. Netscape Communications Corporation*; and Defendant, *Playboy Enterprises, Inc., Plaintiff, V. Excite, Inc.*, Defendant. Sa cv 99-320 ahs (eex); Related case: Sa cv 99-321 ahs (eex).

USDHHS (United States Department of Health and Human Services. Substance Abuse and Mental Health Services Administration) (2005). "Cigarette Brand Preferences," Office of Applied Studies, *THE NESDUH Report: National Survey on Drug Use and Health*.

Vasilash, Gary S. (ed.) (1998). "Building Trucks: Then and Now," *Automotive Design and Production*. <http://www.autofieldguide.com>, accessed November 21, 2007.

Warner, Judith (2005a). *Motherhood in the Age of Anxiety*. New York: Penguin-Riverwoods Press.

—— (2005b). "The Myth of the Perfect Mother: Why It Drives Real Women Crazy, Cover Story," *Newsweek*, US edition, February 21, <http://www.newsweek.com/id/48812>, accessed October 2009.

Waugh, Linda, and Monville-Burston, Monique (1990). "Introduction to the Life, Work, and Influence of Roman Jakobson," in *On Language: Roman Jakobson*. Cambridge, MA: Harvard University Press, 1–45.

Whorf, Benjamin Lee ([1956] 1964). *Language, Thought, and Reality: Selected Writings*, ed. and intro. John B. Carroll. Cambridge, MA: Technology Press of Massachusetts Institute of Technology, 134–59.

Williamson, Judith ([1978] 1998). *Decoding Advertisements: Ideology and Meaning in Advertising*. New York: Marion Boyers.

Wolfe, David (2008). *On Jonas Salk*, April 4. <http://www.agelessmarketing.com>, accessed July 9, 2008.

www.people.com.cn (2004). "China to Tighten Management over TV Commercial," December 10.

XmosBranding (2004). "F-150 Case Study," <http://www.labnet/xmos.com>, accessed March 10, 2006.

Yankelovich, Daniel (1964). "New Criteria for Market Segmentation," *Harvard Business Review*, March–April: 83–90.

Zaltman, Gerald, and Coulter, Robin Higie (1995). "Seeing the Voice of the Customer: Metaphor-Based Advertising Research," *Journal of Advertising Research*, 35/4: 35–51.

—— —— (2000). "The Power of Metaphor," in Cynthia Hoffman, David Glen Mick, and S. Ratneshwar (eds.), *The Why of Consumption: Emerging Perspectives on Consumer Motives*. New York: Routledge, 257–79.

Zhang, Shi, and Schmitt, Bernt H. (2001). "Creating Local Brands in Multilingual International Markets," *Journal of Marketing Research*, 38 (August): 313–25.

Zhao, Xin, and Belk, Russell (2008). "Politicizing Consumer Culture: Advertising's Appropriation of Political Ideology in China's Social Transition," *Journal of Consumer Research*, 35/2 (June): 231–44.

■ INDEX